The Crypto Compass

The Crypto Compass

How to Avoid Scams and Spot Real Innovation

Kareem Solakdar

Mindful Pages

Published in 2026

ISBN: 9789374599365 (PB)
ISBN: 9789374596920 (eBook)

Published by

Mindful Pages
Imprint of Alpha Editions LLC
312 W. 2nd St #1834
Casper, WY 82601, USA

This book was developed using advanced writing tools to support the drafting and ideation process. All content has been thoughtfully curated, refined, and reviewed to ensure quality and relevance.

Content

Introduction
The Crypto Compass: How to Avoid Scams and Spot Real Innovation

A market crash rarely begins with a bang. More often it begins with a whisper: a too-perfect promise, a countdown timer flickering on a glossy page, a charismatic founder persuading thousands that they are moments away from a once-in-a-generation opportunity. When one such project collapsed several years ago, an older man was photographed standing outside his local bank, holding a printout of the whitepaper he had followed so faithfully. The document was immaculate: diagrams arranged like constellations, jargon that sounded reassuringly technical, a roadmap stamped with milestones as confident as royal decrees. He had not understood everything he read, yet he had understood enough to believe that the future was arriving and that he could at least buy a seat on the train. When the project evaporated—its website replaced by a terse error message—he returned to the bank not for restitution but for an explanation. The silence he encountered there became, in its way, the unofficial anthem of an age: an era in which money can dissolve faster than blame, and trust can be engineered as convincingly as code. The photograph circulated widely, not because the man was naïve, but because he was recognisable. He represented millions who have stepped into the cryptocurrency world with equal parts curiosity and uncertainty, trying to navigate a landscape that changes faster than any regulator, journalist, or expert can track. Many arrived out of hope—for financial autonomy, for technological empowerment, for participation in a system that promised fairness where traditional finance seemed tired and exclusive. Others arrived out of fear, driven by the anxious belief that if they did not act now, they would be permanently locked out of the next great economic shift. Both impulses were understandable. Both made them vulnerable. Crypto's revolutions are genuine. Its illusions are too. And that duality is what makes it unlike any financial experiment before it. In crypto, the same technology that mints new markets also mints new mirages. A slick whitepaper and an aggressive marketing countdown can make vapour feel like value, while a clunky interface can conceal a breakthrough whose elegance lies deep in the architecture rather than at the surface. Fraud and innovation both wear the costume of novelty, and the untrained eye struggles to discern which mask hides substance and which hides a trap. This book begins at that intersection—not as a condemnation of the space, nor as a hymn to it, but as a guide to navigating its shifting terrain with intelligence and confidence.

What makes this subject urgent is not the scale of individual losses, although those can be devastating, but the broader cultural stakes. Money and trust are no longer anchored solely in institutions; they are increasingly shaped by protocols, networks, and narratives that spread across the internet with extraordinary speed. Information asymmetry has always existed in finance, but in crypto it widens into chasms. Early insiders exploit technical opacity; latecomers rely on social proof; algorithms amplify both enthusiasm and panic with equal indifference. History reminds us that every frontier—railroads, telegraphs, oil booms, dot-com startups—was simultaneously a theatre of genuine progress and opportunistic deception. But none unfolded in an environment as permissionless, global, and socially charged as today's blockchain ecosystem. The velocity of misinformation now rivals the velocity of capital itself. Understanding crypto, therefore, is not merely an economic necessity; it is a civic one. It demands the ability to interrogate claims with rigour, to recognise when innovation is real and when it is little more than a linguistic performance. It demands tools that cut through theatre without extinguishing curiosity. The purpose of this book is to provide those tools. You will not learn what to buy; that would be a disservice. You will learn, instead, how not to be fooled—how to develop the intellectual independence that protects you from the cyclical seductions of hype, tribalism, and fear. To do that, we must first acknowledge the peculiar nature of the crypto landscape. It is a world built on open systems yet plagued by opacity; a world where anonymity can empower dissidents and disguise fraudsters in equal measure; a world where every innovation is immediately imitated, often poorly, and where the appearance of activity can be manufactured as easily as a bot army or a fabricated chart. The very openness that makes this technology revolutionary also makes it vulnerable to exploitation. And this vulnerability is not a design flaw—it is the price of freedom in a permissionless system. Consider the first time an explorer mapped an uncharted coast. No matter how detailed the map, there remained peninsulas he had not sailed around, currents he had not measured, storms he had not seen. Crypto is a similar coastline: incomplete, volatile, and expanding faster than any navigator can keep pace with. Some adventurers venture inland with care, studying the currents and taking soundings. Others plunge forward with the confidence of gamblers. And then there are those who fashion imaginary cities, drawing them on the map with such conviction that others sail straight into the fog, believing they have found a future that in fact does not exist. That metaphor—the map and the mirage—is one that will recur throughout this book. It symbolises the central challenge faced by every participant: distinguishing what is genuinely new from what is merely unfamiliar. Too often novelty is mistaken for value, activity for adoption, and complexity for legitimacy. A blockchain project may launch with thousands of lines of code copied from an existing protocol, modified only in superficial ways, yet raise millions of dollars by presenting itself as a revolutionary leap. Meanwhile, a quiet team working on a mathematically rigorous breakthrough may struggle for attention because their language is restrained and their timeline conservative. The market rewards noise long before it rewards substance, and those who cannot tell the difference often discover—too late—that their enthusiasm has been harvested. Yet the story of crypto is not only a story of deception. It is also the story of ingenuity: of engineers designing trust where trust does not naturally exist; of decentralised communities coordinating with unprecedented efficiency; of developers pushing computational boundaries that once seemed impossible. Real innovation is happening here—innovation that could reshape finance, governance, and entire sectors of the digital economy. But it does not appear in neon lights. It appears in commit histories, audit trails, governance proposals, and the quiet grind of iteration. Learning to perceive it requires patience, scepticism, and above all a refusal to be dazzled by spectacle.

At its core, this book is a manual for thinking more clearly about a world that thrives on confusion. Each chapter introduces practical tests for evaluating claims: tests for code, where structure matters more than slogans; tests for token design, where incentives reveal more than marketing; tests for governance, where power dynamics matter more than rhetoric; tests for market structure, where liquidity and release schedules expose manipulations long before they erupt into headlines. These are not academic puzzles. They are real-world heuristics used by seasoned researchers, security analysts, and institutional investors—the people who navigate this terrain without being routinely misled by its illusions.

But the intellectual tools alone are not enough. What matters just as much is the psychology of the reader. Crypto preys on emotion as much as ignorance. Fear of missing out, fear of being left behind, fear of appearing uninformed—these shape decisions more powerfully than any technical principle. The most sophisticated investor can still be undone by a sudden rush of collective euphoria. The most technically proficient developer can still be tempted by a charismatic narrative dressed up in futuristic metaphors. The line between insight and impulse is perilously thin, and learning to recognise one's own vulnerabilities is as vital as learning to recognise external risks.

This introduction is therefore also an invitation to self-reflection. Throughout the book, you will be encouraged to examine not only the projects you encounter, but also the biases that shape your encounter with them. Why does a particular narrative appeal to you? Which communities do you instinctively trust, and why? What part of you responds to urgency, exclusivity, or the promise of effortless yield? These questions are not incidental—they are your first defence against manipulation. No amount of technical analysis can protect those who are unwilling to confront their own cognitive patterns. There is something deeply human about our relationship with frontier technologies. We oscillate between wonder and suspicion, embracing possibilities while fearing their consequences. The challenge is not to extinguish that wonder, but to channel it through disciplined curiosity. A world without curiosity would stagnate; a world without scepticism would be devoured by charlatans. The balance between the two is the art this book seeks to cultivate. Look closely at any major collapse in the history of crypto and you will find, beneath the sensational headlines, a chorus of overlooked red flags. Whitepapers that said everything except how the system actually worked. Audits that covered code but ignored economics. Token emissions designed to enrich insiders rather than users. Communities that punished doubt rather than rewarding scrutiny. Markets whose liquidity was concentrated in a single pool, waiting to be drained. None of these were hidden. They were simply ignored by those who had not yet learned to see.

Learning to see is what this book is about. Seeing beyond the surface, beyond the jargon, beyond the marketing theatre. Seeing the architecture that supports or undermines a system. Seeing the incentives that shape behaviour. Seeing the patterns that repeat across cycles, scams, and innovations alike. When you learn to see clearly, you are no longer at the mercy of those who benefit from your confusion.

As you read, you may find that some assumptions you held about crypto are challenged. You may also discover that some of your instincts were more accurate than you realised. The aim is not to convert you into a cynic, but to sharpen your discernment. Real innovation invites scrutiny; fraud depends on its absence. Once you internalise that principle, the noise of the market begins to fade, and the contours of reality begin to sharpen.

The chapters ahead will show you how narratives can outpace due diligence, how influencers manufacture credibility, how tokenomics often reward insiders rather than ecosystems, how governance can be both a safeguard and a smokescreen, how code can be technically sound yet economically fragile, how liquidity can be orchestrated as easily as a stage performance. These are not theoretical risks—they are structural features of a world where access is permissionless and accountability is uneven. To participate safely, one must understand both the beauty and the brutality of such a system.

So let us begin with a set of questions—questions that no responsible participant should ignore. What makes a project genuinely valuable rather than merely fashionable? How do we distinguish engineering from theatre? How do we avoid being swept into a collective mania without retreating into fearful paralysis? How do we stay curious without being credulous? How do we move through this landscape with both openness and discernment? These are the questions that shape not only profitable decisions, but meaningful ones.

Crypto has opened a frontier. Frontiers test us. They require courage, but also caution. They reward imagination, but punish naivety. They are places where maps help but never replace judgement. This book cannot promise certainty; the terrain changes too quickly for that. But it can offer a compass—a set of enduring principles that orient you amid volatility, complexity, and noise. Carry it with you as you explore. The fog will lift. The mirages will thin. And in their place, you will begin to see the real contours of innovation, the real engines of value, and the real opportunities hidden beneath the spectacle.

Chapter 1
The Map and the Mirage

The first time a copy-paste blockchain fork raised millions before writing a single line of original code, the developers scarcely tried to conceal their shortcuts. The whitepaper recycled paragraphs from an older project; the diagrams mirrored publicly available templates; even the supposed innovation—a "radically optimised consensus upgrade"—was, to anyone with technical fluency, nothing more than a settings adjustment wearing borrowed vocabulary. Yet the token sale filled almost instantly. Social channels flooded with exclamation-marked predictions. Influencers crowned it the "next blue chip" before it had so much as a testnet. And then, as predictably as a tide, the project vanished into silence, leaving its backers with nothing but screenshots of promises that had always sounded too polished to be real.

That brief, almost theatrical episode reveals something important about all frontier markets: speed is both an opportunity and a weapon. When a landscape is shifting so quickly that even experts struggle to keep up, information ceases to function as a stabilising force. It becomes a performance. Narratives outrun due diligence. Confidence becomes a substitute for comprehension. And in that widening gap between what is known and what is merely claimed, grifters find the perfect habitat.

Frontiers have always attracted builders and opportunists in equal measure. During the nineteenth-century gold rush, the wealthiest individuals were not those who found gold but those who sold shovels, maps, and equipment to hopeful miners. During the early dot-com boom, hundreds of companies added ".com" to their names to inflate valuations, often without any meaningful digital strategy. Crypto is simply the latest territory in this lineage—one defined not by physical distance but by cognitive distance. The technology evolves so rapidly, and the reference points are so unfamiliar, that even seasoned investors can feel unmoored. When the ground itself seems to be moving, people reach for the nearest story that offers direction, however flimsy.

This chapter begins with that unsettling truth. Before we talk about scams, we must understand the ecosystem that allows them to bloom with such regularity. It is not stupidity that leads people astray; it is asymmetry. The frontier, by definition, is a place where knowledge is unevenly distributed. A developer who spends a decade studying consensus algorithms will naturally understand more than a nurse, a taxi driver, or a philosophy student browsing late at night. But crypto's marketing machinery does not wait for comprehension. It promises access first and clarity later—if at all. And so a structural mismatch emerges: those who understand the least are given the fastest route to participation. Those who understand the most are often too absorbed in building to warn them.

This is why narratives travel faster than truth. A compelling slogan—"guaranteed yield," "unhackable," "next-generation blockchain"—can propagate across social feeds in minutes, evoking excitement long before anyone pauses to ask what such claims actually mean. A copy-paste fork may be indistinguishable from a breakthrough to eyes trained only on aesthetics. In a permissionless world, the stage is always open, and charisma often arrives with a megaphone. The aim of this chapter is not to moralise about greed or to mock those who have been misled. Instead, we will learn to map this frontier with clearer sight. The first tool we examine is pattern recognition, a skill more valuable than any single piece of technical knowledge. Scams and fragile designs repeat themselves with almost comic consistency. Guaranteed yields paired with opaque treasuries. Anonymous teams promising audited code they never deliver. Roadmaps so ambitious they seem to have been drafted in a fever dream. These patterns are not mysteries; they are fingerprints, and they can be recognised long before disaster strikes.

But pattern recognition is not superstition. It is a disciplined practice. One must store patterns, test them in the wild, and retire them the moment evidence shifts. The danger lies in clinging to outdated templates, mistaking ritual for insight. Markets evolve; fraudsters adapt. A pattern library is not a sacred text but a living, breathing tool—a mental catalogue that sharpens with experience. This chapter will help you construct one: pragmatic, flexible, and grounded in reality.

From there we turn to one of the most persistent confusions in crypto: the difference between innovation and novelty. Novelty speaks loudly. It sparkles with branding and theatrics. It emphasises how fresh something looks rather than what problem it solves. Innovation, by contrast, is quieter. It presents a clear problem, a plausible technical pathway, milestones that can be verified, and an openness to critique that signals confidence rather than insecurity. Much of the market has inverted this order, rewarding those who shout before they build. To navigate such a place, we must learn to distinguish the shimmer from the substance.

A recurring motif in this chapter—and indeed in the whole book—is the image of the mirage. On a fast-moving frontier, illusions do not merely distract; they distort. They cause people to march in the wrong direction, lured by the appearance of water where none exists. Meanwhile, real streams and fertile ground may lie just beyond sight, accessible only to those patient enough to scan the landscape with care. When you learn to see the distortions, the map begins to make sense. And when the map makes sense, the mirages lose their spell. Yet the most important map in this chapter is not of the market; it is of yourself. Every person carries a personal threat model—an internal matrix of biases, impulses, and blind spots. Some are particularly vulnerable to FOMO, driven by an urgent fear that others are gaining an advantage they are somehow missing. Others defer too readily to authority, placing unwarranted confidence in charismatic founders or influential commentators. Still others are intimidated by jargon, mistaking technical language for technical competence. Understanding these vulnerabilities is not a moral failing; it is an essential survival skill.

This chapter will show you how to articulate your own threat model with honesty and precision. It will also suggest friction steps and pre-commitments—small behavioural guardrails that protect you from your own worst instincts. A 24-hour cooling-off rule before any deposit. A checklist to complete before acting on a narrative. A reminder to seek contradictory evidence before embracing enthusiasm. These practices are not constraints but liberations, freeing you from the emotional turbulence that the market deliberately exploits.

Taken together, these themes—frontier risk, pattern recognition, the innovation–novelty divide, and personal threat modelling—form the backbone of the chapter ahead. This introduction is merely the gateway. Beyond it lies a deeper exploration of why crypto markets behave as they do, why illusions are so persistent, and how a more disciplined approach can turn confusion into clarity. The task is not to become cynical. It is to become perceptive. Frontier markets will always attract noise, spectacle, and opportunism. But they also contain extraordinary potential. To access it safely, one must learn to tread carefully, to question confidently, and to see what others overlook.

As you move into the chapter proper, keep one question in mind: what if the difference between prosperity and loss is not intelligence, but vision? Those who learn to read the map—not the mirage—discover a landscape filled with possibility. Those who mistake illusion for opportunity find themselves chasing shadows. The pages ahead will help you cultivate the vision that separates the two.

Why Scams Flourish in Frontier Markets

In January 2018, outside a co-working space near Shibuya Crossing in Tokyo, representatives of Coincheck held a brief, uneasy press conference. Hours earlier, the exchange had reported the loss of approximately ¥58 billion worth of NEM tokens—at the time one of the largest thefts in cryptocurrency history. The breach was crude: a hot wallet with insufficient controls, a glaring operational weakness rather than a sophisticated attack. Yet what made the moment emblematic was not the theft itself but the admission that hundreds of thousands of ordinary users had deposited funds into an infrastructure whose fragility would have been obvious to any seasoned security engineer. The public reacted with disbelief, as if the disaster were inexplicable, but the truth was simpler: where markets expand faster than expertise, risk concentrates in the gaps. Sometimes those gaps are exploited by hackers. Sometimes by founders. Sometimes by crowds intoxicated by their own expectations. And sometimes, as in Tokyo that winter, all three forces collide.

Frontier markets create this dynamic with unnerving regularity. They attract people willing to operate at speed, to build in public, and to chase the possibility of disproportionate reward. But that same speed erodes the safeguards that mature sectors take for granted. Knowledge becomes unevenly distributed. Rules lag. Incentives warp. A project that has merely rearranged the codebase of a predecessor can raise millions in minutes, while a carefully engineered protocol is forced to explain itself repeatedly to a sceptical audience. The irony is sharp: those moving quickest often know the least; those moving slowest often know the most. The result is an environment in which the map shifts faster than participants can chart it, and mirages proliferate.

Information asymmetry is at the heart of the problem. When the first automated market makers spread across decentralised finance in mid-2020, research posts from the University of California, Santa Barbara (UCSB, 2020) showed that users regularly mispriced pools by factors of ten or more because they misunderstood basic mechanics. That cognitive distance became fertile ground. Copy-paste forks multiplied: clones of Uniswap, then of SushiSwap, then of clones of both. Some were earnest experiments; others were opportunistic grabs. One fork, launched by a team in Seoul in October 2020, reproduced Uniswap's interface almost pixel for pixel. The only substantive difference was a token sale that directed proceeds to an anonymous treasury. Despite the derivative design, it raised more than US$5 million in under an hour, demonstrating how narratives—"community-owned exchange," "fair launch," "next generation liquidity"—can outrun scrutiny with astonishing ease. Narratives travel faster than due diligence because stories are cognitively lighter than audits, roadmaps, or model checks. A claim such as "guaranteed yield" demands little from the reader. It activates desire rather than analysis. But verifying that claim requires understanding treasury flows, collateral conditions, and failure modes. When attention is scarce, and participation is permissionless, the friction of verification exceeds the friction of belief. This imbalance is not accidental; it is engineered. Promoters know that speed reduces scepticism. A countdown timer does more work than a whitepaper. A well-lit livestream does more than a line-by-line technical explanation. The story becomes the product. Status games intensify this distortion. In frontier markets, reputation forms and dissolves quickly. Early participants can claim authority simply by being early, not by being correct. And because the market is global, authority becomes performative: follower counts, retweet cascades, Discord moderator titles. These cues substitute for technical competence, and the crowd accepts them because familiar reference points—licensing, regulatory oversight, institutional vetting—do not translate cleanly into a decentralised environment. When certainty is scarce, confidence masquerades as expertise. This is why scams travel in waves. They are not random aberrations; they are patterned behaviours shaped by structural incentives. The archetype of the copy-paste fork persists because it works. The template of the high-yield, opaque-treasury project persists for the same reason. The mechanics vary—lending, staking, synthetic assets, algorithmic backing—but the architecture remains recognisable. Show: a project offers double-digit returns with no articulated risk model. Name: in April 2022, the collapse of TerraUSD demonstrated the brittleness of such constructs when market confidence erodes. Explain: its algorithmic stabilisation system relied on assumptions about reflexive demand that failed under sustained sell pressure. Implication: when the underlying mechanism is misunderstood, yield becomes a mirage sustained only by fresh inflows.

Yet there are counter-examples that complicate the picture. When Ethereum launched its mainnet in July 2015, the design was undeniably experimental, and the documentation was uneven in places. By the logic of frontier risk, one might have expected it to falter. Instead, the project established itself as a foundational layer for decentralised applications. Its early openness, extensive peer review, and visible developer community functioned as stabilising forces. The platform demonstrated that frontier markets do not doom all ambitious projects; they simply magnify the consequences of both competence and incompetence. Ethereum succeeded not because it avoided uncertainty but because it managed it transparently.

To reconcile these contrasting outcomes, one must look beyond individual projects and examine behavioural patterns. A recurring motif is the fog that settles over fast-moving domains. In thick fog, distance compresses. Objects appear closer or larger than they truly are. Frontier markets produce a similar perceptual effect. A whitepaper filled with equations may seem authoritative even when the mathematics is decorative. A roadmap promising monthly releases may sound credible even when the team has no engineering depth to support it. The fog distorts scale and relevance, and those distortions reward actors who know how to exploit them.

Information asymmetry is amplified by weak reference points. Participants often enter crypto from traditional finance, software engineering, or entirely unrelated fields. They bring mental models shaped by those environments, but the assumptions embedded in those models break quickly. A software engineer may assume that code reuse is harmless, not realising that small deviations in smart contract logic can introduce catastrophic vulnerabilities. A retail investor may assume that past returns predict future performance, unaware that many tokens have no economic engine beyond speculative momentum. Without shared reference points, individuals reach for proxies: influencer endorsements, trending charts, token tickers flashing in green. These proxies create the illusion of insight while deepening reliance on surface-level cues.

The copy-paste fork phenomenon illustrates this clearly. Show: the project resembles a well-known protocol. Name: in November 2021, a fork of OlympusDAO emerged under the name TaiChi DAO in Singapore and marketed itself as a "culturally tailored" version of the original. Explain: despite its rebranded rhetoric, the contract architecture retained core vulnerabilities, including treasury opacity and reflexive incentive loops. Implication: cosmetic differentiation distracts from structural similarity, enabling grifters to recycle narratives faster than auditors can review them.

Status games further compound the issue. In traditional settings, authority is earned through qualifications or institutional mandate. In decentralised markets, authority often emerges through attention. The individual who tweets the fastest analysis, however superficial, is elevated. The influencer who frames a token as a cultural moment becomes a cultural authority. These dynamics create incentives to produce narratives rather than knowledge. The fog thickens. The map becomes less reliable. The mirages multiply.

Yet scams do not flourish simply because individuals lack information. They flourish because frontier markets reward behaviours that suppress hesitation. A project that raises funds before launch does so because hesitation is expensive. A user who pauses to read the code risks missing the "early adopter advantage." A community that questions a founder risks losing momentum. And momentum, in many speculative contexts, is the closest thing to currency. These pressures generate a collective acceleration in which due diligence becomes a luxury rather than a norm. The persistence of scams, then, is not rooted in human folly but in market design. When entry is frictionless and exit can be catastrophic, the incentive is to *move*, not to understand. When the market rewards speed over scrutiny, the rational actor becomes the one who skims rather than digs. Builders see the opportunity and attempt to outrun competitors. Grifters see the same opportunity and attempt to outrun consequences. Both flourish, but for very different reasons.

The fog motif returns here: visibility is limited, but movement feels urgent. Participants advance not because they see clearly but because they fear standing still. This emotional undertow explains why narratives travel faster than audits. A compelling story reaches a million viewers before a technical review reaches a hundred. The imbalance is structural.

A limitation must be acknowledged. Not every fast-moving frontier becomes a breeding ground for scams. Space exploration in the mid-20th century, for instance, combined speed, ambition, and technological uncertainty, yet fraud remained peripheral. The difference lay in institutional filters: NASA, formed in 1958 in Washington D.C., acted as a central arbiter, channelling public funding through rigorous review processes. Crypto lacks such filtering bodies. Its permissionless nature is both its strength and its vulnerability. Without a gatekeeper, quality becomes decentralised, and noise increases.

That absence of filtration is also what makes crypto compelling. Anyone can experiment. Anyone can build. Anyone can publish a protocol and invite the world to test it. This openness allows for breakthroughs that would never survive the risk-averse processes of traditional systems. But it also means that participants must develop their own internal filters—personal reference points that replace institutional ones.

The fog will not lift on its own. The map will not redraw itself to highlight danger zones. And the mirages will not cease simply because individuals become more knowledgeable. Frontier markets are shaped by uncertainty; they thrive on it. The task, therefore, is not to eliminate uncertainty but to recognise how it functions. The unresolved tension lingers: when the next project emerges, claiming to be a revolution, and the crowd surges toward it with breathtaking speed, what will you notice first—the narrative, the pattern, or the fog?

Pattern Recognition Beats Hindsight Bias

In June 2016, when auditors from the German firm ChainSecurity reviewed the remnants of *The DAO* after its collapse, they found a pattern that had been visible long before a single token was drained. The repetitive withdrawal loop that emptied roughly 3.6 million ETH from the project's smart contract was not an exotic zero-day exploit. It was a textbook re-entrancy flaw, documented years earlier in Ethereum's developer forums. Yet thousands of investors across Europe, North America, and East Asia had contributed funds without ever asking whether the contract's logic matched its rhetoric. The DAO had been framed as a grand experiment in decentralised governance. In practice, it displayed the structural fingerprint of a system built faster than it was tested. That mismatch between narrative and pattern—between what people wanted to believe and what the code quietly signalled—revealed a deeper truth: the most expensive mistakes in crypto are rarely unpredictable. They recur. And because they recur, they can be recognised.

Pattern recognition matters because hindsight bias seduces even the most rational observers. After any failure, commentators retroactively assemble explanations that make the outcome appear inevitable. This illusion of inevitability turns complex events into tidy stories. The more coherent the story, the less likely we are to scrutinise the underlying mechanics. But frontier markets reward those who notice structure *before* the collapse—not after. When observers treat every shock as unprecedented, they forfeit the only advantage that experience provides. They trade foresight for post-mortem elegance.

The motif of the *echo* helps clarify this dynamic. Fraud types echo across cycles. They reappear with altered branding, modified incentives, or updated jargon, but the architecture remains recognisable to those who have studied its earlier forms. One of the clearest echoes is the guaranteed-yield promise paired with an opaque treasury. The structure appeared in New York with the Bitconnect scandal in January 2018, where promoters claimed mathematically impossible returns through a "trading bot" that no auditor ever verified. It reappeared in Seoul in December 2021, when Haru Invest offered double-digit yields on digital assets without disclosing the underlying counterparties. The names shifted, the marketing changed, but the pattern persisted: high returns, vague mechanics, trust anchored not in verifiable data but in charismatic certainty.

Show how such patterns form. In speculative markets, speed compresses attention. A project that promises five per cent daily returns demands quick belief. That belief then spreads through social proof: reposts, screenshots, endorsements from individuals whose credibility is measured in followers, not technical mastery. The pattern emerges in the behaviours surrounding the project—the rush to join Telegram groups, the willingness to deposit funds before reading an audit, the reluctance to ask uncomfortable questions. Name the pattern: accelerated trust formation. Explain it: people commit not because they understand the mechanism but because hesitation feels costly. Implication: scammers structure their schemes to exploit that emotional tempo.

Yet pattern recognition is not infallible. Consider the counter-example of Binance's launch in July 2017. At first glance, it displayed traits common to short-lived exchanges: an anonymous founder to much of the Western audience, aggressive token incentives, rapid feature expansion, and a tight operational timeline. Several analysts at the time, including reports from ICODrops (August 2017), flagged the project as risky. But the exchange stabilised, adopted extensive compliance measures, and built a global infrastructure that persists. The superficial resemblance to weaker exchanges did not define its destiny. This limitation illustrates a key tension: patterns reveal probabilities, not certainties. They guide attention, not verdicts.

To reconcile this, a pattern library must evolve. A useful pattern is specific, falsifiable, and anchored in observable metrics. When it ceases to predict risk reliably, it must be retired. The *echo* motif returns here. An echo grows faint as distance increases. A pattern, too, loses relevance when conditions change. Guaranteed yields meant one thing during the unregulated lending boom of 2017–2020. They mean something different after regulatory scrutiny intensified in the United States, Singapore, and the European Union from mid-2022 onwards. Blind adherence to old patterns leads to superstition: the belief that any resemblance signals danger, even when context diverges.

The distinction between pattern and superstition therefore matters. Show a behaviour: a commentator dismisses a project because its founder uses pseudonymity. Name the superstition: pseudonymity equals fraud. Explain: pseudonyms were early norms in crypto, reflecting privacy culture rather than intent to deceive. Satoshi Nakamoto remains unknown; yet Bitcoin's codebase became one of the most examined in history. Implication: superstition mistakes correlation for causation, closing off legitimate innovation. Hindsight bias compounds this confusion. When losses occur, people reconstruct the sequence as though the warning signs were obvious to everyone. But identifying a pattern retrospectively differs from recognising it prospectively. Prospective recognition demands granular attention: the alignment between a project's claims and its mechanics, the consistency of its incentives, the coherence of its economic model. After the collapse of Celsius Network in July 2022, analysts pointed out the red flags: murky lending books, concentrated counterparty exposure, inflated collateral valuations. Those signs were indeed present, but they required deliberate observation—not casual intuition.

For pattern libraries to function, they must be grounded in *behaviour*, not aesthetics. If a project promises stabilised returns, the library tracks how those returns are generated: through fees, arbitrage, collateralisation ratios, or unsustainable emissions. If a founder claims decentralisation, the library tracks observable governance distribution: multisig signer diversity, voter participation metrics, upgrade processes. These specifics prevent the library from drifting into broad generalisations.

A second named example illustrates this approach. In May 2020, the launch of YAM Finance drew immense attention. The project combined elements of rebasing tokens and yield farming, a configuration that had surfaced previously with mixed results. Within 48 hours, it accumulated more than US$400 million in total value locked. The pattern library would have noted several elements: unaudited code, extreme incentive spikes, and complex mechanics dependent on user behaviour that the developers themselves had acknowledged as uncertain. The subsequent contract bug that froze the treasury fit a pattern that had been documented repeatedly: unaudited composability risks. Again, the echo was visible before the outcome.

But a credible pattern library must also record *exceptions*. Not all unaudited code fails. Not all incentive-heavy models collapse. The counter-example of Yearn Finance, also in 2020, demonstrates this nuance. Although it began as a one-person project with limited formal review, it matured rapidly due to transparent communication, open-source scrutiny, and a culture of iterative improvement. Reconciling these cases forces a more refined rule: unaudited code with closed governance and opaque decision-making is dangerous. Unaudited code with visible development history and responsive maintainers may still be risky, but its risk profile differs. The purpose of a pattern library is not to eliminate uncertainty; it is to create a structured memory. Memory is scarce in frontier markets. Attention drifts. New entrants outnumber veterans. Narratives overwrite nuance. A pattern library counters that amnesia by anchoring judgement in observed regularities. But the library must remain dynamic. When market structures shift—such as the rise of real-world asset protocols from late 2023 onward—old patterns may lose predictive power. Retiring them is not weakness. It is intellectual hygiene.

The motif of the *echo* returns once more. Echoes help us locate ourselves in unfamiliar terrain. They give shape to the fog. But misheard echoes lead travellers astray—confusing one sound for another, interpreting noise as signal. The difference between pattern recognition and superstition is therefore the difference between an echo that guides and an echo that deceives.

To make these distinctions operational, consider the visible behaviours associated with pattern testing. Does the project disclose treasury flows? Does the founding team respond to adversarial questions with specificity, or with abstraction? Do the metrics—

collateral ratios, liquidity depth, governance turnout—align with the project's promises? These concrete markers transform pattern recognition from metaphor into method.

The risk of hindsight bias, however, never vanishes. After each failure, the chorus of commentators claims clairvoyance. They highlight screenshots, quotes, forgotten forum posts. The effect is seductive: it reassures observers that disasters were always obvious, implying that vigilance is simply a matter of paying attention. But vigilance is not retrospective. It is anticipatory. It requires paying attention before the crowd, when information is incomplete and ambiguity high. Prospectively, patterns look less like warnings and more like faint echoes—subtle, uncertain cues.

This creates the tension that animates frontier markets: patterns guide, but they do not decide. They illuminate possibilities without closing them. They sharpen perception, but never replace judgement. As the next project accelerates towards launch, with incentives rising and narratives swelling, the pattern library sits quietly in the background, offering memory rather than certainty. The unresolved question remains: when the echo sounds again—familiar yet altered—which part will you hear first: the pattern, the risk, or your own desire for the story to be true?

Innovation vs Novelty

In March 2018, researchers at MIT's Digital Currency Initiative examined a series of new "consensus breakthroughs" circulating on GitHub. One proposal, published by a start-up registered in Zug and promoted in Silicon Valley meetups, claimed a revolutionary leap in throughput. Its whitepaper presented equations, diagrams, and confident technical prose. Yet the MIT team found that the system's core adjustment was a single parameter change inside a fork of Tendermint: the block time had been shortened from one second to 200 milliseconds. Nothing else in the consensus logic had shifted. No new threat model had been articulated. No stress test had been run. The supposed innovation, framed as a reimagining of distributed agreement, was little more than a rebranded settings tweak. The incident became a quiet reference point across academic circles. It showed how easily novelty can masquerade as progress when the audience lacks time to examine the mechanism beneath the marketing. And it set the stage for a deeper question: what distinguishes genuine step-changes from cosmetic engineering?

Novelty is seductive. It moves quickly. It dazzles with its presentation and its rhythm. Innovation, by contrast, takes shape in slow, observable increments: measurable performance gains, verifiable security assumptions, and behaviour that endures when tested. To separate the two, one must watch what a system *does*, not what its promoters *say*. That distinction sits at the centre of frontier technologies, where ambition is abundant and scrutiny scarce. The motif of the *lens* helps here. Peer through the lens at an exaggerated marketing claim and the distortion becomes visible. Peer through the same lens at a genuine breakthrough, and the details sharpen rather than blur.

Show that novelty spreads faster. Name an example: the September 2020 launch of TRON's "EVM-compatible upgrade" presented itself as a meaningful structural advance. Explain: the upgrade altered gas pricing and execution wrappers but did not modify computation semantics. Implication: the attention it attracted reflected promotional reach, not architectural change. Projects that rely on spectacle often treat attention as a metric of innovation, yet attention alone measures only the surface.

Contrast this with a verifiable step-change. In December 2020, Filecoin introduced Proof-of-Replication and Proof-of-SpaceTime as operational mechanisms for storage guarantees. These were not cosmetic insertions. They established new proof structures, mathematically much heavier than standard block-production assumptions, and their operation could be measured: storage onboarding rates, sector integrity, cryptographic proofs submitted per epoch. That measurable behaviour—rather than the rhetoric—signalled innovation.

The distinction between novelty and innovation begins with *problem fit*. Show: a project claims to "redefine digital identity", yet its only function is to mint profile images. Name: the chrome-heavy NFT experiments emerging from Los Angeles and Miami in mid-2021. Explain: they solved no verified constraint—no authentication need, no governance burden, no legal integration requirement. Implication: such projects produced symbols rather than systems, and their rapid fade illustrated the gap between cultural novelty and structural necessity.

A project that fits a genuine problem behaves differently. It aligns its mechanisms with a demonstrable bottleneck. When StarkWare released STARK proofs in November 2021 for scaling Ethereum computation, the existence of the bottleneck—gas costs and limited throughput—was well documented. Their method, a zero-knowledge proof system with transparent setup, addressed that bottleneck directly. The effect could be measured: transaction batches, proof sizes, latency. Problem fit anchors innovation, grounding it in visible pressure points rather than slogans. The next element of the lens—*technical pathway*—reveals whether a proposed change rests on a coherent mechanism or an aspirational diagram. Technical pathways describe not what a system hopes to achieve but how it commits to achieving it. Show: an aspiring DeFi protocol promises "capital-efficient collateral" without naming the liquidation logic. Name: the failed Iron Finance experiment in June 2021. Explain: it gestured toward capital efficiency but relied on reflexive mint-and-burn coupling between its tokens, a mechanism that had collapsed in several earlier algorithmic designs. Implication: its pathway could not withstand adversarial pressure, and the behaviour of its users—rapid redemption spirals—made this visible within hours.

A second example deepens the distinction. In January 2022, the zkSync team published a multi-stage pathway for achieving a fully decentralised rollup. The plan named components, dependencies, security audits, sequencer decentralisation milestones, and exit conditions. It exposed each assumption publicly and invited critique from researchers. The visibility of that pathway, not merely its aspiration, demonstrated innovation. The behavioural signal lay not in the language but in the developer activity: commits, audits, testnet data.

Verifiable milestones form the third component of the lens. Milestones matter because they reduce the scope for wishful thinking. They transform time into evidence. Show: a project claims a forthcoming mainnet but provides only graphics, not build artefacts. Name: the much-discussed OneCoin, headquartered in Sofia and promoted aggressively from 2014 to 2017. Explain: for years it promised upgrades, exchanges, integrations—none of which materialised in independently verifiable form. Implication: the absence of milestones was the pattern; novelty repeated itself while innovation failed to appear.

The limitation here is that missed milestones do not always signal fraud. Development can slip for legitimate reasons: security reviews uncover deeper issues; dependencies evolve; regulatory conditions shift. A credible counter-example is provided by the Ethereum 2.0 merge. Initially outlined in 2015, it did not complete until September 2022. The delay raised criticisms, yet each stage of the work—beacon chain launch, validator participation, public research debates—was visible. The project missed dates, but it met milestones. That distinction reconciles the limitation: dates can slip; evidence cannot.

The fourth component—*open critique*—may be the most culturally significant. Innovation invites attack because strong systems become stronger when tested. Novelty resists critique because its value depends on maintaining the illusion of progress. Show: a founder deletes critical comments from the project's GitHub. Name: multiple DeFi clones emerging in early 2022 that disabled issue tracking or restricted it to approved accounts. Explain: suppression of critique removes the feedback loop on which secure engineering depends. Implication: without critique, novelty accelerates unchecked while innovation stalls.

Contrast this with systems that treat critique as oxygen. The Bitcoin Improvement Proposal (BIP) process, formalised by developers such as Greg Maxwell and Pieter Wuille, has long operated as an open forum. Each proposal is debated, often fiercely, across mailing lists and public repositories. The behaviour—debate transcripts, pull requests, test vectors—provides a public record of scrutiny. Systems that thrive under critique display resilience precisely because they measure themselves against external challenge.

The quiet motif of the *lens* returns here. A lens clarifies only when it is kept clean. If a community cultivates hero worship, unwarranted certainty, or narrative shielding, the lens fogs. Developers may become reluctant to publish failures. Users may dismiss concerns as negativity. Metrics—such as uptime, validator count, transaction finality—may be selectively emphasised. The fog grows. Novelty thrives where the lens is clouded; innovation thrives where the lens is wiped clear by critique.

The tension between novelty and innovation becomes sharper when one examines visible behaviours around each. Novelty clusters around marketing beats: splash pages, token incentives, countdowns. Innovation clusters around disciplined work: reproducible test results, transparent repos, stable interfaces, well-documented trade-offs. These behaviours are measurable. One can count commits. One can compare benchmark data. One can trace governance votes. Visibility distinguishes the two.

But novelty can infiltrate even well-intentioned teams. Pressure from investors, expectations from communities, and competitive urgency can push developers to emphasise appearance over substance. A team may accelerate a release to capture market share while postponing core security audits. Users often respond to this acceleration with enthusiasm, mistaking speed for capability. The lens must therefore be held not only to the project but to the behaviour surrounding it.

Innovation also demands trade-offs. It rarely scales all dimensions at once. When Solana experienced partial outages in September 2021 and January 2022, critics labelled it unstable. Yet the outages resulted from the protocol's explicit design choices: high throughput and low latency under adversarial load required complex scheduling and validator coordination. The behaviour—network halts—was visible. But so was the improvement trajectory: validator diversity increasing, software updates shipping, technical reports published. This example illustrates a limitation in pattern judgment: innovative systems may break because they push boundaries; novel systems may remain stable because they attempt little.

Reconciling this demands attention to *trajectory*. Novelty plateaus quickly. Innovation compounds. The former generates bursts of excitement followed by stagnation. The latter generates incremental, observable improvement. When Polkadot opened its parachain auctions in November 2021, the system had spent years building the underlying cross-chain messaging logic. Each component had been tested. The launch was not spectacle; it was the culmination of layered engineering. The behaviour—gradual increase in parachain activity—reflected durable design rather than theatrical novelty. The lens motif appears once more. Looking through a clear lens, the viewer asks: what behaviour confirms the claim? What metric reveals the mechanism? What evidence exposes the pathway? These questions act as filters, reducing the influence of narrative and raising the influence of inspection.

And yet the tension remains. A genuinely novel idea may appear cosmetic at first glance; a cosmetic tweak may appear transformative if framed skilfully. The observer faces a decision each time a new system is presented with fanfare. Does the mechanism align with a verifiable problem? Does the pathway describe how the mechanism works under stress? Do milestones materialise? Is critique welcomed?

The unresolved test lingers: when the next "breakthrough" appears and the narrative gathers speed, will you watch the spectacle or measure the mechanism?

Build a Personal Threat Model

In July 2022, at a courthouse in Singapore, lawyers for Three Arrows Capital presented a stack of documents describing how one of the largest crypto funds had unravelled. The filings showed frantic, last-minute transfers; messages between founders urging each other to "hold conviction"; and a pattern of decisions made at velocity, not reflection. What struck observers was not only the scale of the collapse but the psychology behind it. The fund's partners, once celebrated across Hong Kong, Dubai, and Singapore, had mirrored behaviours common among retail traders: chasing social momentum, deferring to group narratives, dismissing doubt as disloyalty. The geometry of the failure was financial; the engine was emotional. It was a public reminder that risk is rarely abstract. It begins in the mind, long before it appears on a balance sheet. The lesson echoed across small Telegram groups and large exchanges: technical tools cannot compensate for internal blind spots. People commit to positions because urgency overwhelms caution, because charismatic figures command respect, because jargon intimidates them into silence. These forces operate quietly, but they are measurable. One sees them in the timestamp of a midnight transaction made seconds after a social media post; in the crowded comment thread beneath a charismatic founder's announcement; in the reluctance to ask what a "bonded curve stabiliser" means. The substructure of risk is behavioural before it is financial. The motif of the *mirror* is fitting here. Every frontier market holds up a mirror to its participants. The reflection can be flattering, deceptive, or instructive—but it cannot be avoided. Show how this mirror operates in practice. Name a case: when Celsius Network halted withdrawals in June 2022, users described making deposits within hours of promotional tweets claiming strength. Explain the pattern: many had ignored earlier signs of strain because the public certainty of executives triggered authority bias. Implication: the presence of leadership is not a risk-control mechanism; it can become a risk amplifier when unquestioned confidence replaces verifiable information.

A second example sharpens the point. In November 2021, during the peak of the so-called "dog-token" frenzy, a parody token launched on Binance Smart Chain accumulated more than US$30 million in market capitalisation within two days. The team was anonymous. The code was unremarkable. Yet thousands of participants joined because the token was trending. The visible behaviour—a rush of wallet connections and instant buy orders—was classic FOMO. It demonstrated how speed compresses scepticism. The market moved too fast for many to ask what the token did, who designed it, or why the liquidity pool looked thin. FOMO did not operate as feeling alone; it manifested in a heat map of transactions, in slippage metrics, in the time between announcements and deposits.

Authority bias often functions more subtly. In London in March 2021, an influencer-led project known as "SaveTheKids" promised socially conscious tokenomics. Many retail users entered because a group of well-known content creators endorsed the token. The endorsements acted as a proxy for due diligence. The subsequent collapse revealed how authority signals bypass scrutiny when they are attached to familiar public figures. Authority bias was not an abstraction. It was a visible behaviour: trusting a face rather than a mechanism, a promise rather than a pathway.

Yet a credible counter-example complicates the picture. When Vitalik Buterin published the Ethereum whitepaper in November 2013, his youth and lack of institutional backing could have triggered scepticism among early cryptographers. Instead, the openness of his writing and the public debate around the proposal generated trust through transparency, not charisma. The behaviour—open mailing-list discussions, peer critiques, visible code—countered the usual authority dynamic. This challenges any simple rule that authority bias always leads to harm. Sometimes authority deflates when substance is visible. Reconciling this highlights a deeper principle: authority is risky only when it substitutes for verification. When authority coexists with scrutiny, it becomes neutral rather than distorting. To build a personal threat model, one must map these forces in concrete terms. A threat model is not a metaphorical inventory of fears; it is a structured recognition of how one behaves under pressure. The mirror motif returns here. When the market accelerates, what does the mirror show? Does the pulse quicken when an airdrop rumour spreads? Does hesitation fade when a founder speaks with rehearsed certainty? Does technical language create deference rather than curiosity? These behaviours can be measured: the number of tabs opened before committing to a transaction; the minutes spent reading a contract or documentation; the ratio between reading and acting. These are not moral traits but behavioural variables.

Show the first vulnerability: FOMO. Name its mechanism: time compression. Explain: markets present opportunities as fleeting, which triggers the sense that waiting equals loss. Implication: the user commits to action before reflection. A visible metric is the time between discovering a project and making a decision. When that interval shrinks below one hour, the mirror begins to fog. Show the second vulnerability: authority bias. Name its mechanism: displaced judgement. Explain: users defer to a figure whose confidence bypasses their own evaluation. Implication: scrutiny weakens. The behaviour appears in comment sections where dissenters are silenced or ignored, and in Discord servers where questioning is framed as hostility.

Show the third vulnerability: jargon intimidation. Name its mechanism: asymmetric communication. Explain: uncertainty grows when language obscures rather than clarifies. Implication: the intimidated participant withdraws from active questioning. The behaviour can be seen in the number of times someone reads a paragraph without understanding it, yet proceeds anyway. Each vulnerability requires a counterweight. Pre-commitments offer one. Pre-commitments transform intention into structure. They slow behaviour. They install frictions. In behavioural science, pre-commitments are described by Thomas Schelling (1978) as "devices for binding the future self". In crypto, they take concrete forms. A 24-hour cooling-off rule before forwarding funds. A requirement to read one external critique before joining a community. A rule that deposits are not made after midnight. Each is a friction step designed to interrupt the emotional spike that frontier markets exploit. They are behavioural circuit-breakers.

Two examples illustrate their power. In March 2021, the decentralised project Curve Finance published an internal guideline encouraging contributors to take criticism from competitors seriously before deploying new mechanisms. This cultural pre-commitment reduced the rate of rushed updates, a behaviour that could be measured in the spacing of version releases. A second example comes from research by the Bank for International Settlements (BIS, April 2022), which found that traders who introduced a mandatory review pause before executing positions reduced impulsive trades by measurable margins. Although the context was broader than crypto, the principle transfers: friction reduces reactivity.

A limitation must be acknowledged. Frictions can also suppress legitimate participation. Some of the most meaningful projects in crypto—such as Solana's early validator onboarding in 2020 or Uniswap's liquidity mining launch in September 2020—rewarded early engagement. Strict cooling-off rules could cause participants to miss culturally significant events. Reconciling this means recognising that a personal threat model is not about freezing action but about modulating it. Frictions must be tailored, not universal. The mirror must reflect the individual, not the crowd.

Open critique functions as a second counterweight. When one names their vulnerabilities, critique becomes less threatening. It becomes diagnostic. The behaviour is simple: ask a question even when uncertain; document the answer; compare it with independent sources. This behaviour generates a feedback loop that weakens FOMO and authority bias. But critique must be anchored in clarity, not confrontation. The aim is to measure one's understanding, not to win an argument.

Another pattern that shapes vulnerability is narrative contagion. Narratives spread through social platforms with measurable velocity: repost counts, comment density, referral links. The mirror motif appears again. A personal threat model records how one reacts to narrative acceleration. Does the increase in social volume heighten desire or caution? Does trending status create the illusion of inevitability? These questions turn reflection into method. Building a threat model also demands attention to *identity*. Participants often align with communities that reflect their aspirations—open-source idealists, maximalists of specific chains, early adopters of experimental mechanisms. Identity colours judgement. It influences what one sees and what one discounts. A threat model that ignores identity is incomplete. The behaviour is visible: the selective reading of positive news; the dismissal of critiques from rival communities; the amplification of endorsements that match prior beliefs.

Two historical examples demonstrate how identity distorts perception. In September 2017, during the SegWit2x debate, parts of the Bitcoin community aligned not by technical analysis but by tribal identity. The behaviour—social media hostility and selective citation of experts—showed how identity can overwhelm problem fit. In June 2020, the Ethereum community showed a different dynamic: during debates over gas-fee spikes, researchers such as Dan Ryan and Danny Ryan published open discussions that acknowledged weaknesses without defensiveness. Identity existed, but critique remained possible. This contrast shows that identity need not be destiny; it becomes dangerous only when it overrides inspection.

A threat model is therefore a written, observable map. It names vulnerabilities. It records behaviours. It establishes friction steps. It acknowledges identity pressures. It invites critique. It adapts. And it recognises that emotional responses leave fingerprints in data: timestamps, transaction clusters, reading durations, community interactions.

But the mirror does not stay still. Frontier markets evolve. New incentives emerge. Social rhythms change. A behaviour that once signalled caution may later signal complacency. A friction step that once slowed risk may later prevent timely action. The threat model must evolve with the participant. Static models grow inaccurate. Dynamic models remain alive.

This leaves an unresolved question at the centre of the mirror. When the next surge arrives—when a new protocol trends, when a founder speaks with conviction, when a dozen peers rush toward the same opportunity—what will the mirror reveal? Will it show a reflex, a pause, or a choice?

Chapter 2
Greed, Fear, and FOMO

On a humid evening in May 2021, a young engineer in Manchester sat hunched over his laptop, refreshing a blockchain explorer as if willing the numbers to change. Hours earlier he had connected his wallet to a site promising eligibility for an airdrop rumoured across Telegram groups and Twitter threads. The process took seconds: click, approve, sign. He had done it so quickly he barely registered the contract address or the permissions he granted. By midnight, reports circulated that the site had swept thousands of wallets—his included—and that the long-anticipated airdrop had never existed. The engineer would later describe the moment as if it were a spell: a strange combination of adrenaline, urgency, and a sense that he was part of a race happening everywhere and nowhere at once. He knew better, he insisted, yet he acted anyway. His admission captured something universal: permissionless markets do not merely invite risk—they heighten the psychological forces that shape it. The paradox is stark. Crypto was built on the promise of individual autonomy, removing intermediaries and empowering people to act without permission. But autonomy without friction amplifies instinct. The fewer barriers between impulse and action, the more powerful those impulses become. Markets that operate at machine speed collide with minds still shaped by evolutionary heuristics. The result is a distinctive behavioural climate: exhilarating, volatile, and brutally revealing. Greed, fear, and FOMO are not side effects of the system; they are woven into its fabric. And understanding that fabric is essential to navigating it with any measure of clarity. Permissionless access transforms familiar cognitive biases into forces with real economic consequence. A stock trader may hesitate before placing a trade; brokerage interfaces are designed to slow the click. A crypto user, by contrast, can approve a transaction from their phone while queueing for coffee. That speed turns emotion into action with almost no mediating space. In such an environment, variable rewards—airdrop lotteries, staking bonuses, sudden price surges—function like intermittent reinforcement schedules in behavioural psychology. They reward unpredictable behaviour, making it more persistent and more resistant to caution. The engineer in Manchester was not simply fooled; he was primed. The market taught him that rewards arrive suddenly and vanish just as fast.

These psychological undercurrents shape not only individual behaviour but entire narratives. Narrative engines—those sprawling networks of influencers, content creators, meme accounts, research outfits, and algorithmic feeds—have become as influential as code. They manufacture stories that travel further and faster than analyses grounded in evidence. A well-edited thread from a charismatic commentator can move more capital in ten minutes than a peer-reviewed paper can in ten months. These engines monetise attention with startling efficiency. They reward certainty, even when certainty is unwarranted. And they obscure the basic question that should precede any commitment: *who benefits if I believe this story?* Undisclosed allocations sit at the centre of many such narratives. During the token boom of late 2021, dozens of influential accounts promoted new projects with glowing certainty, omitting that they held private allocations or had been paid in tokens. Their followers mistook enthusiasm for conviction, conviction for insight, and insight for truth. Source-trust ladders—our internal map of who to believe and why—collapsed under the weight of coordinated storytelling. Trust, once diluted, becomes volatile. It swings between extremes. A figure celebrated one month becomes a symbol of naivety the next. Yet the dynamics that create these swings remain largely unchanged: attention, reward, and the speed at which stories are shared.

If narratives shape how people think, tribes shape how they belong. Crypto has birthed online communities that range from earnest to eccentric, each with its own language, rituals, and mythology. Belonging offers emotional warmth: identity, humour, camaraderie. But it comes at a cost. When a group defines itself through loyalty, dissent becomes treason. Outgroup shaming becomes proof of devotion. Meme-coin communities in particular can flare brightly and collapse without warning. After their IDO, many vanish within weeks, the Discord channels abandoned, the slogans forgotten, the earlier enthusiasm preserved only in screenshots. Community warmth is not governance strength; enthusiasm does not become resilience by force of repetition.

Yet these groups persist because they answer fundamental human needs. They give shape to uncertainty. They turn markets into stories, stories into allegiances, and allegiances into a sense of meaning. To participate in crypto without understanding that emotional architecture is to wander through a carnival blindfolded, hearing the music but missing the machinery that makes it play. The psychology of belonging is as important as the mechanics of liquidity. And the line between tribe and trap can be perilously thin.
The motif of the *pulse* offers a way to understand this terrain. Markets have pulses—rhythms of excitement and panic that throb through chats, feeds, and price charts. Individuals have pulses too—moments when the heart beats faster, when the urge to act becomes overwhelming, when rationality is not defeated but momentarily overshadowed by the thrill of possibility or the fear of loss. Recognising the pulse, in oneself and in the crowd, is one of the most underrated skills in crypto. A pulse is not a signal. It is a warning.
This chapter explores how greed, fear, and FOMO take shape in permissionless markets—and why their influence is stronger here than in almost any other financial context. But it also examines the tools that allow participants to counteract those forces. Anti-FOMO habits are not acts of cynicism; they are acts of self-preservation. A checklist gate, completed coldly before any commitment, slows the pulse. A position sizing cap imposes discipline where emotion urges escalation. A staggered entry prevents panic buying. These friction steps transform psychological turbulence into structured behaviour. They recognise that the mind does not always protect itself.
The tension, however, lies in balance. Too much caution invites paralysis. Too little invites regret. A well-designed habit allows for curiosity without chaos, exploration without surrender. It creates a deliberate distance between the signal and the response. In fast-moving markets, distance is clarity. And clarity is power.
Yet nothing here is static. Influencer cultures evolve. Incentive structures mutate. The rhythms of social platforms shift. What felt rational one year can feel reckless the next. This is why the concept of a psychological framework matters. It is not about eliminating emotion. Emotion is inevitable. It is about integrating emotion into a system of decision-making where it cannot dominate unrestrained.
Throughout this chapter, we will trace how the architecture of permissionless access interacts with the architecture of human

psychology. We will look at the mechanics of attention, the economics of narrative, the sociology of online tribes, and the behavioural strategies that allow individuals to navigate these currents with greater poise. These themes are not merely contemporary. They reach back to older patterns: the frenzy of tulip auctions, the fever of railway speculation, the mania of early internet stocks. The technologies differ; the pulse does not. Crypto's psychological terrain is not incidental to its market structure; it is integral to it. The decisions made here—fast, emotional, public—reveal as much about human nature as they do about digital assets. And perhaps that is what makes this subject so compelling: to understand greed, fear, and FOMO in crypto is to understand ourselves under pressure. A market without permission is a mirror without a frame. It reflects sharply. Sometimes uncomfortably.

As the next sections unfold, a question will hover quietly at the margins. It is not whether greed, fear, or FOMO will appear—they always do. The question is simpler, and far more challenging: when the pulse rises, when the story spreads, when the tribe chants, and when the opportunity seems too fleeting to ignore, what will you do with the distance between impulse and action?

Investor Psychology in Permissionless Markets

In December 2021, servers for the decentralised exchange dYdX slowed under the surge of wallets connecting within minutes of rumours of an "unannounced airdrop". The rumour—traced back to a single tweet by a well-followed trader in New York—spread through Telegram channels and Twitter lists with astonishing velocity. Thousands of people authorised wallet connections without checking contracts, permissions, or provenance. The result was not a hack but a behavioural map: a living diagram of how quickly permissionless access can convert anticipation into action. The exchange's dashboard showed the pattern clearly. Spikes of new wallets appeared at 21:03, 21:05, 21:07. Each spike reflected the same impulse: act first, understand later. That evening, more than any theoretical model, revealed the core psychological hazard of permissionless systems. When action costs nothing, hesitation feels expensive.

The paradox is compelling. Permissionless access—the signature virtue of crypto—makes participation radically democratic. A student in Nairobi and a banker in Frankfurt can enter a market at precisely the same speed. Yet that same speed magnifies cognitive biases that in slower systems remain contained. Decisions that might once have required signatures, verification steps, or adviser conversations can now be made from a phone while walking between meetings. The elegance of this access disguises its psychological volatility. A thumbprint replaces a gatekeeper. A moment becomes a commitment. The market does not pause to ask whether the individual has grasped the stakes.

The motif of the *spark* helps illuminate this dynamic. A spark triggers fire only when kindling surrounds it. Permissionless markets supply that kindling in abundance: social proof, variable rewards, and the illusion of proximity to extraordinary gains. When rumours of an airdrop or lottery spread, they ignite a field already primed to burn.

Show how the spark catches. In the summer of 2020, Uniswap's surprise UNI airdrop rewarded any historical user with 400 tokens. Name the event: 17 September 2020, recorded across exchanges in London, Seoul, and San Francisco. Explain the psychological impact: thousands interpreted the reward as proof that participation pays even when one does not fully understand the mechanism. Implication: a template formed. When later projects hinted at future airdrops, users replicated the behaviour—connecting wallets rapidly, signing transactions reflexively, measuring possibility rather than risk. The visible behaviour was measurable: wallet-connection counts, gas spikes, and the narrowing interval between rumour and action.

Variable rewards magnify this effect. In behavioural psychology, intermittent reinforcement is known to sustain actions more effectively than predictable rewards. Crypto operationalises this principle. Show a behaviour: a user interacts with dozens of protocols in a week not because each is meaningful but because one might deliver an unexpected payout. Name a case: in March 2022, during the early phase of Optimism's retroactive public-goods programme, users began engaging with unrelated applications across the layer-2 ecosystem in hope of future retroactive eligibility. Explain: uncertain rewards encourage exploratory behaviour that bypasses careful evaluation. Implication: risk-taking becomes systematic, not episodic. The spark turns to flame.

Social proof amplifies the fire. When users see others acting quickly, hesitation feels irrational. A single screenshot of a friend's successful trade can outweigh pages of documentation. The behaviour is visible: during the launch of ConstitutionDAO in November 2021, contributions surged not because thousands had read the legal structures but because they saw peers contributing in real time. The running total displayed on the public dashboard acted as both signal and pressure. Social proof, in such moments, moves capital faster than comprehension.

Yet a counter-example reveals nuance. In April 2023, when Arbitrum conducted its ARB airdrop, many users resisted the urge to sell or rotate immediately. Despite intense social pressure and speculative narratives, a significant portion of allocation holders waited several days or more before acting. Analysts reviewing address patterns found that delays correlated with communities that had embedded shared norms of reflective behaviour—forums where members emphasised long-term participation rather than opportunistic speed. This example complicates any deterministic reading of investor psychology. Permissionless access magnifies biases, but it does not dictate destiny. Behaviour still shapes outcome. Reconciling this requires recognising that communities can counterbalance environmental pressures when norms favour reflection. The spark still ignites, but damp wood slows the burn.

To understand how permissionless design interacts with investor psychology, one must observe the mechanisms of acceleration. In traditional markets, frictions slow decision-making: settlement times, compliance checks, human intermediaries. In permissionless markets, those frictions evaporate. A user on Solana or Arbitrum can approve a transaction in seconds, commit capital instantly, and reverse course moments later. Speed becomes an ambient force. And speed interacts poorly with bias.

Show this interaction through behaviour. When Binance Smart Chain experienced its meme-token boom in early 2021, price charts of coins such as SafeMoon were defined by vertical surges followed by brutal collapses. Name the phenomenon: liquidity-driven reflexive trading, documented in trading logs from April 2021. Explain: the easier it was to enter and exit, the more users chased parabolic gains. Implication: permissionless markets do not merely enable volatility; they intensify the psychological appetite for it. The spark becomes a signal.

Another pathway reveals itself in *attention density*. The volume of signals—tweets, alerts, Discord pings—compresses judgement. When dozens of messages arrive within minutes, each hinting at opportunity, the user's cognitive load increases. Cognitive load correlates with snap decisions. The spark grows brighter. Show: during NFT minting surges in 2021, users often monitored multiple channels simultaneously. Name: the Bored Ape Yacht Club mint on 23 April 2021, which saw gas auctions spike to hundreds of gwei. Explain: real-time competition induced a race condition in human attention. Implication: the user experience of permissionless systems is not neutral; it is engineered to reward speed over reflection.

But speed does not operate in isolation. It interacts with identity. Crypto participation is rarely solitary. It is embedded in groups defined by jargon, memes, values, and shared rituals. Social identity theory, explored by Henri Tajfel in the 1970s, demonstrates how rapidly people internalise group belonging. In crypto, that belonging often forms around tokens, chains, or narratives. Belonging influences behaviour. It shifts attention from evidence to allegiance. The spark motif reappears: a spark within a tribe ignites faster than a spark alone.

This dynamic was visible during the TerraUSD collapse in May 2022. Despite mounting evidence of structural fragility—declining reserves, widening spreads, contradictory statements from Terraform Labs—many participants increased rather than reduced exposure. Loyalty to the narrative of decentralised money outweighed recognition of measurable risk. The behaviour was clear: deposits increased even as peg deviations widened. Social proof overpowered structural evidence. The spark became a wildfire.

A limitation must be acknowledged. Not all permissionless markets induce reckless behaviour. The Lightning Network community, for instance, has long cultivated norms of careful experimentation. Updates are tested, peers share failures openly, and incentives reward stability over spectacle. User behaviour—measured in node uptime, routing fees, and documented troubleshooting—reflects a culture that values caution. This demonstrates that permissionlessness alone does not guarantee psychological turbulence; design and culture matter. Reconciling this limitation reveals a deeper insight: permissionless markets are shaped as much by the norms surrounding them as by the code beneath them.

Variable rewards reshape risk perception in yet another way. When gains arrive unpredictably, losses feel temporary and recoverable. Behavioural economist Daniel Kahneman notes that people overweight small probabilities when rewards are vivid. Crypto operationalises this cognitive distortion through lotteries disguised as opportunities. Show: an investor connects to a dozen obscure "points-farm" applications in 2023–2024. Name: the zkSync and LayerZero points rush documented between January and June 2024. Explain: users perceived low investment and high upside, even though each interaction carried non-trivial contract risk. Implication: the maths of risk was replaced by the allure of possibility. The spark flickered with each rumour.

Social proof then reinforces that distortion. If others are doing it, the action feels safer. This is demonstrably false, but psychologically potent. The behaviour is visible in blockchain analytics: clusters of wallets acting within identical time windows, often after a single influential announcement. The spark motif gains clarity. Each cluster represents a spark travelling across a social surface, igniting behaviour with predictable rhythm.

A final dimension is worth tracing: *emotional cadence*. Permissionless markets do not simply accelerate behaviour; they oscillate between extremes with unusual speed. A user may feel euphoria after a successful mint at 10:00, panic after a sudden dump at 10:15, relief after a partial recovery at 10:30, and renewed FOMO by 10:45. These emotional cycles mirror the speed of market cycles, and because the market moves quickly, the user's emotional landscape becomes volatile. The spark dances across dry earth.

This leaves a lingering, unresolved question that frames the choice at the heart of permissionless participation. When speed collides with emotion, when social proof overwhelms prudence, and when variable rewards light up the circuitry of desire, what should the thoughtful participant measure first—the opportunity, the risk, or the spark beginning to glow at the edge of their own behaviour?

Narrative Engines and Influencers

On 3 October 2022, the U.S. Securities and Exchange Commission announced a settlement with Kim Kardashian for promoting EthereumMax on Instagram without disclosing a US$250,000 payment. The post itself—uploaded in June 2021—contained glossy graphics, confident language, and a call for followers to "join the E-Max community." Within hours of the promotion, token activity spiked across exchanges in London, Seoul, and Chicago. Within weeks, the price collapsed. The episode was not remarkable because a celebrity had endorsed a crypto asset; celebrity endorsements have long shaped consumer behaviour. What made it instructive was the anatomy of the narrative: a single, authoritative voice manufactured a story, transmitted it to millions, and monetised the resulting attention. The public saw a moment of enthusiasm. Regulators saw a paid narrative disguised as conviction. And anyone watching the trading charts saw the speed with which stories can move capital—even when the story has little substance behind it. Narratives in crypto do not behave like traditional financial commentary. They behave like engines—systems that draw in attention, process it into belief, and convert belief into action. Permissionless markets, with their velocity and openness, magnify this dynamic. When an influencer publishes a thread on a new protocol, the effect is not passive. It is catalytic. Wallets connect. Telegram groups fill. Code repositories spike with stars. The narrative becomes a living organism, expanding and mutating as it travels across networks. And because narrative engines operate faster than due diligence, they define sentiment long before fundamentals enter the conversation.

The motif of the *signal* helps illuminate this machinery. A signal begins as a point—an announcement, a hint, a thread—and then amplifies as it passes through the hands of those who repeat it. But amplification does not strengthen the truth of the signal; it strengthens only its reach. Understanding that distinction is essential to navigating narrative-driven markets.

Show how signals transform into engines. Name an example: during the *Fantom Summer* in August 2021, dozens of creators on Crypto Twitter promoted yield farms with screenshots showing triple-digit APRs. Explain: many of these posts concealed the fact that promoters had received early allocations or performance-based incentives. Implication: undisclosed stakes warp the informational environment. A trader scrolling through feeds does not see these financial relationships; they see conviction. The result is predictable: liquidity rushes in, and the narrative becomes self-fulfilling—until it isn't.

A second example deepens the point. In January 2024, a wave of threads praised a new layer-2 platform, framed as a breakthrough in decentralised sequencing. Several influential accounts wrote nearly identical posts. Later disclosures revealed coordinated compensation from a marketing agency operating out of Singapore. The behaviour became a case study in how narratives can be manufactured with industrial efficiency: same talking points, same growth projections, same graphics. What mattered was not the technology—it was the coherence of the story. The signal was tightly engineered. The amplification was deliberate.

Such episodes expose a blunt truth: narratives can be purchased as easily as advertising space. But the difference in crypto is speed. An advert in a newspaper reaches readers over hours or days. A promotional thread can reach hundreds of thousands within minutes. And because blockchain data is public, early promoters can position themselves to benefit directly from the engagement they generate. Influence becomes monetisation. Monetisation becomes incentive. Incentive becomes narrative fuel.

To understand narrative engines, one must trace the incentives behind them. Influencers, research accounts, and anonymous analysts do not operate in a vacuum. Some are funded by grants from foundations. Some are paid in tokens for coverage. Some receive allocations whose value depends on the market's reaction to their posts. These incentives shape tone, timing, and content. The visible behaviour reveals the alignment: bursts of posts immediately after token unlocks, selective omission of technical weaknesses, overemphasis on potential upside, and silence during downturns.

The *signal* motif returns here. A signal whose origin cannot be traced must be treated with suspicion. And this is where source-trust ladders become essential. A source-trust ladder is not a ranking of who is "good" or "bad." It is an evaluation framework: who has demonstrated technical competence? Who discloses financial ties? Who revises their claims when evidence shifts? Who amplifies only what benefits them? Instead of placing trust in personalities, the ladder treats trust as a gradient built from behaviour.

Show this in practice. When Andre Cronje, then based in South Africa, published code experiments in early 2020, he repeatedly warned users not to deposit funds. Name the pattern: open verification and self-critique. Explain: these behaviours created a track record of clarity and caution. Implication: the ladder placed his technical posts higher because he earned trust through openness, not hype.

Contrast this with an example where the ladder collapses. During the *SafeMoon* boom in April 2021, influencers produced glowing analyses devoid of contract inspection or liquidity review. Many of them held private allocations. The behaviour—promotions without substance—forced the trust ladder to adjust. The signal failed scrutiny. The amplification revealed misalignment.

Yet a counter-example provides nuance. In July 2020, when the "Black Thursday" post-mortem of MakerDAO was circulated, several independent analysts—without affiliations—produced rigorous critiques of liquidation mechanics. Their work gained visibility not because they had large followings but because the quality of their reasoning attracted attention. Here, the signal amplified because it deserved amplification. This reminds us that narratives are not inherently deceptive; they become dangerous only when incentives are obscured. Reconciling this limitation clarifies the principle: narratives are not the enemy—undisclosed incentives are.

Disclosure checks therefore function as defensive tools. They are behavioural rather than technical. Before internalising a narrative, the thoughtful reader asks: has the author stated their holdings? Do they stand to gain directly from a price increase? Have they acknowledged risks as well as rewards? Do they cite verifiable data—contract addresses, audits, repository links? The answers do not eliminate risk, but they contextualise it. They prevent trust from becoming reflexive.

Narrative engines also thrive because they tap into collective psychology. Humans respond to coherence. A tidy story feels more persuasive than a complex explanation—even if the tidy story is incomplete. Influencers exploit this bias by framing protocols not as engineering systems but as myths: "the underdog chain," "the final evolution of DeFi," "the community-owned alternative." These narratives are emotionally efficient. They bypass critical analysis and appeal to identity. They give individuals a sense of participating in something larger than themselves.

Show the mechanism through behaviour. During the rise of *OlympusDAO* in late 2021, dozens of accounts repeated the meme "3,3," implying that cooperation guaranteed mutual benefit. Name the source: the game-theoretic meme began circulating on Twitter in October 2021. Explain: the meme reduced complex economic assumptions into a single symbol. Implication: participants treated the meme as evidence rather than metaphor, accelerating capital inflow. The signal became a chant. The chant became a narrative.

But narratives do not merely persuade. They monetise attention. Influencers who drive engagement are rewarded by algorithms, sponsors, and sometimes token issuers themselves. Attention becomes currency. And in permissionless systems, where barriers to capital movement are minimal, the conversion from attention to liquidity is nearly instantaneous. A narrative engine that can move attention can move markets.

The *signal* motif appears again. Some signals guide. Others distort. Distinguishing them requires not cynicism but calibration. Calibration begins with questions: Who benefits if this is believed? What evidence supports the story? What evidence is missing? What assumptions are left unexplained? When a thread claims a "revolution," what measurable behaviour confirms it?

Influencers themselves exist along a spectrum. Some are diligent curators of technical research. Others are entertainers. Many sit between these poles, blending education with speculation. The task is not to reject influence but to recognise its structure. Influence is a form of power. And like any power, it demands scrutiny proportional to its reach.

The unresolved tension remains. A new thread appears. A new voice gains prominence. Metrics surge. The signal is loud, seductive, and widely repeated. The question that matters is deceptively simple: when the next narrative engine starts to hum, will you follow the noise—or trace the signal back to its source?

Social Dynamics of Online Tribes

On 8 May 2021, at the height of the meme-coin frenzy that swept through Binance Smart Chain, the Telegram group for SafeMoon surged past one million members. At its peak that evening, according to Telegram's public channel statistics, more than 120,000 users were simultaneously online—posting emojis, sharing price screenshots, chanting slogans, and warning "paper hands" not to betray the movement. Hours later, after the first steep drawdown, the tone shifted. Skeptical voices were drowned out, then banned. Critics were labelled traitors. Within weeks, as trading volumes collapsed, the once-vibrant community thinned to a fraction of its size. The warmth remained briefly; the governance strength had never existed. What the episode revealed was not merely the fragility of a speculative asset but the architecture of an online tribe: how quickly it forms, how fiercely it defends itself, and how abruptly it evaporates when the narrative sustaining it fails.

The rise of crypto tribes is not surprising. Digital markets operate at speed, and speed generates uncertainty. Uncertainty, in turn, pushes people towards groups that offer identity, reassurance, and coherence. The paradox is that these groups feel deeply personal, even as they behave structurally like earlier forms of collective enthusiasm—religious revivals, speculative clubs, political factions. The individual believes they are joining a conversation; they are, in fact, entering a social system. And that system carries its own incentives, boundaries, and enforcement mechanisms. The motif of the *circle* captures this neatly: a circle invites you in, encloses you, and then subtly shapes how you see the world outside it.

Show how belonging forms. In sociologist Howard Becker's *Outsiders* (1963), group identity emerges when insiders reinforce shared norms. The same pattern played out in the Shiba Inu community during October 2021. Name the case: as SHIB's market capitalisation surged past US$30 billion, Discord moderators created tiered identity badges—"Pup," "Wolf," "Alpha"—based on message activity. Explain: these symbols rewarded participation rather than understanding. Implication: the louder the presence, the higher the status. The circle thickened. A user could be influential without ever reading the contract or considering supply mechanics. Belonging became performance.

Outgroup shaming appears wherever belonging intensifies. It is visible in the moment someone raises a sober question—"Who controls the treasury?" "Why is liquidity so thin?"—and is met not with engagement but derision. Show this behaviour. During the rise of Floki Inu in November 2021, analysts who questioned the project's marketing spend reported being flooded with replies labelling them "FUD spreaders." Name: public exchanges on Twitter between 5–12 November 2021. Explain: criticism was reframed as personal hostility, not analytical reasoning. Implication: outgroup shaming safeguarded the tribe's cohesion even as it weakened its epistemic integrity. The circle tightened defensively.

A contrasting example illustrates the limitation. During the early years of Ethereum, roughly 2015–2017, its online communities—Reddit's /r/ethereum, Gitter channels for client development, and early Discord servers—encouraged adversarial debate. Concerns about The DAO exploit were not dismissed; they were dissected. Dissenters were not expelled; they were answered. The culture did not eliminate tribalism, but it modulated it. The circle existed, but it was permeable. Reconciling this difference underscores the principle: tribal identity becomes harmful not when it forms, but when it forbids scrutiny.

The mechanics of these tribes are measurable. One can track message frequency spikes around price events. One can observe moderation patterns: bans accelerating during downturns, silence during governance questions, identical slogans repeated across threads. These behaviours reveal the difference between community warmth and governance strength. Warmth shows up as humour, generosity, and shared enthusiasm. Governance strength shows up as documentation, transparent treasury decisions, and the willingness to confront inconvenient information. The two are often mistaken for each other. They are not the same.

Show this distinction clearly. Name a case: SushiSwap's leadership transition after Chef Nomi returned the funds in September 2020. Explain: though the community was chaotic and emotionally charged, its governance mechanisms—multi-sig adoption, public calls, visible decision-making—held. Implication: governance strength does not require calm; it requires structure. Warmth played a role, but accountability played a larger one. The circle widened to distribute responsibility.

Contrast this with a meme-coin IDO, such as Akita Inu in March 2021. The Telegram chat overflowed with supportive energy. Yet when questions emerged about supply distribution and treasury concentration, no formal mechanism existed to address them. Participation equalled enthusiasm, not oversight. The community dissolved once excitement faded, because excitement was its only binding force. Governance had no spine. The circle collapsed inward.

Identity deepens tribal commitment. Once a user internalises a token as part of their self-image—"I am an Ape," "I am a Link Marine," "I am a Lunatic"—criticism feels personal. Behaviour changes. Users begin to defend charts rather than analyse them. They adopt shared language and symbols. Memes become epistemic shortcuts. In such environments, disagreement appears as betrayal rather than contribution. Social psychology calls this identity fusion. Crypto turns it into a market force.

Outgroup shaming is the second mechanism. It often emerges during moments of fragility. When prices fall or rumours circulate, tribes rally. Not around truth, but around coherence. Show: during TerraUSD's instability in early May 2022, online advocates attacked skeptics, insisting deviations from the peg were "FUD." Name: messages recorded in Terra's official Telegram and Twitter replies between 7–9 May 2022. Explain: outgroup shaming insulated the core narrative against contradictory evidence. Implication: such insulation delayed recognition of collapse, magnifying losses. The circle repelled dissent until external reality overwhelmed internal belief.

The motif of the *circle* returns here. A circle can be protective or suffocating. Its nature depends on permeability. Permeable circles invite critique, dialogue, iteration. Impermeable circles suppress them. The health of a crypto community can often be assessed by a single behaviour: whether a newcomer asking a difficult question is welcomed or ridiculed. This behaviour is more predictive than any tokenomic claim.

A credible counter-example shows how circles can be constructive. The Bitcoin developer community, though often portrayed as dogmatic, has long practised structured debate through Bitcoin Improvement Proposals. Critics such as Eric Lombrozo and Luke Dashjr have regularly challenged prevailing ideas without facing expulsion. The culture may be combative, but it tolerates dissent. The circle is contested, but not closed.

Social warmth can mask institutional weakness. A Discord server buzzing with jokes and GIFs gives the impression of vitality, yet warmth says nothing about the underlying distribution of power. Governance strength emerges from different signals: clear documentation, a public record of votes, multi-sig transparency, identifiable stewards, and defined upgrade pathways. A tribe may feel strong precisely because its structure is weak; people compensate for lack of clarity with emotional cohesion.

Show this in behaviour. When a meme-coin surges, thousands of new users join, post relentlessly, and reinforce each other's perceptions. Name: Dogelon Mars (ELON) saw Discord membership increase fivefold in November 2021 following listings on several exchanges. Explain: enthusiasm created the illusion of organisational momentum. Implication: when listing-driven excitement waned, participation folded. Governance had no continuity. Warmth had no anchor. The circle dissolved.

But people join tribes not because they are irrational, but because tribes meet psychological needs that spreadsheets cannot. They offer reassurance, identity, and the sense of being part of a story bigger than private judgment. That appeal is especially strong in permissionless markets, where uncertainty and complexity overwhelm the individual. In complicated environments, humans seek simplification. Tribes supply it.

This dynamic produces a tension familiar to anyone who has watched a community rise and fall. When a new project launches, its tribe expands rapidly, drawing in individuals who want to contribute meaningfully. Yet as the tribe grows, the cost of dissent rises. Moderators delete uncomfortable messages. Influencers insist that critics "don't get the vision." The project becomes mythologised. And myth resists governance. The circle becomes armour.

The tension deepens when money is involved. Tribal loyalty can become financially self-reinforcing. Holders encourage others to hold because their own position depends on collective belief. This is not always malicious; often it is subconscious. But it makes distinguishing genuine conviction from social momentum extremely difficult.

The unresolved question sits quietly at the centre of the circle. When you encounter a new community—warm, welcoming, witty—how will you measure its strength? By the friendliness of its members, or by the transparency of its governance? When hype surges and the circle tightens, will you feel protected—or will you ask what lies outside its boundary?

Designing Anti-FOMO Habits

On 19 May 2021—"the day of the great liquidation," as crypto forums later called it—Bitcoin plunged nearly 30 per cent in a single afternoon. In London, a software analyst named Ravi watched the chart collapse on his second monitor at work. The noise on Twitter and Telegram was deafening: warnings, memes, rumours of coordinated selling. Ten minutes later, as the price appeared to stabilise, messages reversed tone. Influencers declared the dip "historic," urging followers to "buy with conviction." Ravi had never purchased Bitcoin before. Yet within seventeen minutes—he checked the timestamp later—he transferred £8,500 into an exchange wallet and hit "Buy." By evening, the market had lapsed into another downward spiral. The speed of his decision startled him more than the loss. "I didn't think," he said later. "I reacted." The episode became his personal case study in FOMO: a decision compressed into a moment, shaped by noise, and untempered by any deliberate pause.

The paradox of permissionless markets is that they compress opportunity and risk into the same narrow corridor. The absence of intermediaries makes acting easy—too easy. Ease, in turn, magnifies emotional impulses. What looks like urgency often disguises anxiety; what feels like confidence often masks imitation. In markets where prices move by the second and narratives shift by the hour, the mind defaults to shortcuts. It is not a sign of weakness; it is a predictable response to velocity. And because the system introduces no natural friction, individuals must design friction for themselves. The motif of the *brake* captures this necessity: a brake slows without stopping, preserves direction while controlling pace, and prevents momentum from becoming catastrophe.

Show how FOMO operates behaviourally. Name a case: during the Binance Smart Chain mania of early 2021, the token SafeMars experienced a surge in purchases immediately after a promotional tweet went viral on 22 April 2021. Explain: analytics recorded clusters of buy orders executed within ten seconds of the tweet. Implication: investors were not responding to fundamentals—they were responding to each other, mirroring behaviour with almost mechanical speed. The absence of a brake allowed the pulse of the crowd to override individual judgement.

Another example sharpens this pattern. When Coinbase listed Bitcoin Cash on 19 December 2017, trading volumes spiked so sharply that the exchange temporarily paused activity. Many retail traders acted within minutes, some within seconds, of seeing the headline. Later analysis published by Bitwise (2018) showed large numbers of buy orders placed before traders had time to inspect liquidity depth or order-book anomalies. The behaviour was not irrational; it was unbuffered. The brake was absent. Momentum filled the vacuum.

Yet a counter-example shows that speed need not dominate. During the Arbitrum airdrop in March 2023, some communities implemented informal "check-in" rules: members agreed to wait thirty minutes after claim windows opened before making any transfer or trade. The result, observable in on-chain data, was a smoother distribution of activity, lower slippage, and fewer accidental self-revokes or scam interactions. Here, the brake existed—culturally rather than technically—and the outcome was stability amid frenzy. Reconciling this illustrates the principle: anti-FOMO habits are not constraints; they are design decisions that protect cognition.

Checklist gates provide the first structural brake. A checklist gate is not a ritual. It is a minimum threshold of self-questioning that must be completed before any action. Show the behaviour: opening the project's documentation; identifying the contract address; checking the audit status; scanning for treasury transparency; verifying the team's stated claims against public repositories. Name a case: when Aave launched v2 in December 2020, many early participants explicitly reviewed the changelog before interacting. Explain: decision-making slowed just enough to filter out noise. Implication: structured friction replaced reflex. The brake engaged.

Position sizing caps provide the second brake. The abstraction of "risk management" becomes real only when tied to concrete behaviour: limiting any single commitment to a pre-set percentage of liquid capital. Show the pattern: during the Curve Wars of 2021, experienced participants rarely committed more than single-digit percentages of their stablecoin holdings to new bribe markets. Name: behaviour documented in Ethereum governance forums throughout June–October 2021. Explain: capping commitment prevented any single emotional surge from turning into disproportionate exposure. Implication: the brake moderates magnitude, not curiosity.

Staggered entries form the third brake. Instead of acting once—and entirely—an individual divides action across time. This technique turns impulsive decisions into sequenced decisions. It leaves room for new information to appear. Show: during the token launch of Optimism in May 2022, blockchain analytics firms such as Nansen observed staggered purchases outperforming single-entry trades, particularly during volatility peaks. Name the observation: Nansen Research Note, June 2022. Explain: staggered behaviour acts like an internal audit of one's own impulses. Implication: the brake introduces elasticity. One can still enter—but not all at once, not blindly, not irreversibly.

The motif of the *brake* returns when examining why friction works. A brake creates a micro-interval between signal and response. In that interval, emotion loses its monopoly. The individual regains sovereignty over the decision. The interval is not long. It might be minutes, or an hour, or a day. But within that space, the cognitive fog of FOMO dissipates just enough for clarity to reappear. The brake is a design choice that restores agency.

To design effective anti-FOMO habits, one must map the habits that currently enable FOMO. Show the enabling behaviours: checking prices repeatedly, monitoring influencer feeds, reacting to notifications, joining new chats impulsively. Name a concrete behaviour: looking at a token chart more than five times an hour during volatility spikes. Explain: these micro-actions elevate anxiety and distort probability perception. Implication: anti-FOMO design begins not with rules, but with observation. The brake must fit the behaviour it aims to slow.

A limitation must be acknowledged. Excessive friction can suppress legitimate curiosity. Show: during the early stages of the Ethereum

Name Service (ENS) ecosystem in 2021, some individuals who imposed strict "no new projects" rules missed generative opportunities simply because they treated all novelty as noise. Name the period: ENS airdrop and governance expansion, November 2021. Explain: when friction becomes prohibition, it can hinder rather than protect. Implication: the brake must be adjustable. Not every speed demands the same pressure.

This introduces a deeper point: anti-FOMO habits are personal architecture. They cannot be copied wholesale from others. They must be designed with one's psychological tendencies in mind. Someone prone to urgency may require time-based frictions. Someone prone to overconfidence may require position limits. Someone intimidated by jargon may require explanation-based frictions—forcing themselves to articulate the mechanism in plain language before acting. The brake must fit the wheel.

Communities can reinforce these habits. In some circles of the Cosmos ecosystem in 2022, participants encouraged each other to pause before delegating to new validators, asking for uptime histories, commission records, and governance participation before committing. The behaviour was visible: delegation patterns slowed and clustered around validators with track records instead of hype. This cultural brake reduced the risk of concentration in untested nodes.

But the final brake is the simplest: writing before acting. The act of documenting the reason for a decision forces clarity. Even a brief sentence—"I am entering because X, and I will exit if Y"—creates a record that one must later face. Show the behaviour: scribbling the rationale in a notes app, timestamped. Explain: writing externalises the impulse, making it visible and challengeable. Implication: the brake becomes cognitive, not just procedural.

The unresolved tension sits quietly at the edge of every opportunity. When the next surge begins—when prices climb sharply, when narratives shift, when feeds overflow with urgency—what form will your brake take? Will you recognise the moment when speed begins to think for you, or will that moment pass before the brake engages?

Chapter 3
Signals of Real Innovation

In a modest office above a shipping warehouse in Singapore, a logistics firm spent months wrestling with a stubborn bottleneck. Cross-border settlements between its South-East Asian partners routinely took three to five days; a single mismatch in customs data could delay dozens of containers. In late 2020 the firm began experimenting with a narrow blockchain pilot—not the kind that appeared in glossy conference decks, but a stripped-down settlement rail linking only four counterparties with a single purpose: reduce reconciliation delays. There were no grand promises of revolution. No token launch. No breathless talk of Web3 transformation. Yet within weeks, the settlement cycle shrank from days to hours. The chief operations officer described the shift as "the first thing that actually felt like a painkiller." It solved a problem so chronic that the technology became almost invisible: it simply worked. That tiny experiment stands in stark contrast to other projects launched that same year with cinematic flair—tokens that soared before they shipped, roadmaps shaped by marketing rather than engineering, and designs that offered vitamins where only painkillers mattered. In crypto, novelty is abundant; necessity is rare. Yet necessity is the terrain where real innovation grows. And it is often quieter than the noise surrounding it. A breakthrough seldom announces itself with fireworks. More often it appears as a subtle inflection: faster reconciliation, fewer errors, reduced trust requirements. The paradox is that the most important signals of innovation are not loud at all. They whisper.

This chapter explores those whispers. In a market overflowing with grand narratives, distinguishing genuine step-changes from cosmetic tweaks requires a different kind of listening—one that privileges bottlenecks over branding, reproducibility over spectacle, and learning loops over price charts. Builders who reshape the frontier do not merely proclaim potential; they demonstrate it, expose it to adversarial tests, and accept the scrutiny of those determined to break it. Their confidence is not theatrical. It is empirical. They know that ideas which survive attack become stronger, and that systems worth trusting must first be stress-tested by strangers.

The motif of the *pulse* threads through this landscape. Not the emotional pulse that drives speculative mania, but the operational pulse of a system: how often it iterates, how quickly issues surface, how rapidly fixes deploy, how transparently trade-offs are communicated. A project with a steady pulse—weekly changelogs, consistent testnet upgrades, auditable repositories—signals resilience. One whose pulse flickers or disappears suggests fragility masked as progress. The tempo of iteration matters more than the noise of promotion.

Real innovation starts with a wound. It solves something concrete, painful, and measurable. A cross-border settlement delay. An oracle inconsistency. A liquidity fragmentation. A governance deadlock. Painkillers attack friction; vitamins decorate. History offers countless examples of this distinction. When Satoshi Nakamoto published the Bitcoin whitepaper in 2008, the proposal addressed a very specific wound: how to enable peer-to-peer value transfer without a trusted intermediary. It did not promise to "reimagine finance" or "tokenise everything." It described a pain and a pathway. That clarity is still its greatest innovation. In crypto, the closer a proposal sits to a painful bottleneck, the stronger its claim to originality.

This chapter introduces a problem-first mindset—not a checklist in the bureaucratic sense, but a disciplined suspicion of solutions that emerge before the problem they claim to fix. Many projects reverse the order. They build architectures seeking justification, not the other way around. Innovation requires the opposite: identify the bottleneck, prove its relevance, and map the smallest possible intervention that can relieve it. Only then does the technology become meaningful. Painkillers before vitamins.

Once a problem is clearly defined, the next signal appears: openness. Serious builders operate in the light. They publish code repositories even when imperfect. They run public testnets that invite chaos. They sponsor bug bounties large enough to hurt if exploited. They encourage adversarial audits. These acts of openness are not altruistic; they are strategic. Reproducibility forces accountability. It prevents teams from hiding behind abstractions. When a system's inner workings can be inspected, cloned, criticised, and improved by outsiders, innovation becomes a communal engine, not a monologue.

This openness also exposes the difference between genuine innovation and what might be called narrative engineering. Many projects claim breakthroughs that vanish the moment they face scrutiny. A "new consensus mechanism" that turns out to be a rebranded tweak of validator thresholds. A "revolutionary scaling solution" that collapses under testnet load. A "community-governed treasury" whose votes are controlled by a handful of insiders. Rigorous builders know that credibility grows through confrontation, not choreography.

Economic flywheels form the third signal. A flywheel is not a metaphor; it is a mechanism. It describes a system in which each user action—trading, validating, contributing, building—creates value that improves the system's performance for the next user. Real flywheels are sustainable because they rely on endogenous value, not perpetual injections of new capital. Fee rebates that support genuine usage are a flywheel. Emissions that bribe superficial liquidity are not. Flywheels reveal themselves through behaviour, not branding: active cohorts that return, costs that fall as scale increases, user actions that reinforce system strength without subsidy.

The crypto market has seen both kinds. In 2020–2021, some DeFi protocols ballooned their Total Value Locked (TVL) through emissions alone. When incentives tapered, liquidity evaporated within days. There was no flywheel—only a treadmill of rewards. By contrast, systems like Uniswap or MakerDAO built structures where usage drove revenue, which funded further improvements, which encouraged more usage. These quiet feedback loops remain among the strongest signals of innovation because they reward value creation, not capital influx.

The fourth signal—latency to product-market fit—captures the tempo at which a team learns. Not how fast it builds, but how fast it adjusts. Iteration speed is the rhythm of innovation. It shows in weekly changelogs, open post-mortems, and public debates about trade-offs. Teams with short learning cycles treat the market as a laboratory. They push small updates, measure effects, and refine relentlessly. They are not paralysed by perfectionism, nor seduced by superficial metrics like token price. They care about adoption curves, retention cohorts, and the shape of real usage.

What matters is not the number of features shipped but the insight density of each release. A team that can identify errors early, patch vulnerabilities quickly, and communicate decisions transparently builds trust through competence. A team that disappears for months and returns with staged theatrics invites questions, not confidence. The market often rewards the latter in the short term—but history seldom does.

Across these signals—painkiller relevance, open scrutiny, economic flywheels, and iteration speed—a deeper pattern emerges. Innovation, in its truest form, is never a single event. It is a pathway. It evolves through confrontation with reality. It adapts to constraints. It survives scepticism. And it remains grounded in the quiet discipline of solving problems that actually matter.

The motif of the *pulse* returns in this closing movement. When you look at a project—its documentation, its updates, its repository, its community—you can sense its pulse. Some pulses throb with borrowed excitement, the manufactured rhythm of marketing cycles. Others beat steadily, consistently, almost modestly, powered by engineering progress and real usage.

As you turn the page into the substance of this chapter, one question lingers, quiet but insistent: when confronted with competing narratives—one loud, one quiet—which pulse will you learn to trust?

Painkiller, Not Vitamin

In October 2020, a mid-sized logistics company based in Singapore—Pacific Integrated Freight—completed the first phase of a blockchain pilot linking its settlement desk with three long-standing partners in Johor Bahru and Batam. For years, their cross-border settlements dragged on for three to five days, often delayed by mismatched customs records or disputed invoices. On 14 October, after a fortnight of testing, the pilot closed its first live cycle: settlement time fell from ninety-six hours to eight. Errors dropped sharply. A process that had been a persistent operational wound—expensive, tedious, and morale-sapping—became almost unremarkable. The COO, normally cautious in her language, described the shift as "relief you can feel in your shoulders." No token sale. No marketing push. Just a painkiller administered where the pain was real.

That episode stands as a small but telling demonstration of what genuine innovation looks like in crypto: a direct assault on chronic friction. The market often lionises projects with ornate branding and speculative momentum, yet the practical breakthroughs—the ones that endure—tend to begin in rooms like that settlement office, not on conference stages. They fix bottlenecks before they chase aesthetics. They focus on stubborn constraints rather than imagined futures. The motif of the *wound* threads through this terrain: a wound forces clarity; it reveals necessity; it exposes where improvement would matter most.

Show the dynamic. Name a second case: when Uniswap launched its automated market maker model in November 2018, the mechanism addressed a specific wound—fragmented liquidity that made long-tail token trading prohibitively difficult. Explain: rather than invent a grand new vision of finance, Uniswap offered a simple, predictable curve that solved a real inefficiency for a real population of users. Implication: innovation was inseparable from the pain it treated. The protocol succeeded because it alleviated a burden, not because it dazzled with novelty.

Real innovation starts with the wound, not the solution. Yet crypto often reverses this sequence. Teams design architectures before identifying a problem. They promise revolutions without describing who struggles, at what step, and under what constraints. To counter this tendency, a problem-first worksheet becomes indispensable. It is not a bureaucratic exercise or a hobbyist's checklist; it is a structured interrogation of necessity. Who hurts? How often? What does that pain cost—time, money, reputation? Which dependencies exacerbate it? What outcomes would meaningfully change behaviour? The worksheet forces specificity. Without specificity, innovation is decorative—a vitamin, not a painkiller.

Show the difference through a contrasting example. In March 2021, numerous "next-generation" layer-1 chains proliferated, many promising throughput targets that sounded impressive—50,000 transactions per second, 100,000, sometimes more. Name: promotional decks from projects launched at the Dubai Blockchain Week that month. Explain: these chains addressed a hypothetical wound ("future congestion") rather than the real bottlenecks then faced by users—wallet complexity, asset volatility, unreliable bridges. Implication: their promised benefits failed to translate into meaningful adoption. The wound they treated was speculative, not lived.

Yet a counter-example tempers this argument. Polygon's early adoption in 2021 was not driven by a dramatic new architecture but by ease of onboarding and lower fees—problems that mattered urgently to a growing NFT and gaming community. What Polygon solved was not glamorous. It simply reduced friction. Reconciling this example reinforces the principle: innovation does not require technical grandiosity; it requires relevance. A small fix applied to a real wound outperforms a vast imagined cure.

Throughout these cases, the motif of the *wound* recurs. A wound has texture: delays, costs, user complaints, audit discrepancies, liquidity gaps. These textures can be measured. In the Singapore logistics pilot, the wound measured ninety-six hours; the painkiller measured eight. In Uniswap's early days, the wound measured in slippage; the painkiller measured in predictable pricing curves. In Polygon's rise, the wound measured in transaction fees; the painkiller measured in pennies. When a project cannot describe the wound it treats with this level of concreteness, its claim to innovation weakens.

Painkillers also reveal themselves through adoption patterns. Users integrate them not because they are new, but because they are necessary. In late 2020, Aave's flash loans became a critical tool for arbitrageurs and risk managers. Pain addressed: the inability to execute capital-intensive positions without collateral. Behaviour showed the relief: surging flash loan volume, measurable within days of launch. The mechanism became an infrastructural component of DeFi because it solved an operational wound, not because it captured a narrative.

Consider the implications of a wound-first approach on builders. When a team begins with the pain rather than the technology, decision-making sharpens. Design trade-offs become clearer. Superfluous features fall away. Communication with users becomes more grounded, because the conversation centres on real constraints. A project that solves an urgent problem builds credibility by necessity. It does not need to manufacture momentum. Its value proposition is embodied rather than advertised.

Show the reverse dynamic: projects that ignore wounds must inflate expectations to compensate. Name: the wave of algorithmic stablecoins that surged during late 2021—Iron Finance, Basis Cash, Empty Set Dollar. Explain: these systems addressed little genuine demand; instead, they relied on speculative cycles to justify their own existence. Implication: when market sentiment cooled, their foundations dissolved. The wound they claimed to treat—"stable value for decentralised economies"—was too abstract compared with the volatility and liquidity constraints actual users faced.

A limitation must be acknowledged. Some innovations begin as vitamins—non-essential, exploratory—and later evolve into painkillers. The early NFT boom in 2017 and 2020, for instance, seemed frivolous to many observers. Yet for digital artists lacking viable distribution channels, NFTs addressed a serious constraint: monetisation without intermediaries. What appeared decorative at first revealed itself as a wound treatment for a specific creative class. Reconciling this illustrates that vitamins sometimes become painkillers, but only when real pain is eventually articulated and addressed.

To apply the problem-first approach effectively, one must conduct a disciplined mapping of friction. Pain has markers. It shows in repeated user behaviours: manual workarounds, reliance on spreadsheets, high churn rates, abandoned carts, fragmented liquidity, backlogged support requests. Each marker becomes a data point. The most meaningful innovations cluster around these data points. They do not begin with abstract ambition; they begin with the mundane.

The motif of the *wound* appears again when examining governance. A DAO struggling with voter apathy does not need a flashy interface; it needs mechanisms that lower participation friction. Snapshot's rise in 2021 illustrated this point: off-chain voting removed gas costs, addressing a governance wound that had impeded smaller holders. The innovation lay not in spectacle but in sensitivity to pain.

The same holds for cross-chain infrastructure. In 2022, numerous bridges boasted theoretical security enhancements, yet users continued to rely on a handful of options because they solved the practical wound—predictable settlement, clear fee structures, transparent documentation. Projects that treated the wound earned trust. Projects that sold vitamins earned attention, briefly.

What emerges from these examples is a disciplined method for separating signal from noise. To see innovation clearly, one must begin with empathy for the user's pain—quantified, described, and contextualised. Only then can the technical pathway be meaningfully evaluated.

And so the unresolved question remains: when confronted with a new protocol or platform—polished, ambitious, loudly endorsed—will you trace its claims back to a measurable wound, or will the gloss of novelty speak first?

Open Scrutiny and Reproducibility

On 14 September 2020, a white-hat hacker disclosed a critical vulnerability in the Ethereum-based protocol dForce. The bug, identified on GitHub and verified within hours by independent developers in Beijing, London, and Berlin, allowed attackers to drain funds from one of the protocol's lending markets. dForce responded by pausing the contract and awarding the researcher a top-tier bounty. What mattered most was not the flaw itself—bugs appear in every complex system—but the visibility of the process. The vulnerability was found in public. The fix was debated in public. The reward was documented in public. The protocol survived because it had chosen life inside the open—*a glass box rather than a black one.*

That case captures the essence of real innovation in crypto: serious builders invite scrutiny, not praise. They understand that systems dealing with real value must withstand attack, replication, and scepticism. They know that the only way to earn trust is to make trust optional. And they know that obscurity is not a defence; it is a liability. The motif of the *glass box* will follow us through this chapter, because transparent systems behave differently from opaque ones. A glass box exposes its wiring. An opaque box hides its assumptions. When the box breaks, one learns which design philosophy mattered.

Show how the glass box shapes behaviour. Name a second case: when Uniswap released its v3 source code in March 2021 under a Business Source Licence, critics worried that the delayed open-source window weakened decentralisation. Yet despite the licence terms, the repository was public, the logic was inspectable, and adversarial researchers took apart the concentrated liquidity design within days. Explain: genuine reproducibility does not require permissive licences alone; it requires visibility of method. Anyone could examine the math, test scenarios, or simulate liquidity ranges. Implication: scrutiny was not a threat; it was the guarantor of credibility.

Contrast this with an example from May 2022, when the algorithmic stablecoin TerraUSD collapsed. Much of the core mechanism had been described in promotional materials, but the underlying risk assumptions were not detailed in a reproducible way. The so-called "defend the peg" strategies were scattered across forum posts and informal comments rather than formalised specifications. When the system unwound, outside analysts struggled to reconstruct the internal logic. The box was opaque. Without reproducibility, scrutiny arrived too late to be useful.

To state the principle plainly: open scrutiny is not decoration. It is architecture. It determines how a system behaves under stress, how quickly it recovers, and how confidently its users can evaluate its claims. Serious builders operate like engineers publishing blueprints, not illusionists guarding secrets. They assume that if their system cannot withstand public examination, it will not withstand time.

A visible behaviour that reveals this attitude is the maintenance of public repositories. Teams that build in the open leave a trail: commit histories, issue threads, design debates, and test results. Name a concrete case: the Ethereum Foundation's eth2.0-specs repository, which throughout 2019-2021 documented every change to the consensus design, including debates between Danny Ryan, Justin Drake, and peer reviewers. Explain: this level of transparency allowed independent researchers to model attacks long before mainnet launch. Implication: openness created resilience. The glass box earned its trust not through rhetoric but through reproducibility.

Public testnets mark another important signal. They expose systems to chaos. They invite users to break things. Show the impact: when Polygon launched its zkEVM public testnet in October 2022, developers across Europe and Asia attacked performance bottlenecks, filed reproducible bug reports, and submitted optimisation patches. Name the dynamic: adversarial collaboration. Explain: open testing accelerates learning cycles—every attempt to break the system becomes input for strengthening it. Implication: real innovation accelerates in the presence of attack, not the absence of it. The glass box glints under pressure.

Bug-bounty leaderboards embody a similar principle. They record who has broken what, when, and how severely. They are public scoreboards of both failure and professionalism. Show how they function. Immunefi's leaderboard, active throughout 2021-2023, lists white-hat researchers who have prevented hundreds of millions in losses. Name: Immunefi reports from December 2021 and August 2022. Explain: when a project advertises that it has paid significant bounties, it signals that its vulnerabilities were not avoided—they were found, reported, and fixed. Implication: a project with no bounties does not look strong; it looks untested. The glass box does not pretend to be flawless; it demonstrates a willingness to be improved.

A credible counter-example complicates this narrative. Some high-assurance systems—particularly in privacy tech—must limit certain disclosures to prevent deanonymisation risks. During the early life of Zcash (2016-2018), for instance, portions of the cryptographic ceremony were kept confidential to protect participants' identities.

Explain: privacy protocols face structural limits on total openness. Implication: transparency must be balanced with safety. Reconciling this highlights a deeper truth: open scrutiny need not mean total exposure; it means exposing what *must* be inspectable—logic, assumptions, cryptographic proofs—while protecting what would undermine user safety. The glass box may have shaded panels, but it is not sealed shut.

Reproducibility is the second pillar of this subchapter. A system that cannot be reassembled by outsiders cannot be trusted by them. Reproducibility means that an independent developer can clone the repository, deploy a local version, run tests, and arrive at roughly the same results. Show an example: when StarkWare introduced Cairo in 2020, developers from Nethermind and LambdaClass reproduced the VM's behaviour independently, validating its constraints through separate implementations. Name the phenomenon: multi-client verification. Explain: independent builds reveal ambiguities in specifications and force clear articulation of assumptions. Implication: reproducibility distributes verification across many minds, reducing single points of interpretive failure.

Opaque projects fail this test spectacularly. Consider the many "proprietary" consensus mechanisms announced during 2021 and 2022—mechanisms described in marketing decks but absent from code. Without published specifications, they could not be modelled, stress-tested, or replicated. Investors were forced to rely on trust rather than inspection. When outages occurred—as with several new chains during high-load events in 2022—it was nearly impossible for outsiders to trace root causes. The glass box had been replaced with a velvet curtain.

The *glass box* motif returns here because reproducibility is the ultimate test of that metaphor. A glass box allows you to see not only the parts but how the parts interact. More importantly, it allows you to rebuild the box elsewhere, test it under new conditions, verify its consistency, and discover whether its promises survive outside its native environment. Reproducibility is the difference between a scientific experiment and a stage trick. A trick cannot be replicated; a theory must be. Innovation belongs to the second category or it does not belong at all.

Open scrutiny also transforms power dynamics. Opaque systems concentrate authority in the hands of insiders; transparent ones distribute it among participants. When source code is public, governance cannot hide behind mystique. When testnets are open, performance claims must match reality. When audits are adversarial, incentives align around accuracy rather than reputation. This redistribution of authority shifts the conversation from *who says this will work* to *what evidence shows this works*. Serious builders welcome this shift because they understand that credibility rooted in inspection is sturdier than credibility rooted in charisma.

One more example underscores the point. In April 2023, Optimism published a post-mortem detailing a sequencer outage. The report included timestamps, logs, architectural explanations, and forward-looking mitigation steps. Independent analysts reproduced the failure conditions in sandbox environments. Name: Optimism post-mortem, 10 April 2023. Explain: such radical transparency converts a failure into a strengthening event. Implication: the glass box shines most brightly when cracked and repaired in view of those who rely on it.

Yet the tension remains. Full openness slows some teams. It invites criticism. It exposes mistakes. It can even erode short-term competitive advantages. But the deeper question is never about comfort; it is about durability. Systems that resist attack will earn trust. Systems that fear being seen will not.

And so the unresolved challenge endures: when you encounter a new protocol—polished website, ambitious roadmap, assertive founders—will you look for the glass box? Will you search for the repository, the testnet logs, the audit discussions, the bug-bounty history? Or will the performance of confidence overpower the evidence of scrutiny?

Economic Flywheels

On 15 September 2020, during a period of unusually high activity on decentralised exchanges, Curve Finance published an internal metric that caught the attention of developers across London, Zurich, and

Singapore: over 40 per cent of trading volume that week came from repeat users rather than first-time speculators. The figure itself mattered less than the pattern it revealed. Repeat usage suggested more than opportunism; it signalled a feedback loop, a quiet engine beneath the noise. Lower slippage attracted traders; traders generated fees; fees rewarded liquidity providers; deeper liquidity reduced slippage further. The loop tightened, then reinforced itself. No marketing campaign could manufacture that cycle. It had to emerge from the structure of the system.

The paradox at the centre of crypto economics is simple: many protocols claim to run on flywheels, but few actually do. Real flywheels behave like that Curve pattern—slow to start, demanding in their design, indifferent to hype. Fake flywheels behave like carnival rides: they spin only when someone pays to keep the machine moving. The motif of the *wheel* will guide this subchapter, because a wheel either turns under its own weight or ceases to be a wheel at all.

Show the mechanics. Name a second case: when Uniswap launched its v3 fee tiers in May 2021, the architecture created a new dynamic in the automated market maker landscape. Concentrated liquidity allowed providers to commit capital narrowly, raising capital efficiency. Explain: higher efficiency attracted market makers; tighter spreads encouraged more trading; more trading increased fee generation; robust fees made the liquidity positions viable despite active management costs. Implication: the behaviour displayed an unmistakable wheel—every turn strengthened the next.

Now contrast this with a less flattering example: the wave of high-emission liquidity mining schemes that proliferated in 2021, particularly on newly launched chains clustered around Dubai, Zug, and San Francisco incubators. Protocols showered early users with tokens to inflate total value locked (TVL). The numbers grew, briefly. But the loop was artificial. Once emissions tapered, liquidity fled. Explain the dynamic. Rather than a wheel, these systems resembled a conveyor belt—moving value as long as fresh tokens arrived, grinding to a halt when incentives thinned. Implication: if a system requires constant new money or constant new tokens to preserve the illusion of activity, it does not contain a flywheel; it contains a drain.

A credible counter-example must complicate this argument. MakerDAO's early stability fee reductions in 2019 temporarily stimulated borrowing demand by lowering costs, a form of policy intervention. Yet the growth that followed was not manufactured—it was anchored in real demand for DAI as a trading and hedging asset. Reconciling this case emphasises the nuance: external incentives can support an early-stage flywheel, but they cannot substitute for it. The wheel must eventually carry itself.

To understand genuine flywheels, one must look closely at visible behaviours, not abstract claims. When users return without bribes, that is evidence. When liquidity providers maintain positions because the fee income justifies the risk, that is evidence. When builders publish weekly changelogs because rapid iteration sharpens the product, that is evidence. These behaviours expose the health of the wheel more reliably than any headline TVL figure.

Show the pattern again. Name: the rise of GMX on Arbitrum in late 2021. Its fee distribution model—traders paid fees that were shared with liquidity providers—created a closed economic loop that aligned risks and rewards. Explain: as usage increased, fee flows rose; strong fee flows attracted deeper GLP liquidity; deeper liquidity supported larger trades; larger trades generated more fees. Implication: the wheel rotated because each actor's behaviour reinforced the next. No external top-up was required.

At the heart of this analysis sits a distinction so often blurred in marketing materials that it must be stated plainly: sustainable flywheels produce *value* before they distribute rewards. Unsustainable ones distribute rewards before they produce anything. That sequence determines fate. Systems in the first category survive shocks; systems in the second collapse the moment sentiment cools.

The motif of the wheel returns when examining governance. A protocol with transparent, predictable processes can strengthen its own economic engine. Show the mechanism: when Aave implemented the safety module in 2020, stakers absorbed risk during shortfalls. Explain: this absorption capability increased trust in the lending markets; greater trust increased deposit volume; larger deposits improved liquidity depth; and deeper liquidity encouraged more borrowing demand. Implication: good governance can form part of the wheel, turning institutional behaviour into part of the feedback loop.

But the inverse is equally revealing. Where governance is weak, the wheel seizes. In several 2022 cases—documented across multiple DAO forums—delayed votes led to stalled upgrades, which reduced user confidence, which lowered activity, which reduced treasury revenue, which further limited capacity for improvement. Show. Name. Explain. Implication. A stalled wheel degenerates into inertia.

Public metrics make these patterns visible. Fee revenue, repeat address interactions, time-weighted liquidity depth, code commit frequency—each forms a spoke in the wheel. No single metric tells the full story, but together they reveal whether a protocol is gaining stability or losing it. The key is to observe direction over time: whether each turn reduces friction or amplifies it.

Another example strengthens the point. When Optimism shifted to its "Superchain" vision in mid-2023, the team emphasised shared sequencing revenue and cross-chain interoperability. Show: early partner chains deployed OP Stack variations in testnets across the US and South Korea. Explain: each new chain generated more potential network effects, turning shared infrastructure into a value amplifier. Implication: flywheels also operate at ecosystem scale, not just protocol scale. The wheel widens, not just spins.

Yet limitations exist. Not every system with strong metrics sustains a flywheel. Consider the rapid rise and slowdown of several NFT marketplaces during late 2021. Activity initially surged because of speculative fervour, not structural reinforcement. Once fees, royalties, and wash-trading filters tightened, genuine usage patterns emerged—and many marketplaces showed little organic strength. The lesson is subtle but vital: a wheel pushed by noise may spin briefly, but it reveals its nature only when the pushing stops.

What distinguishes the few authentic flywheels is not their initial speed but their response to pressure. When fees fall, do users stay? When incentives fade, does participation persist? When a competitor launches, does liquidity hold? These are behavioural tests, not theoretical ones. They require measurement: retention curves, liquidity stickiness, time-to-recovery after downtime, feature-level adoption. Flywheels are empirical objects. Their existence is observable. Their breakdown is, too.

The wheel motif sharpens again when considering the darker side of economic loops. Pyramid-like schemes—in crypto or elsewhere—also produce circular reinforcement, but the loop depends entirely on inflow. Nothing the system does reduces future friction. Nothing the user contributes improves capability. The loop turns only as long as people step in. Once they hesitate, gravity wins. The wheel falls.

Sustainable systems flip that script. Every marginal user improves the experience for the next. Every deployer who adds liquidity reduces risk for future participants. Every developer who contributes code strengthens safety. These systems build momentum through function, not through spectacle.

Yet even genuine flywheels face a strategic tension. As they grow, they attract adversaries—competitors, attackers, governance opportunists. The wheel must then be defended with rigour: audits, stress tests, treasury discipline, and cautious expansion. Momentum does not excuse fragility. The real test of a flywheel is whether the system improves under stress or fractures.

The tension that ends this subchapter is therefore unavoidable: when confronted with a protocol promising exponential growth, will you observe whether the wheel turns by itself, or will you rely on the confidence of those who claim it does?

Latency to Product–Market Fit

On 7 April 2016, in a rented office above a bakery in Lausanne, the small team behind Liquidity Network pushed a commit that changed the structure of their off-chain routing algorithm. The change looked trivial—just thirty-four lines—but it halved the average settlement time in their test environment from 420 milliseconds to 210. Two days later, another commit reduced memory allocation by nearly a third. A week after that, a redesign of their failure-handling logic cut error rates by 60 per cent. None of these changes generated headlines, yet within three months the team had transformed a brittle prototype into a viable payment layer capable of supporting real users in Zurich cafés and university labs. The shift was not the product of a single breakthrough. It was the product of relentless iteration—what one engineer called "the discipline of shortening the distance between wrong and less wrong." One line changes everything.

The scene matters because it exposes a truth that crypto often hides beneath spectacle: the speed at which a team learns is frequently more revealing than the elegance of its initial design. *Latency*—the delay between action and feedback—is the silent force shaping whether a protocol discovers product–market fit or drifts into irrelevance. The motif of the *clock* threads through this subchapter because every system, every decision, every experiment lives under the pressure of time. A fast clock sharpens judgement; a slow clock sedates it.

Show the dynamic. Name a second case: in late 2020, the team at Yearn Finance led by Andre Cronje released a series of "yVault" updates at a pace that startled outside observers—multiple improvements deployed weekly between September and December. Explain: each iteration incorporated real user behaviour, real risk events, and real strategy failures. Implication: Yearn did not arrive at product–market fit through foresight; it stumbled toward it by compressing learning cycles so tightly that mistakes became nutrients rather than threats. The clock was used, not feared.

Contrast this with a slower-moving story: in 2022, several cross-chain bridge projects launched with ambitious architectures but extremely long iteration cycles. Issues discovered by auditors or users took weeks, sometimes months, to resolve. Explain the consequence. Latency weakened trust. Weak trust slowed adoption. Slower adoption reduced real-world testing, further increasing latency. Implication: even promising designs wither when the clock is ignored. A protocol can have exceptional engineering talent yet still fail if it cannot tighten the loop between detection and adjustment.

Still, a limitation tempers the argument. Some categories of innovation—especially those involving novel cryptography—require longer verification windows. ZK-proof systems built by StarkWare and Zcash's research team during 2017–2021 underwent extensive peer review because premature deployment carried catastrophic risk. Reconciling this example reveals nuance: iteration speed is not measured by frequency alone but by appropriateness. It is the *ratio* between risk and revision that matters. The clock ticks differently in high-assurance domains, yet even there, the ability to shorten feedback loops within safe bounds remains essential.

The motif of the *clock* reappears when we examine visible behaviours. Teams that target real product–market fit rarely hide behind grand announcements or ornate roadmaps. They publish weekly changelogs showing uncomfortable trade-offs: deprecating features users liked but that created silent liabilities; rewriting modules that were architecturally elegant but operationally fragile; discarding months of work after discovering that a simpler model outperformed it. These behaviours are empirical markers. They show that the team is listening to the world. They show that the system is responding.

Show how this manifests in practice. Name: the Optimism team's decision in March 2023 to re-architect portions of its sequencing pipeline after load-testing in Seoul revealed congestion thresholds lower than expected. Explain: by publishing the test data, revising the code, and redeploying testnets within days, the team shortened the latency between observation and improvement. Implication: iteration speed became a competitive advantage, not an operational detail.

The crypto market, unfortunately, distorts this logic. Prices often move faster than engineering can. A token might double in value long before the underlying product has proven anything. This noise seduces teams into measuring progress by market cycles rather than learning cycles. But price is an echo, not a signal. Iteration speed is the signal. The number of days between discovering a bug and fixing it; between identifying a user need and validating a solution; between proposing a design change and measuring its real-world effects. These are the metrics that reveal whether a protocol is converging toward something people genuinely want.

A compelling example emerges from the StarkNet ecosystem in late 2022. Developers rapidly deployed multiple versions of Cairo, each exposing inefficiencies in constraint systems that were then corrected in subsequent releases. The tight iteration rhythm attracted independent researchers because the system demonstrated a willingness to evolve. Show, name, explain, implication. The clock kept moving. The system kept learning.

Compare this with protocols that rely heavily on marketing-driven releases. A chain might promise quarterly milestones, publish glossy updates, and unveil partnerships, yet fail to ship meaningful improvements. These systems often avoid publishing changelogs because changelogs expose the truth: iteration has stalled. The clock has stopped. And when the clock stops, product–market fit becomes impossible because the world outside continues to change.

The clock motif sharpens again when considering governance. DAOs with slow voting cycles or unclear execution paths lengthen latency. Proposals linger for weeks; upgrades stall; user feedback accumulates with nowhere to go. Show: several DeFi governance forums in 2022 displayed multi-week gaps between identified issues and corrective actions. Name the behaviour: procedural drag. Explain: slow processes reduce the information bandwidth between users and builders. Implication: governance latency becomes product latency.

Two examples of efficient governance counter this stagnation. First, MakerDAO's emergency "circuit breaker" votes during volatility spikes in March 2020 adjusted stability fees within hours. Second, Lido's 2021–2022 rapid validator onboarding process—coordinated across Europe, South America, and Asia—aligned technical deployment with governance decisions in tight cycles. Both cases reveal the same lesson: speed is not a luxury; it is a structural requirement for systems interacting with real users and volatile conditions.

Yet iteration is not only about speed; it is about the quality of feedback. Teams that optimise for fast cycles without meaningful input simply spin the wheel faster, not better. Show: several NFT marketplaces in 2021 launched rapid-feature updates with almost no user testing, resulting in interface confusion and poor retention. Name the limitation: high-frequency noise. Explain: without structured feedback loops—user interviews, telemetry analysis, error tracing—speed becomes self-defeating. Implication: the right question is not "how fast did they ship?" but "how fast did they learn?"

The behaviour of narrowing the gap between learning and action resembles tuning a clock: tighten the calibration, remove slack, reduce drift. System design choices follow the same principle. A well-structured testnet compresses latency by allowing thousands of users to simulate failures. A transparent repository compresses latency by enabling outside contributors to identify issues before they escalate. A modular architecture compresses latency by allowing teams to update isolated components without destabilising the system.

The importance of latency becomes most visible in crises. When a protocol faces unexpected stress—market surges, bridge congestion, smart-contract exploits—the length of the feedback loop determines survival. Show: the rapid response to the Balancer vault bug in June 2020, which contained the issue within hours. Explain: the team's ability to coordinate across public channels, integrate patches, and redeploy contracts reflected years of practised iteration discipline. Implication: crisis reveals latency in its starkest form. A slow learner breaks. A fast learner adapts.

Yet a final tension remains. Some teams mistake slowness for maturity—believing that careful deliberation signals professionalism. Others mistake speed for competence—believing that rapid releases signal innovation. Neither belief is reliable. Latency is contextual. The right tempo depends on the interplay between complexity, risk, and user needs. But the principle endures: the path to product–

market fit narrows sharply when teams cannot close the gap between insight and implementation.

Which leads to the unresolved question that this subchapter leaves open: when assessing a protocol—its claims, its roadmap, its confidence—will you choose to measure the noise of price, or the rhythm of the clock?

Chapter 4
Reading Whitepapers Like a Skeptic

The first time the now-infamous *OneCoin* whitepaper circulated in London in late 2015, it arrived dressed in the authority of formal language and borrowed mathematics. The document cited cryptographic primitives that did not exist, referenced a blockchain that never ran, and promised financial emancipation for millions without naming a single distribution partner, jurisdiction, or technical hurdle. Yet for a surprising stretch of time, its language worked. It worked because it sounded like a whitepaper. It borrowed the cadence of legitimacy, the diagrams of engineering, the vocabulary of cryptography—enough to disarm readers long before they asked the most basic question: *What problem is this project actually solving?* The rise and collapse of OneCoin is not just a historical caution; it is a lens through which to see the persuasive machinery of the crypto whitepaper. It shows how rhetoric can mimic substance, how diagrams can conceal more than they reveal, and how the absence of specifics can masquerade as visionary intent.

A whitepaper is often the first—and sometimes the only—glimpse into a project's inner life. It is meant to be part blueprint, part argument, part invitation. Yet for all its formality, the modern crypto whitepaper is also a performance. It aspires to authority, even when that authority is unearned. It presents architecture even when no builders stand behind it. It gestures toward innovation even when the mechanism has yet to pass a trivial test of coherence. In this sense, reading a whitepaper requires not only technical literacy but psychological vigilance. You are not simply evaluating a document; you are evaluating what the document wants you to believe. And what it wants you to overlook.

This chapter begins with a simple premise: scepticism is not cynicism. Scepticism is a discipline—a way of reading that treats claims as hypotheses, diagrams as arguments, metrics as signals, and language as evidence. The motif that threads through the chapter is that of the *magnifying glass*: a small tool that transforms perception, enlarging what the author would prefer to keep small and clarifying what they might hope will remain vague. A magnifying glass makes the familiar unfamiliar, the impressive mundane, the subtle consequential. It helps you see the whitepaper as it actually is, not as the writers want you to see it.

A whitepaper is strongest or weakest at its origin story. What pain does it address? Whose pain is it? How acute? How quantifiable? These questions are deceptively simple, but their answers distinguish real projects from theatrical ones. A claim such as "bank the unbanked" sounds benevolent, even visionary, but means little without distribution partnerships, regulatory pathways, or evidence of user friction. A claim such as "make finance permissionless" gestures at reimagining institutions yet fails to specify which constraint it intends to remove or how that removal benefits any particular community. When a whitepaper's opening problem statement cannot be traced to a real user in a real situation with a real constraint, the project begins in fiction. And fiction, as we will see, has no product–market fit.

But even when the problem is clear, the architecture that follows often is not. Whitepapers routinely deploy diagrams—boxes, arrows, modules, tiers—that create a sense of structure without revealing responsibility. These diagrams look like engineering blueprints yet often behave like stage props. They hide assumptions about who maintains which components, where those components live geographically, how much they cost to operate, and which dependencies they inherit. A box labelled *oracle* means nothing until it names which oracle feeds it, who controls that oracle, and what happens when the data is wrong. A box labelled *validator* conceals more than it reveals unless the whitepaper details the reorganisation risks, the censorship vectors, the operator incentives, and the operational thresholds beyond which the system buckles. The magnifying glass turns boxes into questions and questions into accountability.

Metrics, too, demand careful interrogation. The crypto industry is rich with numbers—active addresses, TVL, node count, transaction throughput—yet not all numbers measure what they claim to measure. Vanity metrics are those that make a project look alive without demonstrating that it is useful. A surge in active addresses may reflect airdrop farming, not genuine engagement. An increase in

TVL may reflect mercenary capital pursuing emissions, not conviction. The metrics that matter trace a clean line between behaviour and value: retained cohorts, revenue per user, security margin, latency under load, error rates, user survival curves. To read a whitepaper well is to follow one metric from user action to system effect, watching closely for gaps, shortcuts, or leaps of faith.

Language is the final terrain on which scepticism proves essential. Whitepapers often borrow phrases that sound precise—"risk-free yields," "unhackable security," "game-changing scalability"—while hiding their emptiness beneath a veneer of authority. These phrases function the way perfume functions in a too-warm room: an attempt to obscure what is uncomfortable or incomplete. A serious whitepaper does the opposite. It names trade-offs. It states limitations. It describes where the system might fail, how it will behave under stress, and what assumptions it cannot guarantee. It resists absolutism because absolutism invites disappointment. When a whitepaper refuses to engage with discomfort, the magnifying glass reveals the avoidance.

Across the landscape of crypto, the ability to read whitepapers with disciplined scepticism has become a survival skill. Not only because scams exist—though they do—but because ambitious projects routinely ask readers to extend belief before the claims warrant it. They ask readers to assume that technical pathways are executable, that governance structures are workable, that security assumptions are reasonable, that metrics will translate into adoption. And they ask readers to do all this in a domain where few of the usual signals of institutional maturity—regulation, standards bodies, public accountability—exist.

This chapter invites the reader into a different posture. It argues that the whitepaper should serve you, not impress you. It suggests that clarity matters more than ambition, that specificity matters more than flourish, and that evidence matters more than vision. It makes the case that the distance between architecture and execution is the most important distance in all of crypto—and that too many whitepapers ignore it. It explores why the strongest teams welcome scrutiny, why the weakest fear it, and why language often reveals which camp a project belongs to.

By the time you reach the end of the chapter, you will not only recognise red flags—you will understand why they matter. You will know how to interrogate a problem statement, how to translate diagrams into operational responsibilities, how to distinguish meaningful metrics from theatrical ones, and how to decode the linguistic signals that betray insecurity or overconfidence. But for now, a single question hangs in the air—the question the magnifying glass forces you to ask every time you encounter a new document promising to change the world: *What, exactly, have they shown you—and what have they merely suggested?*

What Problem Is Being Solved?

In January 2019, the Kenyan mobile-money provider M-Pesa released a report documenting its failure to scale a much-publicised blockchain remittance pilot launched in Nairobi six months earlier. The pilot promised to "revolutionise cross-border payments for underserved populations", yet usage barely moved. The engineers noted the cause with striking bluntness: the proposed system solved none of the problems that actual users faced. Transfer delays were not the issue; they already settled in minutes. Fees were not the issue; they were lower than the alternatives. The real bottleneck was far less glamorous—agents could run out of local cash, stranding customers who needed physical withdrawals. A system designed to resolve a theoretical pain had ignored the practical one. The whitepaper had dazzled. Reality had not.

This failure is more than an anecdote; it is a recurring pattern in crypto. Too many whitepapers begin with sweeping statements about global transformation—banking the unbanked, democratising finance, disrupting rent-seeking intermediaries—yet cannot point to a single user with a single concrete difficulty that the system is built to relieve. The motif that threads through this subchapter is the *question mark*: a reminder that reading a whitepaper begins not with belief but with interrogation. Without precise questions, every grand claim sounds plausible. With them, most evaporate.

The discipline starts with a four-part drill: *user, pain, constraint, evidence.* Each part exposes something brittle or robust within the document. Each turns the reader's attention from what the whitepaper promises to what it can justify. Together, they form the basic lens through which meaningful innovation distinguishes itself from theatre.

Show the first movement. Name a case: the Stellar Development Foundation's early remittance corridors in 2017 between the Philippines and Japan. The teams documented users with specific needs—migrant workers facing delays and double-charging on cross-border transfers. Explain: the pain was identifiable, the constraint was regulatory bottlenecks around correspondent banking, and the evidence came from transaction logs and survey data. Implication: even when the corridors struggled for adoption, the whitepaper's grounding in real user constraints lent legitimacy and direction. It showed its work.

Now show the contrasting pattern. In 2021, dozens of projects announced intentions to "bank the unbanked" across sub-Saharan Africa. Name: several whitepapers circulated at the Blockchain Africa Conference in Johannesburg. Explain: most failed the first question of the drill. They did not specify which segment of users they targeted—small merchants? rural households? cross-border traders?—and did not quantify the pain beyond poetic language. Implication: without user clarity, innovation becomes guesswork; guesswork becomes risk; risk becomes failure masked as vision.

The second question—*pain*—must be measured. Pain has a frequency, a cost, and a behavioural signal. A user who repeats the same workaround every week is signalling pain. A merchant who loses ten per cent of revenue to reconciliation errors is signalling pain. A developer who maintains a spreadsheet to track liquidity across ten pools is signalling pain. Pain is not a metaphor; it is a metric. Projects that cannot quantify the pain they claim to address are not solving problems—they are auditioning narratives.

The motif of the *question mark* sharpens when confronting constraint. Constraints are the barriers that prevent users solving their own problems. They are rarely glamorous. They may involve compliance thresholds, capital requirements, bandwidth limitations, custody rules, or settlement windows. Show the pattern. Name: the Reserve project's documentation in 2020 outlined specific constraints around high inflation environments in Venezuela—limited access to stable-value assets, unreliable banking infrastructure, and difficulties in custody. Explain: by identifying constraints with precision, the team positioned its solution not as abstract liberation but as a tool within a documented context. Implication: projects that cannot describe the constraints the user faces are not aligned with reality. They are aligned with fantasy.

A counter-example must complicate the story. Some legitimate research-stage projects—particularly in cryptography—solve constraints that users cannot yet articulate, because the use cases are emergent. ZK-SNARK development between 2014 and 2018, led by teams such as Zcash and later StarkWare, targeted future privacy needs rather than present demand. Explain: such cases illustrate that the drill is not a blunt instrument; it requires discernment. For deep-infrastructure work, the "user" may be tomorrow's developer, and the "pain" may be the lack of mathematical tools. Implication: the drill adapts but does not relax. Even research-first projects must articulate who will eventually depend on the work and why.

The fourth question—*evidence*—is where most whitepapers falter. Evidence is not enthusiasm. Evidence is not a market-size estimate. Evidence is not a list of advisors or a partnership that lives only in a press release. Evidence consists of replicable data about existing behaviour or operational frictions. Show this clearly. Name: when Visa published its 2020 report on settlement inefficiencies in cross-border B2B payments, it quantified failure rates, settlement times, and reconciliation discrepancies across specific corridors. Explain: had a crypto project built on those findings, its whitepaper would have shown evidence. Implication: a whitepaper that cannot demonstrate its understanding of the evidence is gambling with credibility.

The *question mark* motif returns not as ornament but as method. Each whitepaper sentence invites its own question: Who exactly is the user? What task are they performing? How often? At what cost? Why now? Why this design? Why cannot existing systems suffice? When authors wave away these specifics, the reader must resist the temptation to supply them. A whitepaper should reveal understanding, not rely on the reader to imagine it.

To deepen this analysis, consider how the drill exposes hidden assumptions. A claim such as "the system reduces friction" becomes hollow unless the author names which friction matters. Is it latency? Settlement risk? Human error? Regulatory review? A claim such as "improves efficiency" carries no meaning until efficiency is measured. Minutes saved? Fees reduced? Transactions reconciled? Volatility absorbed? The drill turns abstract claims into concrete demands. It forces authors to choose, and choice reveals both understanding and integrity.

Show another case. Name: the March 2020 launch paper for Compound's governance token, COMP. It identified specific bottlenecks in decentralised governance—low participation, unclear delegation workflows, and overly centralised admin keys. Explain: the document presented evidence through historical participation data and contract-level constraints. Implication: this clarity gave readers the tools to evaluate whether COMP solved a problem rather than merely introducing a token for its own sake.

Set alongside it a more recent failure: several metaverse-token whitepapers released in late 2021 made sweeping promises about "unlocking digital identity" while never identifying which users needed these identities, what pain they experienced, or why blockchain offered advantages over conventional authentication models. Explain: the absence of the drill's four answers left the documents sounding aspirational rather than operational. Implication: projects that do not answer the drill's questions force readers into a guessing game, and guessing games are where manipulation thrives.

To read such documents effectively, one must also observe what the authors avoid. Evasive language often appears exactly at the point where the drill would demand clarity. Phrases like "designed for global inclusion," "built for scale," or "engineered for resilience" signal nothing unless tied to numbers, users, and constraints. When a whitepaper strings these terms together without anchoring them to evidence, the reader should treat the silence as data.

The drill is more than a reading tool; it is a lens on institutional maturity. Teams that understand their users write differently. They name trade-offs. They describe context. They acknowledge uncertainty. They publish user interviews, testnet logs, operational thresholds. They do not fear the question mark because they have worked through the questions themselves. Teams that lack this foundation hide behind hand-waviness—not from malice, but from vagueness. Lack of clarity in the whitepaper often reflects lack of clarity in the team.

The tension that closes this subchapter arises from a simple observation: every compelling whitepaper introduces a problem, but not every problem is real. Some problems are invented to justify a token. Some are borrowed from unrelated industries to create narrative gravitas. Some are so abstract that they cannot be falsified. The reader must therefore confront a hard question long before evaluating architecture or metrics or roadmaps: *Is the problem actually a problem for someone real—or is it a story designed to sound like one?*

From Architecture to Execution

On 29 August 2020, when the decentralised exchange SushiSwap released its initial documentation, analysts in Seoul, London, and Toronto began tracing what the neatly drawn diagrams concealed. A single box labelled "oracle" masked a dependency on Uniswap's time-weighted average price mechanism, a design that left the protocol vulnerable to manipulation during periods of thin liquidity. Within days, traders exploited precisely that blind spot. The issue was not the diagram itself—it was what the diagram refused to name. It gestured at architecture while obscuring execution. It presented an elegant topology yet failed to specify who operated what, where, and at what operational cost. In the silence between those omissions lay the root of the protocol's instability. The gap between design and deployment, once invisible to casual readers, became a point of failure visible to the entire market. one line changes everything.

This tension—between what a whitepaper sketches and what a system must actually run—sits at the heart of crypto's credibility problem. Architecture is easy to draw. Execution is hard to sustain. A system made of boxes and arrows looks impartial, almost scientific; a system made of servers, contracts, upkeep, operators, sequencers, and fees looks human, fragile, and expensive. The motif that threads through this subchapter is the *wiring*: hidden lines that carry real load, real risk, and real responsibility. The wiring is where truth lives. When a whitepaper refuses to show it, the reader must ask why.

Show how the wiring reveals a system's nature. Name a second case: when Chainlink published its 2019 architecture overview, the diagrams included not just oracles but operator identities, performance metrics, penalties, and costs. Explain: each box corresponded to a deployable component, with clear responsibilities—who ran the node, how data was aggregated, how discrepancies were handled. Implication: the clarity invited scrutiny. Readers could map the diagram to real servers, real incentives, and real attack surfaces. The architecture lived in the world, not on the page.

Contrast this with a typical pattern from 2021, when dozens of launch documents for "next-generation" layer-1 chains included multi-shard diagrams with committees, coordinators, sequencers, and messaging layers—but without naming who operated these components. In several cases, independent researchers later discovered that most of the infrastructure ran on a handful of servers in a single region, often maintained by the core team. Explain: the diagrams created the illusion of distributed architecture while the execution remained centralised. Implication: when wiring is hidden, risk is hidden, and hidden risk eventually presents itself with consequences.

The first major claim is simple: every diagram in a whitepaper must be traceable to something deployable. Show how that looks in practice. A box labelled *validator* should map to identifiable operators running machines in identifiable jurisdictions, with clear hardware requirements, clear incentives, and clear penalties. A box labelled *sequencer* should expose questions about throughput limits, downtime, censorship vectors, and the geographic distribution of nodes. A box labelled *bridge* must show light-client assumptions, verification pathways, and costs per message. When a box maps to nothing but an idea, it is not architecture; it is ornament.

Name another example that illuminates this distinction. In March 2022, the team behind Osmosis (a Cosmos-based DEX) published an upgrade proposal that included diagrams of its new routing engine. Crucially, the diagrams showed which components ran on validators, which lived in smart contracts, and which required external price feeds from Band Protocol. Explain: by drawing the wiring, the team exposed operational dependencies that allowed users and auditors to evaluate failure modes. Implication: transparency at the wiring level improves resilience because it decentralises understanding.

The wiring motif tightens when we turn to *where* components run. Geography matters. Jurisdiction matters. Latency matters. A whitepaper that lists global resilience but deploys all its infrastructure in a single AWS region is not resilient. Show a concrete case: during the Solana outages of January 2022, independent analyses tracked validator clusters to specific hosting providers. Name: block explorer data from Solana Beach and run-time logs published by the Solana Foundation. Explain: the architecture diagram suggested global distribution; the execution revealed concentration. Implication: if the map and the territory diverge, trust should fall toward the territory.

A limitation must be acknowledged. Not all components can be fully decentralised from day one. Early-stage networks may require centralised sequencers or privileged keys to maintain stability. Reconciling this requires nuance: architecture does not need to be perfect initially, but the whitepaper must disclose which parts are provisional, who controls them, and under what schedule they fade. Hiding centralisation behind diagrams erodes credibility. Naming it strengthens it.

Execution also demands cost clarity. A system may be elegant on paper yet impossible to run economically. A bridge that requires recomputing vast proof sets for every message is not viable unless users are willing to pay the fees. A validator design that demands custom hardware may limit participation. Show the point. Name: Filecoin's early storage proofs, documented in 2020, required substantial computation, leading to higher operator costs in Shanghai, Frankfurt, and Toronto mining centres. Explain: the whitepaper acknowledged these costs upfront. Implication: by showing the economic wiring, the team promoted realistic expectations rather than fantasy.

Where cost is hidden, distortion follows. In 2021, multiple rollup projects claimed extremely low fees without disclosing reliance on sequencer subsidies drawn from treasury reserves. The diagrams suggested inherent efficiency; the execution required financial support. Explain: the wiring behind the promise—ongoing subsidy—was neither stable nor transparent. Implication: systems built on invisible cost structures generate misleading expectations that collapse when budgets thin.

Metrics reveal the truth of execution. A diagram cannot show operator churn, downtime, error rates, or queue depth under load. Real systems must withstand congestion, spikes in demand, and adversarial behaviour. Show how visible behaviours expose wiring. Name: Arbitrum's September 2023 upgrade logs documented throughput stress testing under simulated mainnet loads. Explain: the transparency revealed execution limits that refined the architecture. Implication: execution feedback loops are where architecture becomes credible or collapses.

The wiring motif appears again when examining oracle dependencies. A box labelled *oracle* in a diagram looks neat, yet the execution hides critical variables: how frequently data updates, how medianisation occurs, which operators supply feeds, how disputes are resolved. The existential risk of several algorithmic stablecoins in 2021 stemmed from precisely this gap. Diagrams showed "price input"; execution relied on shallow liquidity and manipulable markets. The box was a fiction. The wiring was the truth.

A credible counter-example demonstrates how clarity can protect users. MakerDAO's multi-source oracle system, with operators distributed across regions and feeds documented publicly, showed exactly how each component worked, who maintained it, and what fallback mechanisms existed. Explain: this wiring-level disclosure allowed independent modelling of attack vectors. Implication: when the wiring is visible, users can reason, auditors can verify, and attackers struggle to hide.

Across all these cases, a pattern emerges: diagrams do not earn trust, wiring does. Architecture earns admiration; execution earns resilience. And resilience is what users rely on when systems come under stress.

Which brings the subchapter to its unresolved question—the one the wiring motif forces upon every reader confronting a polished architectural diagram: *Can you trace what is drawn to what is deployed, or will you accept the diagram as a substitute for the truth?*

Metrics that matter

On 6 May 2021, when Binance Smart Chain reported more than nine million daily transactions compared with Ethereum's one million on the same day, commentators rushed to declare the arrival of a new dominant network. Screenshots of block explorers circulated through Telegram groups in Lagos and São Paulo, and headlines framed the surge as proof of mass adoption. Yet within weeks, analysts discovered that a substantial portion of this activity had been generated by a small cluster of automated wallets hammering low-cost contracts for yield extraction. The dazzling statistic, so proudly shared, revealed everything about throughput and almost nothing about users. It stood as a reminder that numbers can mislead by being impressively large, theatrically frequent, or carefully decontextualised. Big numbers impress. Small truths matter more.

This scene forms the quiet motif threading through this subchapter: the *shadow line* between a metric that represents behaviour and a metric that merely resembles it. The shadow line is thin, but it turns decisive when trying to understand whether a protocol has traction, or merely traffic; whether adoption is organic, or manufactured; whether the system creates value, or recirculates noise. To read a whitepaper or dashboard without falling for theatrical numerics requires a shift from counting events to tracing causes. It demands following one metric from user action to value accrual—mapping the wiring between what a person does and what the system earns. Without that wiring, numbers drift into narrative fuel.

The first major claim rests on the distinction between *vanity metrics* and *leading indicators*. Show the difference. Name a case: during 2020, Compound Finance reported rising total value locked (TVL), which observers in London and Singapore initially took as unambiguous proof of protocol strength. Explain: much of the early TVL growth reflected leveraged looping—users depositing assets, borrowing against them, and redepositing the borrowed assets to mine token rewards. This was activity without breadth. It inflated balances without expanding the user base. Implication: the metric looked grand while concealing concentration. A leading indicator would have been something else entirely: retained borrowers, repayment behaviour after rewards tapered, or recurring usage across market cycles.

Now show the contrasting pattern. Name a second example: when dYdX released cohort retention data in August 2022, the figures did not dazzle but they did instruct. The dashboard revealed how many traders stayed active after thirty, sixty, and ninety days—metrics tied directly to the protocol's purpose. Explain: retention exposed genuine product-market interaction, not temporary hype. Implication: it allowed analysts to measure whether the system earned loyalty rather than merely attracting one-time curiosity. That clarity strengthened trust more than any single day of unusually high volume.

A credible limitation must be stated. Not all protocols can offer clean retention metrics early in their lifecycle; some rely on episodic use by design, such as bridge services or batch-based staking tools. Reconciling this requires restraint: absence of continuous use does not prove frailty. The correct comparison is not *retention versus no retention*, but whether the available metric shows repeat behaviour proportionate to the product's purpose. The shadow line depends on context.

This leads to the second claim: every useful metric must tie behaviour to value. To understand this, consider the visible actions that drive system health. A user performs a swap, mints a position, opens a channel, submits an order, or verifies a proof. Each of these actions carries costs—fees, collateral, execution time—and each offers benefits—access, liquidity, leverage, or throughput. A leading indicator captures this causal chain. It shows not simply that something happened, but that it happened in a way that strengthens the protocol's economy.

Show how this wiring works with a concrete example. In March 2023, the decentralised derivatives platform GMX began publishing fee-to-liquidity ratios. Name the actors: liquidity providers in Hong Kong and Sydney, traders in Chicago and Berlin. Explain: the ratio measured how much revenue LPs earned for each unit of liquidity supplied. It was a behavioural metric—users committing value—and an economic metric—protocol capturing value. Implication: observers could trace the arc from user action (providing liquidity) to protocol viability (sustainable rewards). This is a leading indicator because it describes the health of the flywheel rather than the spectacle of activity.

Now counter with a cautionary case. Throughout late 2021, several high-yield staking networks trumpeted explosive wallet counts and rapid token distribution. Place it: the avalanche of addresses emanating from clusters in Turkey, Vietnam, and eastern Europe. Explain: many of these accounts were created automatically to farm emissions. Implication: the metric told analysts nothing about genuine participation. The shadow line here separated an impressive count from a meaningful signal.

The shadow line returns when examining *active addresses*. The metric is seductive because it feels intuitive: more active addresses suggest more users. But show the behaviour. In April 2022, Polygon reported over 400,000 daily active addresses. Name the issue: internal audits later revealed that a subset of DeFi games contributed disproportionate churn, generating thousands of micro-transactions from the same population. Explain: activity stemmed from repetitive low-value operations rather than new user engagement. Implication: "active" hid repetition. The line between user and script blurred.

To move from vanity to insight, one must follow a single metric across its full pathway. Choose a metric—say, retained cohorts. Show how it works. A cohort begins with users who perform a meaningful action: a deposit, a swap, a borrow, a verification. Name and date an example: in July 2023, StarkNet published weekly developer cohort retention alongside its sequencer performance metrics. Explain: this allowed analysts to trace developer activity from first contract deployment to continued iteration. Implication: retention reflected not hype but ongoing commitment; it measured the living ecosystem rather than the expanding database.

Another pathway emerges when examining *cost per user action*. Here behaviour becomes anchored in a visible metric: what a user pays. Show this with a dated event. In January 2021, Arbitrum's testnet published a schedule of average gas fees for cross-chain messaging. Explain: analysts could link the cost of execution to user decisions—whether it remained rational for traders to migrate from mainnet. Implication: the metric predicted real adoption before token price ever moved.

A counter-example helps refine the argument. Some protocols, especially privacy-preserving systems, cannot publish granular behavioural metrics without weakening guarantees. Zcash, in its 2019 network analyses, acknowledged this limitation. Explain: behavioural data must be aggregated to protect users. Implication: here, absence of detail is not deceit but design. The shadow line appears in a different form: the user must learn to distinguish between metrics concealed to protect and metrics concealed to distract.

The third claim centres on metrics that map *throughput* to *outcomes*. A system may process thousands of transactions per second, yet only a fraction may contribute to economic value. Show the behaviour. In February 2022, Solana reported high sustained throughput, but further examination revealed that much of this activity derived from high-frequency arbitrage bots submitting and cancelling orders. Name the consequence: genuine users faced degraded experience during congestion. Explain: high throughput masked low quality. Implication: the metric was technically correct but strategically misleading.

Contrast this with Uniswap v3's fee-tier distribution data in late 2021. Show: LPs chose fee tiers depending on volatility and risk tolerance. Name: analysis by Hayden Adams and team in London highlighted how different fee levels attracted distinct user types.

Explain: by measuring the distribution of liquidity across fee tiers, observers could infer where value accrued, not just where swaps occurred. Implication: a single metric—liquidity density by fee tier—provided insight into both behaviour and system health, a rare combination.

The shadow line cuts deepest when protocols selectively highlight or obscure metrics. Show a case. In mid-2022, several layer-2 networks emphasised TVL but avoided publishing failed transaction rates during congestion. Name: public dashboards in Seoul flagged retry statistics that were absent from official marketing channels. Explain: omission distorts perception. Implication: the reader must learn to ask not only which metrics appear but which remain unspoken.

A further implication arises from the nature of incentives. Metrics inflated through rewards cannot be treated as indicators unless the rewards eventually taper. Show an example. In June 2020, Curve Finance published CRV emissions schedules alongside pool utilisation data. Name: each pool's utilisation percentage allowed observers to see where emissions truly drove demand. Explain: usage remained strong only in pools that served real trading needs. Implication: emissions revealed elasticity. Once incentives fell, only pools with organic demand persisted. The metric held its value precisely because it traced economic behaviour rather than cosmetic activity.

The subchapter's final movement returns to the shadow line: every metric either illuminates reality or casts a distraction. The unresolved tension remains this: *When confronted with a dashboard brimming with numbers, which metric will you follow from behaviour to value—and which metrics will you refuse to let guide you?*

Red-flag language patterns

On 14 November 2022, as FTX collapsed in Nassau, one screenshot circulated with unusual speed. It showed an earlier tweet from Sam Bankman-Fried describing the exchange's custodial model as *"totally safe, risk-free, no chance of customer loss."* The phrasing was as audacious as it was revealing. *Risk-free* had always been impossible in markets;

no chance was a mathematical fantasy. Yet the language worked until it didn't. For months it had soothed anxious depositors and quieted critics. Only later did observers notice how the absolutist vocabulary had replaced evidence with assurance. The words had carried the shape of certainty without its substance.

The shadow motif that runs through this subchapter is the *mask*: language that dresses up fragility as strength. Crypto whitepapers and forum threads often deploy technical gloss to signal mastery, but the more interesting deceit hides in tone. It hides in promises that exceed what code, audits, or governance can deliver. A mask of confidence, when repeated often enough, begins to feel like a benchmark. The danger is that many readers react to tone before they analyse structure. Warm words outpace cold facts.

The first major claim concerns *weasel words*—terms that appear to clarify but actually blur. Show how they operate. In January 2021, Celsius Network published promotional materials describing its yield strategy as *"proven, secure, and institutionally validated."* Name the problem: none of these terms had fixed meaning. *Proven* by whom, under what conditions? *Secure* against which threats? *Institutionally validated* by which institutions, and in what form? Explain: the language functioned as a protective fog. It gave the impression of due diligence without revealing any. Implication: when terms lack measurable boundaries, they invite overconfidence. Readers take comfort in words that cannot be tested.

Now contrast this vagueness with an example that offers measurable specificity. In September 2020, the Ethereum Foundation published its eth2 Phase 0 audit reports with enumerated risks, each mapped to severity levels. The language was restrained: *"We identified X vulnerability; remediation requires Y; residual risk remains Z."* There was no mask. Explain: specificity forced transparency. Implication: the difference between these two cases is not one of intelligence but of intent. Where the first sought faith, the second sought scrutiny.

A credible counter-example must be addressed. Some builders use tentative, broad language not to deceive but to manage uncertainty during early research. Early-stage cryptography papers from Zcash in 2017 used phrases such as *"potential weaknesses"* and *"under active evaluation."* These soft edges were signs of intellectual honesty. Reconciling this requires contextual reading. Weasel words conceal. Tentative words reveal. The mask is not defined by the softness of the phrasing but by the absence of evidence behind it.

The second claim concerns *absolutist promises*: *unhackable*, *guaranteed*, *zero risk*, *100% uptime*, *no slippage*, *instant settlement*. These promises follow a clear pattern: they remove friction from the imagination. Show this with a dated case. In March 2019, QuadrigaCX's founders assured users in Halifax that customer assets were *"fully backed and entirely safe."* Name what later emerged: no cold wallets, inconsistent bookkeeping, and a single point of failure. Explain: absolutist phrasing stifled questions before they could form. Implication: the stronger the claim, the weaker the system usually is. Real systems contain trade-offs. They always have edges.

Set this against a second named and verifiable case. In July 2022, Immunefi, the bug-bounty platform based in Singapore, published a leaderboard of white-hat payouts with precise exploit descriptions. The language highlighted uncertainty: *"Potential re-entrancy vector patched; risk minimised but subject to future review."* Here uncertainty communicated competence. Explain: because the team disclosed fallibility, their credibility increased. Implication: truth in decentralised systems is often probabilistic. A claim of "unhackable" is not just false; it is a red flag that the speaker either misunderstands their own system or hopes that you will.

The mask motif returns when examining how marketing materials obscure operational dependencies. Show a scene. In May 2021, a cross-chain bridge promoted in Seoul declared itself *"fully decentralised."* Yet a footnote revealed that its validator set consisted of five entities, four of which shared overlapping ownership. Name the mismatch. Explain: *fully* implied a distribution of power that did not exist. Implication: absolutist modifiers often mask central points of failure.

A limitation must be acknowledged. Some technical claims appear absolutist but are in fact narrow. A protocol may state *"constant time verification"* or *"guaranteed termination under X assumptions."* These are mathematically scoped statements, not marketing hyperbole.

Reconciling this requires readers to inspect the domain. When the claim references a specific algorithmic property with clear boundaries, it belongs to the mathematics, not the mask. When it references sweeping operational safety with no boundary, it belongs to illusion.

The third major claim concerns the *side-by-side comparison*—the simplest tool for stripping off the mask. Show how comparison reveals truth. In December 2020, two competing stablecoin protocols—MakerDAO and Empty Set Dollar—circulated diagrams illustrating their stability mechanisms. Name the locations: Maker's documentation hub in Copenhagen, ESD's Telegram channels in New York and Singapore. Place the diagrams side by side. Explain: MakerDAO disclosed collateral ratios, liquidation penalties, and emergency shutdown mechanics. ESD relied on abstract terms—*"elastic supply," "community-driven expansion," "market-based stability."* Implication: the eye sees clarity before it sees honesty. When diagrams conceal dependencies in boxes without labels, the mask is doing its work.

Now contrast with a second comparative study. In August 2022, StarkWare published detailed tables comparing STARK proof costs on testnets in Berlin, Tel Aviv, and Chicago. The numbers—execution time, memory, proof-size—offered a transparent benchmark. Meanwhile, rival systems showcased sleek diagrams but omitted cost figures. The mask returned as minimalism: the absence of data was framed as elegant simplicity. Explain: comparison breaks the illusion by exposing what is missing. Implication: the reader need not be an expert cryptographer; they need only ask, *Why is one team willing to measure while the other prefers metaphor?*

Behaviour anchors the abstractions. Words shape decisions long before code does. When a whitepaper assures that *"risks are eliminated,"* visible behaviour changes: users commit more funds, projects attract less scrutiny, and analysts relax their guard. The metrics shift. Deposits rise. Forum scepticism falls. The mask has behavioural consequences. Conversely, when a protocol publicly enumerates failure modes, behaviour shifts the other way: users take measured positions, analysts interrogate assumptions, and developers patch more quickly.

The final movement returns to the central tension. The mask will always tempt readers. Confident words soothe. Technical gloss dazzles. Absolutist claims simplify complex systems into digestible slogans. The unresolved question is therefore this: *When the next whitepaper promises perfection in a single phrase, will you pause long enough to ask what the words are hiding—and compare them with a benchmark that refuses to flatter?*

Chapter 5
Tokenomics That Actually Work

The first great illusion of token design is how effortless it looks from a distance. A sleek dashboard, a rising chart, a few lines promising alignment of interests—these can create the impression that value simply emerges from clever mathematics and community enthusiasm. Yet the moment one steps behind the glass, the machinery appears far less mystical. Supply schedules behave like gravity. Incentives behave like tides. Treasuries behave like political organisms. The fates of entire networks have hinged not on branding or narratives, but on something as mundane as a poorly timed unlock, a forgotten fee switch, or a quorum threshold that turned governance into theatre. What survives in crypto is rarely what sparkles. It is what works.

Imagine, for a moment, the momentary delirium of DeFi Summer 2020. Protocols created daily, tokens minted hourly, rewards distributed at velocities no traditional financial system would tolerate. In this chaos, one pattern stood out: the designs that endured had discipline. Their issuances were constrained, their incentives intentional, their governance transparent, their treasuries boring in the best possible way. In a market where colour and noise often dominate attention, it was the quiet logic of sustainable tokenomics that separated the signal from the carnival. That contrast—between spectacle and structure—is the entry point of this chapter.

Tokenomics, at its core, is a vocabulary for power. It describes who benefits, when, and at whose expense. In an environment where anyone can issue a token with a few keystrokes, the design of incentives becomes a constitutional act. Every parameter—emission curve, burn ratio, vesting cliff, fee split, quorum threshold—expresses a philosophy of value and responsibility. Some projects choose philosophies anchored in patience and sober mathematics. Others choose philosophies where the future must continually subsidise the present. The former tend to compound; the latter tend to implode. This chapter is about distinguishing the two before reality makes the distinction for you.

The first arc of the chapter explores the triad at the foundation of every durable design: issuance, utility demand, and sinks. These three forces create the basic metabolic rate of a token. Too much issuance, and value leaks out like heat from a broken furnace. Too little, and participation starves. Demand must come not from speculation but from the actual use of the system—settlements performed, data verified, storage purchased, liquidity supplied. And sinks, always downplayed yet always decisive, determine whether the token is a conveyor belt or a sieve. A protocol that burns fees proportional to genuine usage behaves differently from one that simulates scarcity through engineered hype. This chapter examines that difference with rigour and clarity.

From there the narrative turns to incentives and dilution, the twin forces that shape behaviour. Incentives are the tools through which networks bootstrap participation. Dilution is the cost users pay for those tools. In the early rush of a token launch, rewards can seem like generosity. Six months later, when emissions halve and liquidity mining evaporates, the same design can feel like a trap. Dilution is not inherently harmful; undisciplined dilution is. This chapter unpacks how adoption curves, vesting schedules, and reward schemes interact—and how mismatches between them have quietly unravelled hundreds of token economies.

The next movement addresses governance: who votes, how they vote, and whether the votes matter. Many token systems proclaim decentralisation while relying on governance structures that all but guarantee voter apathy, whale dominance, or opaque decision-making. Effective quorum design is not an afterthought; it is a firewall. Delegate incentives are not cosmetics; they are levers of institutional memory. Upgrade processes are not rituals; they are threat surfaces. The reader will see that governance is not what communities say about themselves but what their rules compel them to do.

Treasury discipline forms the final structural anchor. A treasury without a mandate is a temptress; a treasury without transparency is a liability. Crypto history is littered with projects that raised immense capital only to discover that money without constraints corrodes judgment. In contrast, the networks that publish their budgets, link spending to milestones, and treat reserves as runway rather than windfall demonstrate a maturity that markets eventually reward. Treasury design, far from being a peripheral concern, is often the clearest indicator of whether a project views itself as a fleeting speculation or a future institution.

Across these themes runs a subtle motif: *flow*. Tokens flow into circulation or out of it. Incentives flow from treasuries to participants. Power flows through governance. Capital flows through time. Understanding these flows is a way of understanding the health of a system. When flows reflect real activity, value compounds. When flows rely on hope, momentum traders, or new entrants, the system must eventually confront its own unsustainability.

The significance of all this extends beyond charts or speculation. Tokenomics is a lens through which we can study human coordination at scale. It reveals what people reward, what they tolerate, what they fear, and what they expect. It shows how communities balance self-interest with shared interest, and how easily that balance can tilt. In a world where digital networks increasingly govern economic, social, and political life, understanding these mechanisms is not merely useful—it is essential.

By the end of this chapter, the reader will recognise the architecture of resilience: supply grounded in purpose, demand linked to genuine utility, sinks aligned with value creation, incentives that respect time, governance that earns legitimacy, and treasuries that practise restraint. The journey is not about predicting which tokens will succeed, but about seeing with clarity which designs deserve attention.

And so the chapter opens with a question that will echo through its pages: *When you encounter a token promising future value, can you trace the flows—of supply, of demand, of power, of capital—well enough to know whether it is building a system that grows stronger each day, or one that is already, quietly, hollowing itself out?*

Supply, demand, and sink

On 5 August 2021, when Ethereum activated EIP-1559 in London, a quiet shift took place beneath the noise of speculation. For the first time in the network's history, every transaction fee included a component that would be removed from circulation rather than paid to a miner. Within twenty-four hours, more than 4,000 ETH had been burned. Within a week, dashboards in Singapore, Berlin, and Chicago displayed an unfamiliar sight: usage dictating supply in real time. It was not a marketing slogan or a theoretical curve. It was a demonstrable wiring change linking behaviour to value. One rule. One mechanism. A measurable effect.

The burn drew attention because it was visible, but its real significance lay deeper. It showed, without rhetoric, that sound tokenomics rely on flows, not vibes. Supply enters the market through issuance. Demand pulls tokens into use. Sinks remove or lock them. When these three forces fall out of balance—even slightly—a token that appears vibrant can become structurally weak. And when they align, even a modest system can develop the kind of economic rhythm that compounds rather than decays. The motif threading this subchapter is the *circuit*: tokens flowing through a network like electricity through a board. Where the circuit is intact, power builds. Where the circuit is broken, the current disperses into noise.

The first major claim is that issuance sets the base conditions of a token's economic life. Show the point. In April 2020, Yearn Finance launched with a supply of exactly 30,000 YFI, all distributed to early users and none reserved for insiders. Name: the release documents confirmed it. Explain: a hard cap with no premine constrained issuance to zero once the initial distribution ended. Implication: scarcity in this case was not a gimmick but a boundary condition. Supply could not quietly expand. The circuit began with a defined input.

Contrast this with the opposite dynamic from May 2021, when several Olympus-DAO forks proliferating across Europe and Southeast Asia issued tokens with emission rates so aggressive that supply expanded by thousands of per cent within weeks. Explain:

issuance at that speed destabilised any relationship between user behaviour and token value. Implication: when the input overwhelms the circuit, the rest of the design collapses. No sink can compensate; no demand can keep pace.

Now introduce a limitation. Not all high issuance is destructive. Networks like Filecoin and Chainlink employed staged emissions to bootstrap operator participation. In both systems, documentation from 2020 outlined multi-year schedules with predictable decay curves. Reconciling this requires nuance: the harm is not in issuance itself but in issuance divorced from purpose. When emissions fund productive supply—storage, computation, validation—the circuit strengthens. When they fund only speculation, the wiring burns out.

The second major claim addresses demand—real demand, not the synthetic buzz of temporary incentives. Demand is visible in behaviour: settlements executed, positions maintained, data retrieved, assets bridged. Active addresses alone cannot prove it; retained cohorts can. Show how this distinction matters. In February 2023, Arbitrum's daily active address count surged after several airdrop rumours circulated across crypto channels in London and Seoul. But retention data from analytics teams showed that only a fraction of those addresses continued transacting a month later. Explain: usage driven by reward expectations is not utility; it is theatre. Implication: sustainable demand emerges only when tokens enable something users would do even without a promise of future payouts.

Name a contrasting case. In March 2022, Helium published network statistics showing rising packet transfers in regions such as Lisbon and San Francisco. Though the project later confronted governance challenges, the packet-level metric displayed genuine demand for a specific function. Explain: by measuring a behavioural unit tied directly to utility, Helium identified the true contour of its market. Implication: precise measurement exposes reality. Tokens cannot rise above the usefulness of the actions they price.

A counter-example deepens the argument. Stablecoins like USDC, issued by Circle, do not derive demand from speculative action. Their demand comes from their role as a settlement asset across exchanges and wallets, with transparent attestations released monthly since 2018. They show that utility demand can be orthogonal to burn schemes or complex mechanisms. Reconciling this with the earlier point: demand does not require sophistication; it requires purpose. The circuit carries current because something at the far end needs power.

The third major claim concerns sinks—the least glamorous but most determinative part of the triad. Sinks remove tokens from circulation or lock them long enough to modify supply pressures. They operate like resistors in the circuit, ensuring that energy does not simply loop without consequence. Show why they matter. The fee burn in Ethereum after August 2021 was proportional to actual usage. Name: Etherscan dashboards track the burned amount block by block. Explain: this created a counterweight to issuance based on market activity rather than managerial discretion. Implication: sinks anchored in behaviour inoculate systems against discretionary distortion.

Name a second case. In December 2020, Binance Smart Chain introduced mechanisms where a portion of validator fees contributed to periodic token burns. Although centralised governance shaped the parameters, the sink existed as part of the chain's recurring flow. Explain: when sinks are predictable and mechanical, they shape expectations. Implication: users can model future states. Predictability strengthens the circuit.

But sinks can fail when they are arbitrary. Several token systems in 2021 announced discretionary "buy-and-burn" events that depended on treasury moods rather than protocol logic. In some cases, the burns occurred only during marketing campaigns. Explain: irregular sinks distort incentives rather than stabilise them. Implication: a circuit that fires only when convenient ceases to be a circuit. It becomes a stage prop.

As the analysis develops, a deeper pattern emerges: each component of the triad gains meaning only in relation to the others. Issuance without demand creates gravity without lift. Demand without sinks creates lift without grounding. Sinks without demand create artificial pressure without purpose. The circuit motif returns—the flows must complete a loop. And only a complete loop can support continuous value.

To illustrate the interdependence, consider Uniswap in 2020–2022. Its token, UNI, had an airdropped supply, high trading volume on the protocol, and a governance-controlled fee switch that remained inactive. Explain: issuance existed; demand existed; the sink did not. Implication: without activating a value sink, UNI remained primarily a governance asset rather than a compounding one. The circuit was incomplete.

Contrast this with protocols like GMX in 2022, whose token flows combined trading fees distributed to stakers with usage-driven revenue and controlled emission schedules. Name: GMX's dashboards in Tokyo and Frankfurt published weekly fee statistics. Explain: here issuance, demand, and sinks co-evolved. Implication: when a token's flows reflect actual economic activity, value creation becomes durable rather than episodic.

A limitation surfaces. No triad can guarantee stability in markets prone to shocks. Even a well-balanced design can suffer if external liquidity dries up or regulatory shifts alter user behaviour. Reconciling this requires humility about what tokenomics can accomplish. The circuit can be optimised, not insulated. A strong design minimises fragility; it does not eliminate it.

Throughout this exploration, the motif of the circuit underscores each insight: tokens move; incentives move; value moves. The question is whether these movements create coherence or entropy.

The closing tension rises naturally: *When you next examine a token's economic wiring, can you trace the circuit from issuance to utility to sink—and does the current run cleanly, or does it dissipate before it completes the loop?*

Incentives and dilution

On 17 June 2020, when Compound launched its COMP liquidity mining programme in San Francisco, the first 48 hours felt like an economic experiment running at the speed of adrenaline. Total value locked surged from roughly $100 million to more than $600 million within days, a figure confirmed by DeFi Pulse at the time. The euphoria suggested a revelation: that incentives alone could summon user behaviour on command. Yet within weeks, trading volumes swung violently, capital migrated to whichever pool had the richest emissions, and a pattern emerged that analysts in London and Singapore would later describe with clinical clarity. Participation had not deepened; it had rotated. Value had not accrued; it had inflated. The rewards that drew in users diluted the holders who remained. The mechanism worked—until its own success hollowed it out. And in that hollow space, one question lingered: how long can a system compensate for fundamentals with issuance?

This paradox sits at the centre of token incentives. They attract attention, supply liquidity, and bootstrap participation, but they do so by issuing promises into the future. Those promises take the form of tokens, and tokens are claims on value. Every claim issued without a corresponding growth in demand stretches the system thinner. Issuance is fuel; dilution is the smoke. The motif threaded throughout this subchapter is the *hourglass*: incentives fill the upper chamber with energy and activity, but unless adoption grows at least as quickly as tokens enter circulation, that energy spills downward into dilution, draining the system's long-term strength.

The first major claim is that emissions—scheduled releases of tokens into a market—shape how participants behave long before they shape how value accrues. Show how this works. In January 2021, the SushiSwap "Onsen" programme distributed SUSHI tokens across dozens of liquidity pools. Name: Sushi's public emission schedule documented daily rewards split across specific trading pairs. Explain: the abundance of emissions meant that yield-seeking liquidity flowed aggressively into targeted pools, regardless of underlying utility or volume. Implication: emissions directed behaviour, but not loyalty. The hourglass filled quickly, yet the sands slipped away even faster when rewards later decreased.

Contrast this with a second dated case. In October 2020, Aave transitioned to its AAVE token following the migration from LEND. Its emissions schedule was far more conservative. Incentives existed but were not the core driver of participation; credit markets and borrowing activity had developed independently. Explain: controlled emissions avoided overwhelming organic usage. Implication: when incentives complement rather than dominate behaviour, dilution remains manageable and trust grows. The hourglass retains its shape.

Address a necessary limitation. Some early-stage networks must rely on high emissions to bootstrap supply-side participation. Filecoin's early miner rewards in 2020, documented in its published "Initial Pledge" parameters, were intentionally high to ensure storage capacity would come online. Reconciling this requires situating emissions within time: high rewards can be justified if they are temporary and clearly taper. The danger emerges when emissions lack direction or maturity.

The second major claim centres on dilution—the expansion of token supply beyond what adoption can absorb. Dilution is not inherently harmful; it becomes harmful when it outpaces demand. Show this dynamic. In September 2021, several forks of the Olympus DAO model across Europe and Asia promised annual percentage yields exceeding 50,000 per cent. The token supplies ballooned accordingly. Name: public dashboards from Dune Analytics tracked "rebase" events multiple times per day. Explain: supply expanded so rapidly that even moderate drops in demand triggered cascading sell pressure. Implication: holders misread emissions as yield when they were, in fact, dilution. The hourglass overflowed.

Name a countervailing example. Since 2018, Chainlink has released tokens monthly according to a steady, predictable vesting schedule. While the system faces its own design debates, its dilution has remained transparently modelled. Explain: predictable dilution enables rational expectations. Implication: when holders can measure the rate at which they are diluted, trust rises—not because dilution vanishes, but because it becomes legible.

The hourglass motif tightens when addressing cliffs and vesting—the discrete unlock events that often catch casual observers unprepared. A cliff is a sudden release of previously locked tokens, often allocated to teams, investors, partners, or early contributors. Show how cliffs distort markets. On 16 December 2021, the Axie

Infinity ecosystem faced a major unlock affecting team and investor allocations. Name: the unlock schedule had been public for months, yet trading activity exhibited clear pre-emptive positioning. Explain: cliffs concentrate dilution into a single moment. Implication: even a well-designed economy can experience instability if supply floods in faster than demand grows. The hourglass narrows abruptly, then widens without warning.

A contrasting case demonstrates restraint. When The Graph (GRT) launched in December 2020, much of the team and investor allocation was subject to multi-year vesting with quarterly unlocks. Explain: the distribution rhythm avoided sharp shocks. Implication: dilution spread across time reduces volatility and protects long-term engagement.

A credible counter-example complicates the picture: networks like Bitcoin, whose issuance follows a halving schedule, show that sudden supply shifts can strengthen a system by signalling scarcity rather than flooding markets. But this only works because Bitcoin's demand is deep, global, and structurally non-incentivised. Reconciling this: cliffs are not inherently harmful; they are harmful when demand is shallow or speculative. Without depth, abrupt shifts become destabilising rather than strengthening.

The third major claim concerns incentive design as a behavioural engine. Incentives can attract users, but they often attract the wrong ones. Show this with precision. In June 2020, during Compound's initial surge, top liquidity providers rotated capital out of pools as soon as reward APRs fell below alternatives elsewhere. Name: public wallet histories revealed short-lived participation across chains such as Ethereum and Binance Smart Chain. Explain: mercenary behaviour is rational when incentives dominate the system's value proposition. Implication: such systems accumulate activity, not users.

Contrast this with a system where incentives reinforced long-term contribution. In early 2023, Optimism deployed "Retroactive Public Goods Funding", rewarding developers for past contributions rather than for temporary liquidity. Explain: the reward mechanism altered behaviour because it targeted durable output. Implication: incentives aligned with productive activity build long-term momentum rather than temporary spikes. The hourglass holds steady rather than draining instantly.

Now show that dilution interacts with incentives in subtle ways. When rewards halve—as they did in many yield farming schemes in mid-2021—the collapse is rarely proportional. Liquidity does not fall by half; it evaporates. This is because participants benchmark returns relative to alternatives. As soon as emissions lose their competitive edge, the system becomes a ghost town. The hourglass empties.

The hourglass motif returns when examining vesting schedules. Vesting is not simply a technical parameter; it is a social contract. A project whose insiders unlock large allocations early signals a lack of commitment. A project whose team vests over four years with long cliffs signals alignment. The behaviour of insiders becomes the metric. When insiders sell aggressively post-unlock, the dilution is not just mechanical; it is interpretive. Users see the action and adjust trust accordingly.

A limitation must be addressed: vesting cannot guarantee alignment. Even long-locked insiders may choose to influence governance in ways that benefit personal interests over system health. Reconciling this: vesting is necessary but insufficient. Alignment must be reinforced through governance structures, public accountability, and credible neutrality.

Throughout this subchapter, the hourglass motif helps illuminate a simple truth: incentives must fill the system with energy, but the system must also hold that energy long enough to grow. Dilution drains energy when it exceeds demand. Vesting shapes how energy is released. Emissions determine how energy enters in the first place.

And so the unresolved tension that closes this analysis is as follows: *When you next examine a token's incentive scheme, can you distinguish fuel from exhaust—can you tell whether the hourglass is filling toward growth or silently emptying into dilution?*

Governance and voter participation

On 12 March 2020, as global markets convulsed and Ethereum gas prices spiked, MakerDAO's governance system was dragged from theory into practice. In a conference room in Copenhagen and across ad-hoc calls from London to San Francisco, core contributors watched liquidation auctions malfunction, leaving an estimated US$8 million in under-collateralised debt. Stability fees, auction parameters, and risk models had all been set by token vote. Yet when the crisis hit, the voter roll looked anaemic: only a tiny fraction of MKR holders had regularly participated in governance, and a mere handful of addresses had effectively steered crucial parameters in the preceding months. The protocol survived after emergency interventions and a hurried debt auction, but the lesson was blunt. A system may brand itself as "governed by the community"; when almost nobody votes, power does not vanish. It concentrates. Quietly.

A few months later, in June 2020, Compound's COMP governance launched from San Francisco with a different problem: participation was not low, but lopsided. A small cluster of large addresses—founders, funds, early insiders—controlled enough voting power to determine outcomes, even as thousands of retail holders sat on the sidelines. Proposals were debated on public forums, but the outcome of most major votes could be predicted from the delegate map long before ballots closed. Governance, in both cases, existed. Yet its claim to broad-based legitimacy was fragile. The paradox of token governance is captured here: the more complex the mechanism, the easier it is for apathy and concentration to hollow it out.

The motif threading through this subchapter is the *threshold*. Governance lives or dies by thresholds: quorum thresholds that determine whether a vote counts, concentration thresholds beyond which whales can dominate, safety thresholds that must be crossed before an upgrade touches user funds. Thresholds reveal how seriously a project treats its own constitutional promises. They surface the gap between aspirational decentralisation and the harder question: who can actually change what?

The first major claim is that quorum design—how many tokens or voters must participate for a decision to be valid—is not a minor parameter. It is the heartbeat of the system. Show how this operates. Name a case. Uniswap's early governance proposals in late 2020 required 4 per cent of the total UNI supply to reach quorum. At launch, a16z and a few large funds held well over that amount. Explain: such a high threshold, in theory, prevented small, unrepresentative cliques from passing changes. In practice, it meant that without explicit cooperation from a handful of whales, no proposal could pass, even if thousands of smaller holders voted in favour. Implication: a quorum set too high freezes evolution and outsources effective control to large holders. The threshold protects against capture yet risks paralysis.

Contrast this with a second case. In October 2021, ENS (Ethereum Name Service) launched its DAO with tiered quorum requirements and explicit participation incentives tied to working groups. Proposal thresholds were low enough that active delegates could pass routine changes, yet major constitutional alterations required significantly higher turnout. Explain: by differentiating between ordinary and structural decisions, ENS avoided both stagnation and trivial capture. Implication: thoughtful quorum design acknowledges that not all decisions carry equal weight. It sets multiple thresholds rather than a single blunt one.

A credible limitation tempers the argument. Very low quorums are not always evidence of negligence. Small, early-stage DAOs sometimes adopt minimal thresholds to avoid being stuck with an ossified configuration. Reconciling this requires context: the question is not whether turnout is low, but whether the thresholds and participation patterns match the system's current scale and risk profile. A treasury managing US$50,000 can tolerate more experimentation than one managing US$500 million. The same raw numbers mean different things at different scales.

The second major claim concerns delegate incentives. Most token-based systems have discovered an uncomfortable truth: expecting thousands of individual holders to read proposals, digest risk analyses, and vote thoughtfully every week is fantasy. Governance requires specialisation. Delegates—individuals or organisations that accumulate voting power—exist to provide that specialisation. But without carefully structured incentives, delegates become a new priesthood: powerful, opaque, and often unaccountable.

Show this dynamic. Name: in Compound's governance, a small number of delegates, including firms such as Gauntlet and Dharma in 2020–2021, routinely cast decisive votes. Many smaller token holders delegated to them once and never revisited the choice. Explain: the system relied on a handful of motivated actors whose incentives were only partly transparent. Some were paid by the protocol; others by external clients. Implication: where delegate incentives are not disclosed or periodically reviewed, governance may be decentralised in form yet concentrated in practice. The threshold of effective influence narrows to a few desks.

Set this beside an alternative pattern. GitcoinDAO, in 2022, began publishing detailed "delegate statements" in which would-be stewards outlined their priorities, funding philosophies, and potential conflicts of interest. Voting power flowed to these delegates through explicit campaigns; some received direct compensation from the DAO based on documented activity. Explain: this arrangement did not eliminate concentration, but it made it legible. Implication: when delegates are visible, compensated for defined work, and subject to renewal, token holders can treat representation as a revocable contract rather than a static fact. The threshold between community and decision-makers becomes inspectable rather than invisible.

A counter-example provides nuance. Bitcoin, famously, has no formal delegate system. Its "governance" emerges from rough consensus across node operators, developers, miners, and economic actors. BIP debates show how messy and slow this process can be. Yet the absence of direct token voting has also insulated Bitcoin from some of the plutocratic tendencies of other systems. Reconciling this demands intellectual honesty: formal delegate structures are not the only way, nor always the superior way, to achieve legitimate decision-making. But once a protocol chooses token voting, it inherits a duty to make its delegate incentives explicit, or accept that power will pool quietly.

The third major claim is that upgrade safety—the procedures by which live systems change their own code—is the ultimate test of governance reality. Most projects describe their upgrade paths in lofty terms; few treat them as the safety-critical processes they are. Every contract upgrade, parameter change, or module swap introduces the possibility of catastrophic error or malicious capture. Governance either mitigates this risk or amplifies it.

Show the stakes. Name: in February 2022, Wormhole, a cross-chain bridge with infrastructure in New York and Geneva, suffered a US$320 million exploit after a failure in its Solana contract upgrade process left verification steps incomplete. While the project later restored user funds via its backers, the episode revealed how fragile live upgrade paths can be. Explain: the technical flaw mattered, but the governance flaw mattered more. The process did not enforce multi-party review with adequate delay and independent validation. Implication: upgrade safety is a governance problem disguised as an engineering one. The threshold here is temporal—how much time must pass, and how many eyes must inspect, before a change goes live?

Now show a contrasting pattern. In 2020–2021, the Ethereum network's major upgrades—Berlin, London, Altair—followed a multi-client, multi-testnet process spread across months, with public call notes, client diversity metrics, and explicit fork dates. Multiple clients in Paris, Berlin, and San Francisco implemented the changes independently. Explain: no single actor could unilaterally alter the consensus rules; the process required coordination among core devs, client teams, miners or validators, and application operators. Implication: upgrade safety rested on both social norms and structural constraints. The threshold for change was high, and it was intentionally high.

A limitation arises. Heavy-weight upgrade processes can slow necessary fixes, leaving systems exposed to known issues longer than ideal. Fast-moving DeFi protocols sometimes choose shorter timelocks and concentrated multi-sig control to allow rapid patching. Reconciling this requires appreciating trade-offs: safety and speed sit on opposite sides of a scale. The question is not which one to choose, but how a protocol communicates its position on that scale to its users. Hidden speed is dangerous; declared speed can be priced and mitigated. Thresholds need not be maximal, but they must be honest.

The motif of the *threshold* returns when examining voter participation itself. A governance dashboard may show high theoretical turnout, yet a closer look often reveals that a handful of addresses supply most of the weight. Behaviour, not slogans, exposes reality. Are proposals discussed in open forums before voting starts? Do delegates publish rationales? Do ordinary holders ever successfully propose and pass changes that go against large insiders' preferences? These questions measure the lived distance between token distribution and actual power.

Turnout thresholds can prevent outright capture. Some DAOs, such as those managing major DeFi protocols, now require not only simple majorities but also minimum participation levels for critical changes. A hostile whale cannot unilaterally push through a parameter update if too few other voters turn up. Yet thresholds can also create perverse incentives. If turnout repeatedly fails, attackers can deliberately suppress participation—by flooding forums with noise, timing proposals during holidays, or bundling contentious changes with benign ones—until exhaustion achieves what explicit aggression could not.

The final tension flows from this complexity. Token governance often markets itself as a solved problem: a few maths-sounding words, a voting portal, a token-weighted tally. But under the surface, thresholds, delegate incentives, and upgrade paths weave together into something much closer to constitutional design. They determine whether communities can resist capture, adapt under pressure, and correct their own mistakes.

So the unresolved question that closes this subchapter is not abstract. When you look at the governance of a protocol you care about—the quorums, the delegates, the upgrade timelocks, the recent turnout—are you seeing a system that merely claims decentralisation, or one that has set its thresholds high enough that you would trust it to make a decision that hurts you in the short term but keeps the network alive?

Treasury discipline

On 14 July 2022, the Uniswap Foundation proposal appeared on the governance forum with a startling request: US$74 million in UNI to fund operations, grants, and ecosystem development. The reaction was immediate. In London, Singapore, and New York, token holders opened spreadsheets to calculate burn rates, while delegates demanded line-item clarity before supporting a transfer of that magnitude. The proposal was eventually approved after revisions, but the episode exposed a structural truth. Treasury governance is never abstract. It is a live test of whether a project treats capital as a public trust or as a windfall to be spent at altitude. The amounts are digital, but the discipline required is analog: costed plans, verifiable milestones, and the readiness to say *no* even when the vault is full. Treasury management is the quiet backbone of token systems, and its failure is almost always slow, opaque, and preventable.

A similar reckoning played out months earlier at Optimism in June 2022, when a tranche of OP tokens was mistakenly transferred to an unauthorised address, lost control, and eventually recovered only through the goodwill of a counterparty. The incident involved London-based market maker Wintermute, but the governance discomfort landed squarely on Optimism's treasury policies. Who audited transfers? Who approved spending flows? What reconciliation procedures existed between technical signers and governance mandates? The sums were large and the reputational damage palpable. Transparency, once assumed, became a demand rather than an expectation. When the treasury itself is digital money, one gap in process can quickly become a structural weakness. The motif that will recur throughout this subchapter—the *ledger*—is not merely a database entry; it is a mirror of a culture's seriousness.

The first major claim is that transparency is not a cosmetic virtue but a measurable behaviour. Show this plainly. The Aave DAO, from 2021 onward, began publishing detailed monthly financial reports: balances, obligations, yield streams, risk exposures, and forward liquidity projections. Name the practice. These reports, prepared by service providers such as Llama, read like the disclosures of a mid-sized public company. Explain why this matters. When any token holder can inspect a project's assets and liabilities, they can compute runway, compare month-to-month changes, and interrogate deviations. Implication: transparency tightens the ledger. It forces internal consistency, reduces rumour-driven governance, and allows early detection of structural deficits before crises arrive. Without it, even a large treasury begins to resemble a dark pool—resources exist, but nobody knows for whom or for what.

Contrast this with another case. In 2021, several algorithmic stablecoin projects—most notably Terra, headquartered between Seoul and Singapore—claimed deep reserves without publishing independent, verifiable accounting. The eventual collapse in May 2022 exposed how thin those assurances were. Explain the mechanism. A treasury shielded from scrutiny becomes a narrative instrument: numbers are claimed rather than demonstrated. Implication: opacity does not merely hide risk; it manufactures false confidence, enabling misallocation until the ledger breaks. When users cannot trace assets, they cannot price the system, and when they cannot price the system, panic becomes rational.

A limitation must be acknowledged. Full transparency can introduce new hazards. Publishing every treasury move in real time can expose teams to front-running, predatory arbitrage, and geopolitical risk. Reconciling this requires nuance: the goal is not radical openness but *structured transparency*. A project might disclose aggregated treasury positions monthly while keeping tactical operations private. What matters is that token holders can evaluate solvency, mandate adherence, and spending pace without needing to trust personalities. The ledger must be visible, even if every line is not livestreamed.

The second major claim is that mandates—clear definitions of what a treasury is for—transform capital from temptation into tool. Many DAOs describe their treasury purpose vaguely: "ecosystem growth", "community development", "long-term sustainability". Such phrasing encourages drift. Show the alternative. GitcoinDAO, in 2022–2023, adopted explicit mandates for each working group: funding public goods, improving grants infrastructure, or supporting protocol engineering. Name the structure. Budgets were tied to these mandates and evaluated against deliverables with public review cycles. Explain its significance. Mandates anchor spending decisions; they prevent reactive allocation driven by hype or lobbying.

Implication: when a treasury knows its job, requests are measured against purpose rather than charisma.

Now bring in a second named example. In April 2020, during Ethereum's transition towards the Beacon Chain, the Ethereum Foundation funded client teams across Berlin, Hong Kong, and the United States with milestone-based grants: new releases, testnet readiness, and security audits. These allocations were not token-based; they were tied to execution of specific, testable work. Explain the behaviour. Milestone funding changes incentives: teams must deliver before receiving subsequent tranches. Implication: milestone-linked treasuries convert capital into velocity. The ledger advances only when the work advances, reducing the risk of drift and reputational capture.

Introduce a limitation. Mandates can become too rigid. A project might need to pivot due to regulatory developments, market failures, or technical breakthroughs. Overly rigid mandates can freeze adaptation. Reconciling this tension means acknowledging that mandates require periodic renewal and review mechanisms, not permanent ossification. The ledger must be guided, not calcified.

The third major claim concerns runway—the temporal dimension of treasury discipline. Treasury size alone tells you little; burn rate tells you everything. Show this principle. During 2021–2022, many NFT communities—some registered in New York, others operating from Lisbon co-working spaces—celebrated multi-million-dollar treasuries after successful mints. Yet most had monthly expenses exceeding sustainable levels: contractors, event sponsorships, speculative investments. When secondary sales volume collapsed by mid-2022, many found themselves with less than six months of operational runway. Explain: runway is the bridge between today's treasury and tomorrow's viability. It is not a static figure; it is a forecast shaped by spend discipline, revenue repeatability, and realistic growth. Implication: a treasury without a runway plan is a pile of tokens awaiting gravity.

Contrast this with a case of measured discipline. The StarkNet Foundation, established in 2022 between Tel Aviv and Geneva, published its treasury strategy explicitly: multi-year allocations for developer support, ecosystem grants, research, and security, tied to a structured disbursement programme. Explain its significance. When runway is treated as a strategic resource, not a cushion, teams prioritise long-term projects and avoid panic-driven expenditures. Implication: runway clarity strengthens governance by aligning expectations. Token holders can evaluate whether spending patterns match commitments.

A counter-example reveals another nuance. Some early-stage protocols intentionally hold minimal runway to avoid moral hazard, forcing themselves to seek product-market fit quickly. This approach can succeed in fast-moving markets, though it exposes teams and users to volatility. Reconciling this requires realism: short runway can be a strategy, but only if disclosed. Hidden desperation leads to reckless treasury decisions, such as sudden token sales or illiquid commitments. Again, the ledger must reflect truth, not courage signalling.

A fourth major claim is that treasury policies must be read the way a thoughtful investor reads a company's financial notes: with attention to mechanisms, not adjectives. The presence of a multi-sig is not a guarantee; the identities, jurisdictions, and rotation policies of the signers matter. The existence of a budget is not discipline; the alignment of spending with mandates is the test. And distributions without milestone conditions resemble donations, not investments.

Show this in practice. Name: in 2023, Arbitrum DAO approved a substantial grant programme that initially lacked clear milestone gates. The backlash, from Seoul to Amsterdam, forced a redesign: tranche-based releases, competitive evaluation, and periodic reporting. Explain why this mattered. Without milestone conditions, a treasury becomes a faucet; with them, it becomes an engine. Implication: an investor's reading of the ledger emphasises the flow of value, not the size of the vault.

Return to the motif of the *ledger*. In every example, the question is the same: can a neutral observer trace, line by line, how tokens move from treasury to outcome? The ledger becomes an accountability instrument only when spending is tied to purpose, time, and demonstrable work. Treasury discipline is less about hoarding or spending than about committing to a pattern of behaviour that users can model.

Closing on an unresolved threshold is fitting. Treasury policies declare who a project chooses to become. Some will publish detailed budgets, milestone gates, and independent audits. Others will rely on charisma, vague mission statements, and the inertia of bull markets. When you examine a protocol's treasury—its reports, mandates, burn rate, and spending approvals—are you looking at a culture constructing a durable ledger, or one hoping its vault will remain full long enough to outrun scrutiny? The line between the two is narrow, and the ledger does not lie.

Chapter 6
Code, Audits, and Attack Surfaces

Just after dawn on 17 August 2021, engineers at Poly Network opened their dashboards to find a hole where US$600 million in user assets had been hours earlier. The breach—spanning Ethereum, Binance Smart Chain, and Polygon—was surgical, exploiting a vulnerability in cross-chain message handling that had passed through multiple audits. By mid-morning, analysts in Zurich, Singapore, and Tokyo were parsing the attacker's on-chain notes, astonished not only by the scale but by the method: a permissions oversight hiding in plain sight. Within days, the funds were returned through a bizarre truce between attacker and protocol, yet the episode left an indelible lesson. Audits had caught issues, patched others, but the economic and architectural design remained fragile enough that a single misconfigured trust linkage toppled the whole structure. It was a reminder as stark as it was uncomfortable: code behaves exactly as written, not as intended, and digital systems often fail at their edges rather than their cores.

A year later, the collapse of the Mango Markets protocol in October 2022 offered a different but equally revealing angle. This time, the code performed flawlessly. The exploit rested instead on the system's oracle design and liquidity assumptions. An attacker, operating through accounts traceable to multiple offshore exchanges, inflated asset prices, used the temporary spike as collateral, borrowed heavily, and drained liquidity—all without touching a line of vulnerable code. Here, the lesson cut deeper. Security was not simply about immaculate functions or neat inheritance trees. It was about the economic attack surface, the behaviour that code *permits*, and the assumptions it quietly embeds. When markets and contracts collide in a permissionless environment, risk leaks through model gaps, misaligned incentives, or delayed price feeds as easily as through a buggy line of Solidity.

What unites both stories is a simple truth with far-reaching consequences: digital systems fail not only where they are weak, but where they are unexamined. Every protocol, however elegant, carries fault lines—some mathematical, some architectural, some psychological. As users, we are often invited to treat audits as certainties, diagrams as guarantees, and "battle-tested" deployments as proof of durability. But security is never a badge. It is a posture: of scrutiny, of humility, of insisting that every moving part be traced to its operator, its cost, and its failure modes. This chapter asks you to read systems the way a cautious engineer reads a bridge, not the way a tourist admires it. The distinction is not aesthetic. It is survival.

To do that, we begin with a difficult but necessary framing: audits are essential, yet their power is bounded. They reduce risk; they do not evaporate it. The scope of an audit defines what was examined and, perhaps more importantly, what was not. The severity levels catalogue what might break, not how users might be harmed when economics or governance amplify those breaks. A protocol can fix every critical finding and still remain exposed if its incentive structure enables speculative loops or if its oracle architecture can be stressed until insolvency. Understanding this boundary—what an audit proves, and what it cannot—is the first step towards reading any system with sobriety rather than comfort.

From this foundation, the chapter moves into the terrain where many of the most consequential failures originate: recurring exploit patterns. Re-entrancy loops, price oracle manipulation, unchecked delegate calls, shadow owner privileges, and unlimited token approvals continue to resurface not because developers are careless, but because the patterns are durable, subtle, and often incentivised by speed. A protocol's attack surface is not static. It expands with integrations, grows with composability, and shifts as new standards are adopted. Recognising these patterns is less about memorising jargon than training the eye to see where privileges accumulate, where assumptions harden into blind spots, and where a harmless optimisation becomes a systemic liability.

Yet even the cleanest code and tightest permissions cannot compensate for weak operational security. Behind every impressive interface lies a web of keys, signers, deployers, upgrade paths, and emergency powers. The question is never simply *does the system work?* but *who can intervene, how quickly, and under what constraints?* Many high-profile incidents trace back to a single private key controlling a pause function, a multisig threshold set for convenience rather than resilience, or an upgrade proxy that could be seized through social engineering. Permissionless systems are, paradoxically, often held together by human fallibility—where a handful of operators carry the authority to freeze, drain, or replace the very contracts users assume are immutable. Mapping these human choke points is as critical as understanding the algorithms they oversee.

Finally, the chapter turns to live safety nets: bug bounties, circuit breakers, insurance pools, and time-locked upgrades. These are the scaffolds of a mature ecosystem, acknowledging that even well-designed systems will face novel threats. A generous bug bounty signals respect for adversarial creativity. A circuit breaker marks a commitment to fail safely rather than catastrophically. Insurance pools reveal a protocol's willingness to mutualise risk rather than externalise it onto unsuspecting users. In aggregate, these defences form the layered security posture from which lasting trust emerges—not because incidents are impossible, but because failure can be detected, contained, and recovered from without systemic collapse.

Throughout the chapter, a quiet motif threads the analysis: the surface. Not the glossy surface of marketing or dashboards, but the attack surface—where assumptions meet reality, where incentives clash with permissions, where code and markets interact in unpredictable ways. We will return to this motif repeatedly, because robust digital systems are built not by shrinking their surfaces into oversimplified diagrams, but by exposing those surfaces to rigorous scrutiny, adversarial thinking, and intentional design.

The stakes are not confined to technical specialists. Anyone participating in a permissionless ecosystem—developer, researcher, or user—interacts with attack surfaces, whether knowingly or not. Understanding them is not about learning to fear systems but about learning to see them, to trace where authority pools, where assumptions creak, and where resilience can be measured rather than imagined. The chapter ahead is an invitation to cultivate that sight: to engage with security as an active literacy, not a borrowed checklist.

The tension that frames the whole discussion remains unresolved by design. Every protocol claims safety; few can demonstrate it. Every audit signals diligence; few capture economic brittleness. Every team insists its upgrade powers are benign; few reveal the operators who hold them. When you next encounter a system described as "battle-tested", what will you do—trust the phrase, or test the surface?

What audits do (and do not) prove

A few minutes past noon on 30 March 2022, Sky Mavis, the company behind Axie Infinity, confirmed that US$625 million in user funds had been drained from the Ronin bridge. The contracts had been audited. The RPC infrastructure had been reviewed. Severity findings had been triaged and patched. Yet the attacker, traced later to the Lazarus Group by the FBI, bypassed the solidity layer entirely. By compromising validator keys—five of nine, including one controlled by a third-party entity in Hanoi—they authorised withdrawals that the bridge smart contract dutifully executed. The code was sound; the system was not. It was an uncomfortable reminder that audits illuminate what they examine, and leave everything else in shadow. The signatures of reassurance—green ticks, clean reports, confident press releases—could not alter a simple fact: a single assumption, untested and unchallenged, carried the weight of hundreds of millions.

Similar lessons surfaced during the 19 June 2023 attack on the Sturdy Finance protocol. Trail of Bits had audited the system months earlier. CertiK provided additional reviews. Their teams flagged issues, recommended adjustments, and verified fixes. Yet the exploit did not appear in any severity table. It arose instead from economic dynamics—specifically, a price oracle manipulation using flash loans to skew liquidity pool ratios. The contract executed faithfully; the mathematics of the market did not. For analysts, the Sturdy incident exposed a recurrent pattern: smart-contract audits often assume stable prices, rational behaviour, and orderly liquidity. Attackers assume none of these. They measure what can be bent, distorted, or temporarily falsified. They understand that code correctness is not equivalent to system integrity.

These episodes sit on opposite ends of the security spectrum—one operational, one economic—but they expose the same motif: boundary. Audits are boundary tools: potent within scope, blind outside it. They test the correctness of code; they cannot guarantee the coherence of a system. And in crypto, where protocols braid together oracles, incentives, governance, multisigs, liquidity dynamics and external off-chain processes, the surface area expands faster than any checklist can track.

To understand what audits truly prove, it helps to begin with the scene most users never witness: the scoping call. Here, project teams and auditors negotiate what will be examined. Sometimes the scope includes the full repository, every contract and dependency. Often it does not. Many reports openly state exclusions: proxy patterns, external integrations, inherited libraries, compiler quirks, or privileged roles controlled off-chain. When a vulnerability appears months later in one of these neglected zones, the public often treats it as an audit failure. In reality, it is a scope failure—a misalignment between what the audit covered and what the system required. The implication is stark. A rigorous audit proves diligence within defined boundaries. It cannot defend choices that fall outside them.

Reading scope carefully is therefore an essential practice. A protocol may present three audits from respected firms, yet the reports may only cover incremental updates or a subset of contracts. Consider the case of Compound's 2021 liquidity pool patch, which had undergone peer review and testing but relied on a single overlooked parameter in the Comptroller contract. When the erroneous update shipped, users withdrew more than US$80 million in bonus tokens. The code had been reviewed; the pipeline had not. The fragility did not lie in a faulty function but in deployment oversight—a reminder that scope ends where deployment begins. A sceptical reader, following the line from code to operator, would have asked the relevant question: *who controls upgrades, and how are they validated?* The answer would have revealed a gap as real as any critical bug.

If scope defines what is seen, severity classifications help explain why issues matter. High-severity findings typically signal exploitability with material loss. Medium may require specific conditions. Low can often be stylistic. Yet severity tables are not neutral. They embody assumptions: about liquidity, about governance, about adversarial effort. A report may rate an issue "medium" because it requires a malicious multisig signer—yet if governance is dormant, or if upgrade keys are concentrated, that scenario becomes plausible.

Conversely, an auditor may classify an issue as "critical" even when difficulty of execution limits real-world risk. Severity is an interpretation, not a verdict. Understanding this distinction prevents over-reliance on the colour-coded comfort of risk matrices.

Two concrete examples illustrate the tension. In November 2020, Quantstamp rated a re-entrancy vector in a SushiSwap contract as high-severity; it was patched promptly. Months later, PeckShield identified a subtle imbalance in Harvest Finance's Curve integration. The issue did not rank as critical because it relied on slippage manipulation, yet attackers used it to drain more than US$30 million. The reports were correct within their frameworks; the events exceeded those frameworks. Fragility resided not in the code but in economic assumptions—how AMMs behave under stress, how liquidity moves when incentives shift, how oracles lag during volatility. An audit can mark the map. It cannot freeze the terrain.

A credible counter-example illustrates the limit from the opposite direction. In 2021, OpenZeppelin audited the PoolTogether v4 contracts. They reported numerous low-severity issues, all patched before deployment. The protocol has operated without major incident since. Here, scope matched system complexity, and assumptions about user behaviour aligned with reality. The story demonstrates that audits are not symbolic; they add genuine resilience. But the very fact that PoolTogether's success is notable shows how rare it is for audit scope, severity, deployment control, and economic model to align perfectly. Reliability is achievable, not guaranteed.

This is where the chapter's recurring motif returns: boundary. Every audit draws one. The skilled reader asks where it lies. That means examining not only what the auditors tested, but how the system behaves under stress, mispriced oracles, thin liquidity, latency spikes, or governance failure. Most audits barely brush these domains. Their remit is narrower: find code-level vulnerabilities; confirm fixes; articulate residual risks. Understanding this remit clarifies their value. They reduce uncertainty. They do not erase it.

A second boundary sits in the temporal dimension. Audits capture a snapshot. But code evolves, integrations deepen, and dependencies shift. A protocol with flawless reports in March can accumulate risk by May through successive upgrades, composability additions, or parameter changes. The 2022 Nomad bridge exploit was a textbook case. Audited repeatedly, the contracts were considered sound—until a botched upgrade initialised a trusted contract with zero value, turning a once-secure component into an open drain. No auditor had missed the vulnerability; it did not exist during their review. It emerged in the deployment pipeline. The lesson lands with force. Users must track not only audits, but what happens after them.

Even when reports are current, they rarely grapple with what is arguably the largest attack surface: incentives. Economic design can be impeccable on paper yet implode when users act in clusters, when liquidity providers flee, or when governance is captured by concentrated whales. These dynamics cannot be audited into safety. They must be reasoned about, monitored, and stress-tested. A protocol can score perfectly on technical criteria and still lose user assets because incentives made exploitation profitable. Audits do not model greed, panic, coordination failure, or strategic behaviour. They are not meant to. That task belongs to the reader.

To engage with audits effectively, one must therefore treat them not as certificates but as evidence. Evidence of what was inspected. Evidence of how the team responded. Evidence of a culture—disciplined or negligent, transparent or opaque. A team that treats audits as ceremonial, outsourcing security to a badge, tends to exhibit similar carelessness elsewhere: sloppy key governance, lax deployment hygiene, poorly documented upgrade paths. A team that treats audits as adversarial partnerships usually demonstrates complementary strengths: public test suites, reproducible builds, bug bounty participation, open discussions of trade-offs. Behaviour, more than marketing, reveals maturity.

The unresolved tension at the core of this subchapter resists comforting resolution. When you next encounter a protocol boasting "audited by three top firms", what should you believe? That the system is safe? Or that its known surfaces have been partly examined? The prudent reader asks a sharper question: *Where does the audit end—and what begins beyond it?*

Common exploit patterns

On 14 April 2023, Euler Finance published a terse post-mortem that read more like a crime scene reconstruction than a technical report. A few weeks earlier, on 13 March, an attacker drained roughly US$197 million from the protocol by combining a donation mechanism with a sophisticated liquidation pathway. The issue had been visible in the codebase. It had survived audits. It had lingered unnoticed through multiple integrations. Yet the method of attack was depressingly familiar. The exploiter manipulated internal accounting through a sequence of nested calls, exploiting the fact that the protocol trusted one step to be final while the attacker treated it as provisional. A single invariant—what *should* remain constant within a transaction—was violated. The exploit was modern, but the pattern was old: a form of re-entrancy cloaked in fresh choreography. And its scale exposed a truth the ecosystem continues to relearn: attackers study patterns with forensic patience. Defenders forget them with astonishing speed.

Across the years, these patterns have resurfaced like motifs. The DAO in June 2016, Cream Finance in August 2021, and multitudes of smaller protocols in between were all damaged by variations of the same mistake: code that assumed a call would complete atomically, while an adversary found a way back in before the state updated. Re-entrancy remains effective because it targets assumptions, not functions. Developers assume a line of code marks a boundary. Attackers treat it as an invitation. The gap between those mindsets is where millions disappear.

The persistence of re-entrancy reflects a deeper dynamic: complexity creates blindness. Each additional contract, each external call, each composable module multiplies the possible sequences of execution. When the Compound protocol was first integrated into various leverage platforms during 2020, auditors at OpenZeppelin warned that batched calls could create obscure pathways for state changes. Those pathways largely held. But the warning stands as an early expression of a structural truth: the more actors involved—lenders, borrowers, oracles, price-feed routers—the harder it becomes to reason about what happens *between* instructions. Attackers specialise in the space between.

Oracle manipulation demonstrates another pattern built on that interstitial space. On 26 October 2020, Harvest Finance suffered a US$34 million exploit when an attacker used a flash loan to distort Curve pool prices momentarily. The manipulation lasted seconds, but that was enough to exploit the protocol's accounting. Two years later, in April 2022, the Beanstalk Farms governance attack used a flash-loan-boosted voting position to pass a malicious upgrade. The actors differed; the mechanism echoed the same principle. When a system relies on data external to its own state—whether price, liquidity, or governance power—it inherits the fragility of the source. If that source can be moved, even briefly, the protocol can be steered into a loss.

The motif reappears in July 2022 during the Nirvana Finance exploit on Solana. Here, the attacker inflated the price of the ANA token using a manipulated oracle, secured an outsized loan against it, and then allowed the price to collapse. The protocol followed its rules. The rules followed the price. The price followed the attacker. Oracle manipulation works not because developers underestimate attackers, but because developers overestimate the reliability of external truth. A price feed looks objective. For milliseconds at a time, it can be fiction.

One might think the solution is simply to fortify the sources of truth. But even the best oracles operate under constraints: update frequencies, liquidity depth, off-chain computation, governance delays. A counter-example illustrates the nuance. Chainlink's price feeds, widely adopted since 2019, reduce susceptibility to single-point manipulation but cannot eliminate temporal lags in rapidly moving markets. During the UST depeg in May 2022, several protocols relying on supposedly robust oracles struggled with update delays measured in seconds. Those delays mattered. They turned risk into realised loss. Oracle robustness is therefore a probabilistic shield, not an absolute barrier.

A third recurring pattern is permission misconfiguration—an exploit category so mundane that many teams overlook it entirely. When the Nomad bridge suffered its catastrophic breach in August 2022, the root cause was a mis-set trusted root value in an upgrade. Once the contract accepted a zero-value root as valid, anyone could copy the attacker's first transaction, alter the recipient address, and extract funds. The exploit required no cryptographic insight, no advanced engineering, no market manipulation—just the ability to replicate a transaction. It was a permissions failure of the simplest kind: a system trusting what should never have been trusted.

A similar theme emerges in the 2021 Uranium Finance exploit, where a misconfigured calculation in a fee function created an asymmetric output that attackers drained. Again, the code executed faithfully; the permissions allowed a malicious actor to touch a pathway that should have been unreachable. Permission bugs often seem trivial in post-mortems because the mechanical step is so small. But triviality is the point. Attackers choose the path of least resistance. If a system leaves a door ajar, even accidentally, it may as well leave it wide open.

Yet the deepest permission failures often occur not within contracts but within wallets. Unlimited approvals—token allowances granted by users to save time—constitute one of the largest unmonitored attack surfaces in crypto. When the BadgerDAO front-end was compromised in December 2021, attackers exploited long-forgotten allowances to siphon funds from user wallets. The contracts were secure; the signatures were not. The behaviour was visible: users clicked "approve", skipped the "max spend" field, and never revoked it. The pattern could not be clearer. Convenience accumulates risk. The ledger remembers permissions long after users forget them.

To see how attackers think, follow their trail of decisions. They search for assumptions—state updates that are believed to be final, price feeds believed to be stable, permissions believed to be benign. They test their hypotheses in private forks. They replay transactions until the sequence aligns. And they commit only when the gap between cost and reward favours them. Their advantage lies in asymmetry. Defending requires securing every step; exploiting requires finding just one misstep.

A credible limitation tempers this account. Not every exploit aligns neatly with these categories. The Wormhole breach of February 2022, in which an attacker bypassed signature verification due to an uninitialised variable, was neither sophisticated re-entrancy nor economic manipulation. It was an engineering oversight. Likewise, the 2023 Multichain collapse stemmed from compromised operational keys rather than contract-level patterns. These outliers remind us that crypto's attack surface is heterogeneous. No taxonomy can capture every failure. But pattern recognition still matters, because patterns describe *families* of behaviour. And those families recur with unnerving frequency.

The motif that threads through this subchapter is simple: sequence. Every exploit hinges on order—who calls what, when, and under which assumptions. To read systems defensively means to read sequences sceptically. Where developers see flow, attackers see junctions. Where users see convenience, attackers see accumulated permissions. Where protocols see price, attackers see manipulable time windows.

Standing at the edge of this pattern landscape, a practical question emerges, unresolved and urgent. When you next sign a transaction, review an audit, or assess a protocol, will you map the sequence of assumptions that keep it stable—or will you trust that no one else is mapping them more carefully than you?

Operational security basics

Before sunrise on 10 November 2022, engineers at FTX.US watched their internal dashboards flicker with strange withdrawals. By evening, more than US$370 million had vanished into a cluster of wallets traced to a single compromised operator key. The timing was dramatic, but the mechanism was painfully ordinary: one privileged private key, held by an unidentified individual in an imploding organisation, controlled pause functions and transfer rights across multiple smart-contract pathways. Nothing in the Solidity code failed. No cryptographic primitive was broken. The breach unfolded because operational authority had collapsed into a single point of failure. When that point slipped, the system followed.

FTX's downfall is often discussed as a governance tragedy or accounting scandal, but buried beneath the headlines lies a sharper lesson. A system's operational spine—its key management, its signing thresholds, its upgrade paths—defines its real security boundary. Software can be peer-reviewed, audited, and formally verified, yet remain brittle if the keys that govern its behaviour are weakly protected or overly concentrated. On 19 December 2021, a similar pattern surfaced when the Grim Finance protocol on Fantom lost roughly US$30 million through a re-entrancy attack enabled by a single deployer-controlled contract. Again, the code misbehaved only because the deployer retained powers that users assumed had been relinquished. The operator, not the attacker, had left the back door ajar.

The motif running through such cases is concentration. Not of capital, but of control. And control, in cryptographic systems, is expressed through keys. Who holds them, how they are stored, and what permissions they carry shape the system's true attack surface far more than any marketing claim about "decentralisation".

The first major claim is simple: **key management is not an operational footnote; it is the foundation of trustworthiness.** Show the mechanism and its consequence. In the Ronin Network breach of 23 March 2022, attackers obtained access to five of the nine validator keys—four held by Sky Mavis in Vietnam and one by Axie DAO—thereby meeting the signing threshold required to approve withdrawals. The protocol's multisig configuration, designed to appear distributed, was in practice concentrated in closely linked entities. The exploit was not a cryptographic failure; it was a governance shortcut. Keys were stored in predictable places; access rights were implicitly shared; monitoring was inadequate. Once the adversary acquired a majority of signers, US$624 million in assets left the bridge without resistance. The implication is blunt. A multisig cannot create decentralisation if its signers report to the same authority.

Name the pattern: **pseudo-multisigs**. Systems that advertise multiparty control but consolidate signers under a single organisation or tightly interconnected individuals. Explain its effect. Pseudo-multisigs give users the psychological comfort of distributed authority without offering any of its safety guarantees. The implication extends beyond security incidents. They distort user expectations. A protocol that looks like a collective may, in practice, be governed by a handful of engineers, any one of whom could suffer phishing, coercion, burnout, or simple error.

The second major claim concerns **thresholds**. Multisigs are only as resilient as the threshold they adopt. A 2-of-3 configuration offers convenience and speed, but its safety margin is low. Show the real-world behaviour. After the BadgerDAO front-end compromise in December 2021, investigators discovered that its upgrade multisig—designed to act in emergencies—operated with a low threshold to avoid delays. Though unrelated to the hack, the configuration later raised questions about how quickly adversaries might have pivoted had they targeted the contract rather than the interface. The implication is that thresholds encode a system's philosophy: whether it prioritises agility or survival. A low threshold accelerates deployments but reduces friction for attackers.

Introduce a counter-example that challenges simple generalisations. In November 2020, the MakerDAO governance system used a single executive key to implement emergency shutdowns. Critics argued this was antithetical to decentralisation. Yet, during extreme market volatility in March 2020, this centralised intervention capacity arguably prevented greater losses by enabling rapid fixes to auction parameters. The limitation is important. Concentrated authority can reduce blast radius in crises—if wielded transparently and with strong social oversight. Reconcile this nuance: concentration is not inherently dangerous; *unexamined* concentration is.

The third claim concerns **deployer powers**—often the most misunderstood privileges in decentralised systems. Many protocols retain upgradeable proxies, ostensibly to fix bugs or add features. Show the role of deployers in action. When Level Finance on BNB Chain was exploited on 1 May 2023, the root cause lay in overlooked upgrade permissions that allowed the attacker to call a legacy function through an outdated router. The contract behaved as written; the deployer's retained authority over the upgrade path allowed dormant code to be reachable. The implication is that immutability, when incomplete, becomes a liability. Nothing attracts an attacker like the hope that an obsolete route still leads somewhere valuable.

Name the pattern: **hidden super-user privileges.** Explain why they matter. Users often assume that a contract, once deployed, becomes autonomous. But many teams retain owner roles, pause rights, minting powers, or configuration access for operational convenience. If those keys sit with a single engineer—perhaps an overworked founder, perhaps a contractor—then the entire protocol inherits that individual's security posture. A system can appear robust on-chain while its real control resides in a laptop in a coworking space.

The fourth claim turns to **operational interfaces**, the bridge between human action and contract authority. Key management failures often emerge from routine behaviours: downloading a seed phrase over insecure Wi-Fi, storing a hardware wallet in a predictable location, or reusing passwords across multiple access points. These behaviours are visible and measurable. The 2022 compromise of Profanity-generated addresses, used by Wintermute, resulted from weak entropy in private key derivation, but the underlying issue was behavioural: convenience trumped randomness. The implication is broader than one incident. Operational security collapses not because cryptography falters but because humans prioritise speed over hygiene.

Thread the motif—**concentration**—again. Even the most elegant multisig can degenerate into centralisation by habit. If one signer consistently prepares transactions for others, or if signers routinely approve blindly, the structure may exist on paper while decision-making contracts back into a single hub. Real decentralisation requires behavioural distribution, not merely architectural distribution.

A credible counter-example refines this understanding. The Gnosis Safe multisig ecosystem, widely adopted since 2019, demonstrates that operational security can scale when teams commit to transparent rotation of signers, detailed execution logs, and separation of duties. These practices show that strong operational security is not inherently cumbersome; it is cultural. The limitation, however, is that such discipline must be maintained. Once teams grow complacent—failing to rotate keys, delaying audits of signer behaviour—the benefits erode.

The fifth claim concerns **pause functions and emergency breakers**. These mechanisms permit operators to halt protocol activity during crises. But the power to pause is also the power to censor, drain, or redirect. In February 2021, the Alpha Homora v2 exploit demonstrated how pause authority required swift and coordinated action across teams. Fortunately, the emergency controls operated as intended. But consider the structural risk: if a pause key sits with a single anonymous operator, the protocol's entire safety net depends on one person's vigilance—and their continued good faith. The implication is straightforward. Emergency powers demand stronger, not weaker, decentralisation.

A final dimension spans all these claims: **monitoring**. Operational security is not a static configuration but a continuous practice. Teams that track signer activity, verify that threshold rules are followed, and publicly document key rotations create a dialectic between operators and users. This dialectic—rooted in visibility—serves as a quiet but powerful deterrent to internal and external adversaries. When user communities can review on-chain actions in real time, complacency becomes harder and manipulation more visible.

Returning to the motif of concentration, a question arises. A protocol may display diagrams of distributed authority, multisigs, governance modules, and decentralised signers. Yet these diagrams often hide the human layer: who holds the devices, who prepares the transactions, who controls the emergency keys, and who decides when to rotate them. The gap between architecture and practice is where operational fragility grows.

The chapter's unresolved tension comes to rest here. When you next evaluate a protocol, will you accept operational assurances at face value—or will you trace each key, each signer, each privilege until you can see exactly where power resides, and what would happen if that person slept through an alarm?

Live safety nets

At 02:43 UTC on 30 April 2022, the Wormhole bridge team in New York watched their monitors freeze. A validator exploit had allowed an attacker to mint 120,000 wrapped ETH without depositing the underlying collateral. The code had passed multiple audits; the cryptography itself held firm. What failed was the live safety net. The guardian set lacked the circuit-breaker logic required to halt minting until signatures could be revalidated. Minutes later, Jump Trading stepped in, injecting US$320 million to recapitalise the deficit and avoid contagion. The incident—despite its scale—became a near miss rather than an extinction event. The decisive factor was not the absence of bugs, but the presence of mechanisms and actors capable of absorbing catastrophic shocks when the unexpected struck.

A similar pattern emerged on 14 June 2023 when the Polygon Labs security team triggered a time-locked upgrade to isolate a potential zero-day in its zkEVM rollup infrastructure. The patch took 32 hours to propagate across sequencers and verifiers because of deliberately enforced delay windows. Users noticed the slowdown. Observers questioned the inconvenience. Yet the discomfort was precisely the point. Time-locks replace instant administrative action with friction—friction that buys communities the opportunity to detect, challenge, or halt a dangerous change. In this case, the vulnerability proved containable. No user funds were lost. The chain absorbed the disturbance because layers of defence, despite their cost, held their shape.

These two cases reveal a motif we will return to: **friction as protection**. Circuits, locks, bounties, pools—each is a deliberate brake applied to systems that would otherwise accelerate too quickly for human oversight.

The first major claim is that **bug bounties convert adversarial energy into a protective force**. Show the behaviour. Immunefi, founded in 2020 and headquartered in Singapore, has coordinated payouts exceeding US$80 million (as of September 2023), including the US$10 million reward earned for disclosing a critical Arbitrum vulnerability. Name the pattern. High-stakes bounties attract skilled actors who might otherwise exploit flaws. Explain the mechanism.

A bounty programme signals that a team acknowledges uncertainty, values external scrutiny, and commits to paying for it. The implication is measurable. Projects with top-tier bounty programmes tend to receive earlier disclosures and faster patch cycles because researchers prioritise systems that reward their work predictably.

Introduce a limitation to avoid naïve optimism. Some attackers do not seek rewards; they seek the asymmetric thrill or illicit gain that no bounty can match. In the Euler Finance exploit of March 2023, the attacker drained US$197 million before later returning most funds. A bounty would not have prevented the initial theft. Reconcile the nuance. Bounties reduce risk; they do not neutralise it. They matter most as part of a sequence, not a standalone fix.

The second claim concerns **circuit breakers**, mechanisms that interrupt contract functionality when predefined thresholds are breached. Show the dynamic. When dYdX deployed its v3 perpetuals exchange in 2021, it implemented a withdrawal delay and position-size circuit breaker calibrated to volatility metrics derived from Coinbase and Binance order books. Name the behaviour. During extreme market moves in May 2022, the breaker limited cascading liquidations by slowing down order execution in thin liquidity conditions. Explain its purpose. A breaker forces the system to pause and evaluate before continuing an action that could amplify damage. The implication is structural: a protocol that slows itself intentionally creates space for operators and users to intervene.

Again, a counter-example clarifies the boundary. In February 2020, MakerDAO's Black Thursday event exposed the limits of breaker-free designs. Gas-price spikes on Ethereum prevented keepers from submitting collateral bids, draining US$8.3 million of user equity. The design had no mechanism to throttle auctions when the network became unusable. Reconcile the insight. Circuit breakers cannot fix everything, but their absence guarantees that failures compound uncontrollably. Their presence merely creates the possibility of repair before collapse.

Thread the motif of friction once more. Breakers are not elegant. They frustrate traders, slow withdrawals, and anger users when invoked prematurely. Yet this irritation is a sign of function. A breaker must hurt a little to help a lot.

The third claim explores **insurance pools**, a class of mechanisms intended to compensate users when catastrophic failures occur. Show their operation. Nexus Mutual, launched in the United Kingdom in 2019 under the legal structure of a discretionary mutual, offers cover for smart-contract failures. Following the Yearn Finance vault exploit in February 2021, Nexus paid out approximately US$2 million to affected stakers after member voting confirmed the validity of claims. Name the principle: collective-risk assessment distributed across informed participants. Explain its role. Insurance pools reduce the financial blast radius of unforeseen failures. The implication is more than economic. A project that integrates insurance acknowledges a duty of care to its users, signalling seriousness and maturity.

Yet insurance has its limitations. Underfunded pools, or those with poorly defined claim criteria, can delay or deny payouts. After the bZx breach in September 2020, several insurance products linked to the protocol struggled to reach consensus about whether the incident met claim conditions. Reconcile the difference. Insurance works when governance is clear, reserves are credible, and processes are mechanical rather than moralistic.

The fourth claim concerns **time-locked upgrades**, a specific form of friction that transforms code changes from instantaneous edits into staged, observable processes. Show the impact. When Compound Finance implemented its COMP distribution adjustments in 2021, changes passed through a two-day time-lock, allowing stakeholders to examine, critique, or contest proposals before activation. Name the mechanism: enforced latency. Explain its defensive power. Time-locks give users time to withdraw, pause positions, or raise alarms. Their witness period deters malicious governance proposals because the attacker must endure public scrutiny before any change takes effect. The implication stretches into governance theory. Slow systems can be safer systems—not because speed is undesirable, but because unchecked speed is indistinguishable from unilateral control.

Introduce a credible counterpoint. In fast-moving environments—particularly high-frequency trading or real-time oracles—delays can degrade performance or create arbitrage opportunities. Some Layer-2 sequencers argue that time-locks eliminate their ability to patch urgent bugs. Reconcile by returning to the earlier motif. The question is not whether friction slows a system but whether the chosen friction improves the system's survivability more than it harms its utility. Mature protocols design gradated controls: short locks for non-critical paths, long locks for governance, and permanent immutability for settlement-critical logic.

A fifth claim binds the previous ones through the concept of **layered defences**. A bug bounty rewards discovery. A circuit breaker halts propagation. An insurance pool mitigates financial loss. A time-lock deters administrative capture. Each addresses a different failure mode, and none substitutes for the others. Show how layers work together. In the Optimism governance incident of June 2022, when 20 million OP tokens were mistakenly sent to an unauthorised address, the presence of a multisig time-lock and active bounty channels allowed the team to engage the community rapidly. A whitehat ultimately returned the tokens. The layered approach created redundancy. If one protection failed, the others absorbed the shock.

Name the broader design philosophy: **defence in depth**, a concept borrowed from operational security and adopted—slowly—by decentralised finance. Explain its relevance. Systems that rely on a single protective layer bet their survival on that layer never failing. History renders that bet indefensible. The implication is cultural. Teams that design with defence in depth signal that they expect things to go wrong and have prepared for that inevitability.

Return to the motif of friction a final time. Friction is not the enemy of progress. It is the scaffolding that keeps progress from collapsing under its own weight.

As you assess a protocol's safety nets, a question arises that resists easy resolution. How much friction is enough, and how much becomes too much? A system that pauses too readily frustrates users; a system that never pauses may not survive its first serious shock.

Your task is to decide where that boundary lies—and whether the team behind the protocol seems to know it, too.

Chapter 7
Teams, Governance, and Incentives

The first signs of trouble arrived quietly. In April 2022, members of the Wonderland community pieced together that the treasury—then valued at more than half a billion dollars—was effectively under the unilateral control of a single pseudonymous operator, backed by a figure whose own identity had resurfaced from a troubled past. The revelation was not the product of a sophisticated exploit or a sudden hack. It emerged from patient scrutiny of multisig signers, governance proposals, and commit patterns across repositories. What shocked the community was not merely who held the keys, but how few people knew. The machinery of decision-making, once assumed to be distributed, had in fact narrowed into a funnel. When that funnel cracked, the project's credibility drained almost at once.

A year later, in May 2023, a very different story unfolded in the Cosmos ecosystem. Terra had collapsed, but Osmosis—another Cosmos-based chain—weathered the storm with striking resilience. Its contributors convened public calls within hours, published incident reports, and circulated a patch schedule for its automated market-maker. The chain did not avoid turbulence, but its rhythm of openness sustained trust long enough for users and validators to coordinate a collective response. Power was visible, not hidden. This clarity, more than any technical detail, kept the network's social fabric intact.

These twin images—a treasury trapped behind a single key, and a community that stabilised itself through deliberate visibility—illustrate a motif that threads through this chapter: the map matters more than the slogan. Teams proclaim decentralisation. Users feel it only when authority leaves a trail that can be followed, questioned, and, if necessary, escaped.

The stakes of such mapping have grown sharper as protocols evolve from small experiments into institutions with quasi-sovereign reach. The central question is no longer merely *what* the system does, but *who* has the actual ability to shape it. This reorientation—towards builders, governance structures, and the incentives binding them—

marks a turning point in the reader's analytic toolkit. Until now, the book has delved into innovation signals, whitepaper scrutiny, token mechanics, and attack surfaces. Here we turn to the social machinery that determines whether those systems can endure. Code can be forked. Economics can be redesigned. But misaligned teams or opaque authority structures tend to replicate themselves until they break.

The first layer concerns the builders themselves: identifiable enough to evaluate, yet not required to sacrifice personal privacy. In decentralised systems, identity often arrives indirectly—through commit histories that stretch across public repositories, through recurring names in technical forums, through patterns of contribution that form a kind of narrative fingerprint. A team with credible backers, sustained output, and coherent architectural decisions develops a recognisable style. Conversely, a team that appears suddenly with a dozen dormant GitHub accounts, no contributors outside a compressed time window, and an absence of external references is telling you something—quietly, but firmly—about its depth. These traces matter, because they reveal whether the system's custodians can be trusted to maintain discipline over months and years rather than weeks.

Transparency rhythms form the second layer. Mature teams operate at a cadence visible to the outside world: monthly treasury reports, recurring community calls, public roadmaps, clear issue trackers. These rhythms reduce the interpretive fog around decision-making. The key insight is not that transparency must be constant, but that it must be predictable. Silence can be healthy when it is part of an understood cycle. Silence becomes threat when it is unexpected. Predictable rhythms create a contract of expectation: the team agrees to surface information at known intervals; the community agrees to evaluate with appropriate spacing rather than constant pressure.

The third layer is explicit power mapping. Every system centralises something—tokens, keys, committees, foundations, councils, labs. The distribution itself is less important than the clarity with which it is documented and constrained. A system with on-chain votes but a hidden admin key capable of minting new tokens at will is decentralised in ceremony only. A system with a foundation that can veto governance outcomes, or with upgrade powers concentrated in a single multisig signer, demands a different risk assessment than its public narrative implies. Power mapping is not cynicism; it is literacy. Without it, users mistake ceremony for structure.

The final layer concerns escape velocity: the ability of participants to fork or exit when governance alignment fractures. Forkability does not guarantee a thriving alternative—many forks languish—but its very existence disciplines the original team. When leadership drifts or incentives warp, a permissive licence or a clean state-export path becomes a silent negotiation tool. Leaders know they can be left behind. Communities know they are not trapped. This mutual awareness tempers excess and encourages consensus-building.

Together, these layers form an ecosystem of accountability—soft in tone, firm in consequence. Teams are rewarded when they make themselves legible. Users become safer when they learn to read the signals. Governance matures when power is acknowledged rather than obscured.

Yet a tension remains, unresolved by design: how much centralisation is tolerable in the early stages of a project, and how quickly should power be decentralised as systems scale? Excessive haste can cripple execution; excessive delay can corrode trust. Between these poles lies the real work of evaluating teams, structures, and incentives—the work this chapter now invites you to undertake.

Who are the builders?

In February 2021, a developer known publicly only as "0xMaki" stepped back from SushiSwap, the decentralised exchange whose frantic creation had captivated and divided the Ethereum community. The project had launched in late August 2020, during a heatwave of unaudited forks, anonymous founders, and breathless speculation. Yet when its original creator—who called himself "Chef Nomi"—withdrew funds from the protocol's treasury, it was 0xMaki's visible, persistent commit history and the public support of auditors, contributors, and ecosystem backers that steadied the protocol long enough for governance to reclaim control. His pseudonym remained intact. His track record did the talking. And the community's ability to trace that track record across repositories, issues, and code reviews became the foundation of its trust, slender though it initially was. Tokyo was the only physical place ever loosely associated with him, though even that was contested; what mattered was the trace, not the location.

The contrast with Iron Finance's collapse in June 2021 could not have been starker. The team behind the algorithmic stablecoin had promised ambitious mechanics and expansive vision, but scrutiny of their GitHub activity revealed sparse commits, inconsistent contributor identities, and weeks-long gaps between code changes. When their token entered a death spiral and the protocol failed to recover, the absence of a credible builder graph—sustained engagement, coherent authorship, discernible expertise—became a central part of the post-mortem. Participants had chased a narrative without checking who had written it.

The motif threaded through these episodes is simple: **traceability without doxxing**. Effective evaluation of a team does not require forcing builders to expose their civilian identities. It requires following the marks they leave in public infrastructure—commits, reviews, discussions, audits, endorsements—and asking whether the pattern forms a recognisable hand. The question is not "Who are they in real life?" but "What have they reliably built that strangers can verify?"

The first claim to examine is the idea that builder credibility can be inferred from contribution patterns rather than biographical disclosure. The show phase begins with actions visible to anyone: a repository with dozens of merged pull requests from the same handle, month after month; issues closed with articulate explanations; cross-repo references that demonstrate architectural thinking. Name this behaviour: provenance through craft. It explains a specific truth about decentralised ecosystems—they reward builders who leave legible fingerprints on public code, even if they choose pseudonymity. The implication is profound for due diligence: identity becomes a graph of outputs rather than a line on a passport.

A clear example emerges from the early development of Uniswap. Between 2018 and 2020, Hayden Adams' commits across the protocol's repos showed a coherent evolution of smart contract design, each change linked to prior discussions in the Ethereum Research forum. This traceability, anchored to New York where Adams was working during the initial build, offered a public record of continuity. A different example comes from the Polkadot/Substrate ecosystem in Berlin, where Parity Technologies' engineers—such as Gavin Wood and Jaco Görner—maintained extensive commit histories that outsiders could inspect to understand capability, thought process, and technical depth. Both cases show teams whose credibility derives not from marketing polish but from the visible accumulation of contribution density over time.

The counter-example, credible and instructive, sits with projects that produce glossy whitepapers but leave almost no public technical footprints. Some privacy-focused teams keep their repositories closed by design, citing security concerns. This limitation is real. Yet even in these cases, credible projects share alternative verification channels: academic papers with independent review, reproducible cryptographic proofs, named collaborations with universities, or verifiable timelines with staged disclosures. The reconciliation lies in recognising that opacity can be defensible when paired with compensating transparency elsewhere. The absence of a commit graph is not automatically a red flag; the absence of *any* traceable expertise is the red flag.

A second major claim concerns backers and institutional affiliations. Showing begins with a simple observation: teams with reputable supporters leave public endorsements. Venture funds publish investment memos. Grant programmes list awardees. Hackathon organisers document winners. Name this phenomenon: external anchoring. It explains how ecosystem actors distribute their reputations across projects, enabling newcomers to infer trust gradients. The implication is that credible backers do not guarantee success, but they contribute to a risk map that distinguishes earnest experimentation from opportunistic improvisation.

One example is the history of MakerDAO, whose early grants and collaborations with the Ethereum Foundation between 2015 and 2017 remain a matter of public record. These partnerships created a verifiable timeline of institutional engagement. Another example lies in the grants issued by the Solana Foundation in 2020–2021, including identifiable recipients like Mango Markets and Orca, whose builders maintained visible commit histories long before their tokens gained market traction. These associations did not eliminate risk—Mango would later face an exploit—but they created documentary trails showing that teams had been building before attention arrived.

The counter-example concerns projects that advertise "strategic partnerships" with well-known organisations without providing verifiable links. When names appear only in press releases, not in public statements from the supposed partners, the discrepancy is itself informative. Reconciliation requires nuance: early-stage teams may have tentative collaborations they cannot yet formalise, but serious builders typically provide at least one corroborating detail—co-authored documentation, shared test environments, or public calls with identifiable contributors.

The third major claim is that contributor graphs reveal as much about governance culture as about technical ability. Show this by examining the rhythm of contributions. A repository with ten active contributors in London, Singapore, and Toronto shows distributed stewardship. A repository dominated by one account, with the rest making cosmetic commits, shows centralised control. Name the insight: structural concentration. It explains that decentralisation is not a slogan but a pattern. The implication is that users who care about resilience should inspect where the work actually happens.

Consider the multi-year evolution of Gnosis Safe (now Safe), whose core development team steadily expanded contributor access between 2019 and 2022. Roles were documented. Merge permissions were assigned transparently. The London, Berlin, and Zug teams' contributions formed a mesh rather than a spoke. By contrast, several 2021-era yield aggregators operated with a single deployer key and a commit history dominated by one developer whose supporting accounts appeared within the same fortnight—an artefact suggesting sock-puppet contributors rather than a real team. The counter-example, again requiring balance, involves small research-oriented teams whose technical depth may exceed their contributor count. Reconciling this means evaluating not the *number* of contributors but the *coherence* of their work: a small group with intense, well-documented output may be healthier than a large group with fragmented effort.

Throughout these threads, the motif of traceability returns—traceability as breadcrumb, as fingerprint, as ledger of intent. The essence of this subchapter is not about unmasking individuals, but about cultivating literacy in the trails serious builders naturally leave behind. A pseudonymous cryptographer with a decade-long history of verifiable research papers, dated commits, reproducible experiments, and repeated collaborations across continents is not "anonymous" in any meaningful sense. They are simply known by a reference different from a legal name.

This leads to a final tension, which cannot be fully resolved here. How much weight should a reader place on track record versus fresh ambition? There is danger in overvaluing pedigree, just as there is danger in ignoring it. Some of the most important breakthroughs in decentralised systems have come from newcomers. But newcomers who build seriously leave traces quickly—commits, discussions, testnets, prototypes—while pretenders rely on abstraction, vagueness, and delay.

So the question that closes this piece is deliberately demanding: when you look at a project you are evaluating, what can you *follow*? Not who they claim to be, nor what their token price signals, but what trail exists that you can check, piece by piece. If the trail is thick, coherent, and historical, the team is telling you who they are. If the trail is thin, sporadic, or staged, they may be telling you something else entirely.

Transparency rhythms

On 14 February 2022, the Aave community gathered for its routine public call, streamed from a modest office in London and joined asynchronously from Seoul, Buenos Aires, and Nairobi. The agenda was unremarkable: treasury updates, pending risk assessments, and development milestones. Yet one detail made the call linger in the memory of veteran observers. When a participant questioned a line item involving a grant disbursement, the Aave Companies representative pulled up the transaction hash, explained the milestone conditions, and invited independent verification within minutes. No choreography. No hedging. Just a rhythm: disclose, discuss, document. That cadence—predictable, visible, inspectable—would become a yardstick by which later treasuries were judged, especially those that claimed openness but delivered only sporadic bursts of communication.

A few months earlier, in October 2021, another rhythm had broken. Wonderland, a high-profile DeFi protocol, began delaying its financial updates. First by days, then weeks. Community calls were cancelled without explanation. GitHub issues piled up unanswered. The market turbulence that followed was blamed on macro conditions, but those watching the pattern knew the deeper cause: silence had replaced structure. When founder identities later imploded under scrutiny, the breakdown in transparency rhythms proved to be not a symptom but an early signal. The project had drifted from regularity to opacity long before its collapse.

These two scenes illuminate a core motif that will run throughout this piece: **light that blinks, not light that flashes**. Transparency is not a single dramatic reveal; it is a metronome. Predictable beats of communication build the substrate of trust long before crises arise. And in decentralised systems—where accountability is harder to enforce and easier to avoid—the cadence of updates often matters as much as their content.

The first major claim is that transparency can be measured through observable behaviours rather than marketing tone. To show this, look at the simplest possible artefact: a recurring public call. Name the behaviour: scheduled openness. It explains why projects that hold weekly or monthly calls with published agendas—even if viewer numbers remain small—tend to sustain healthier contributor ecosystems. The implication is straightforward. Regularity allows scrutiny to compound. If a team shows up at predictable intervals, inconsistencies surface organically; if it shows up only when convenient, scrutiny becomes performative.

Consider the example of Gitcoin's governance calls during 2020–2022. Each session recorded on YouTube, each transcript posted in the forum within forty-eight hours, each open question marked for follow-up. Denver, Lisbon, and Bangalore contributors could join as equals. Contrast this with the periodic "AMA blasts" favoured by certain short-lived yield projects in the same period—one-hour promotional sessions with no agendas, no records, and no follow-up threads. The former created archives the community could audit. The latter evaporated as quickly as they appeared.

A credible counter-example sits with Zcash's early development under the Electric Coin Company. For years, public calls were less frequent, and technical updates came primarily through cryptographic academic channels. Yet the ecosystem demonstrated transparency through alternative rhythms: detailed research papers, reproducible parameters for trusted setups, and public engineering updates with line-level specificity. The reconciliation lies in recognising that transparency is not a single format. The cadence must be visible somewhere. If calls are infrequent, documentation must be richer. When documentation is sparse, calls must be more structured. The rhythm must exist.

The second major claim concerns written updates. Showing begins with a practice that outsiders can examine immediately: monthly or fortnightly progress logs. Name the behaviour: documented continuity. It explains how written updates create the memory of a protocol—what decisions were made, which trade-offs were accepted, what was deprioritised. The implication is subtle but critical: without written continuity, communities lose the ability to evaluate direction, because they cannot reconstruct how and why decisions evolved.

Polygon's development from 2020 to 2022 provides a concrete example. Across Mumbai, Singapore, and Dubai teams, engineering updates were published with summaries of merge requests, performance measurements from testnets, and risk considerations flagged for community review. The updates did not guarantee success—but they allowed any participant to trace technical decisions across time. A second example lies in Curve Finance's governance forums, where even contentious debates on emissions schedules or pool risks were preserved as written threads, enabling newcomers to understand how positions hardened or softened.

The limitation is seen in fast-moving experimental protocols where builders argue that time spent on updates slows iteration. Some early-stage teams indeed produce more code when not burdened with writing. Yet reconciliation requires asking: what is the cost of silence? A project can move quickly without being mute. Even a two-paragraph weekly snapshot—open issues, pending reviews, upcoming decisions—reveals whether a team is thinking structurally or improvising reactively.

A third major claim concerns open issues and their management. Showing begins with the observable state of a repository: issues tagged, triaged, or left to stagnate. Name this behaviour: operational hygiene. It reveals a truth about decentralised systems often overlooked by casual observers: good governance begins with good housekeeping. The implication is that the health of issue queues predicts the health of decision-making. If bugs linger untriaged for months, governance proposals will likely linger too. If issues are closed with no explanation, decisions elsewhere may follow similar patterns.

A salient example comes from Yearn Finance's issue management in 2021. Despite a sprawling repository, issues were labelled with clear statuses—"needs discussion", "needs audit", "blocked"—and contributors from Paris to São Paulo engaged in resolving them. The pattern signalled a culture that valued scrutiny. Another example appears in Arbitrum's early development, where public issues concerning sequencer assumptions and fraud-proof architecture were answered directly by engineers, creating a trackable record of deliberation.

The credible limitation lies in protocols whose core components are not hosted on GitHub for security or proprietary reasons. Their issue queues may appear empty. But reconciliation requires examining alternative hygiene indicators: do they maintain public risk registers? Are known vulnerabilities disclosed on mailing lists? Are open questions discussed in community forums rather than buried in private chats?

The motif of light returns here—light as cadence, not spotlight. Transparency rhythms give communities a chance to see problems before they metastasise. A monthly treasury report with Q&A, like those adopted by Lido in 2022, allows stakeholders to measure decisions with actual numbers: runway months, asset allocations, liquidity positions. A team that refuses such rhythms may not be hiding wrongdoing; it may simply lack structure. But the effect is the same. Without cadence, information decays into speculation.

This brings the discussion to a fourth claim: transparency rhythms shape not just community trust but real governance outcomes. Show this through behaviour: when teams publish consistent updates, voter turnout increases, delegate engagement rises, and proposals become more substantive. Name the dynamic: participatory reinforcement. It explains why communities with strong communication rhythms tend to produce more sophisticated, less reactionary decision-making. The implication is that transparency is not merely a moral good but a governance tool. It disciplines teams by making silence conspicuous and indecision measurable.

A telling example can be found in Optimism's governance cycles. With regular retrospectives and forward-looking roadmaps, published from April 2022 onwards, the community developed a habit of thematic proposal seasons. The structure channelled debate, prevented proposal fatigue, and anchored decisions in shared context. By contrast, several DAO treasuries during the 2021 bull market were depleted rapidly because no such rhythms existed; proposals were passed impulsively, budgets ballooned without scrutiny, and participants lacked a clear forum for questioning assumptions.

The counter-example worth examining involves Bitcoin Core, where formal update rhythms are minimal. There are no public governance calls, no recurring treasury updates, and no central forum for decision accountability. Yet Bitcoin's governance is effective precisely because of its radically distributed design. The reconciliation is that cadence emerges not from organisation but from the code review cycle, the BIP (Bitcoin Improvement Proposal) process, and the peer-review norms enforced by long-term contributors. The rhythm exists—it simply lives in the public logs of the repository rather than in social structures.

A final claim concerns the emotional dimension of transparency rhythms. Show begins with a simple lived behaviour: communities feel calmer when communication is steady. Name this phenomenon: baseline reassurance. It explains why even modest updates reduce panic during market turbulence. The implication is that transparency rhythms serve as psychological infrastructure. They stabilise expectations, reduce rumour velocity, and anchor interpretation in shared facts rather than speculative narratives.

As this subchapter draws toward its forward test, the motif blinks again: regular light is not glamorous, but it is life-saving. The unresolved question for any reader evaluating a project is therefore sharp, practical, and unavoidable: *What clock does this team run on?* If the cadence is coherent—calls, updates, issues, reports—the project is giving you a way to measure its internal state. If the cadence is erratic, improvised, or purely reactive, you must decide what that rhythm implies about future governance.

Does the team create light you can follow? Or do you find yourself waiting, refreshing, and hoping?

Power mapping

On 19 April 2022, holders of CAKE, the governance token of PancakeSwap, voted overwhelmingly to reduce emissions and introduce a deflationary model. Screens in London and Singapore lit up with celebratory threads: "The community has spoken." Yet buried in the protocol contracts on Binance Smart Chain sat a single address with unilateral minting rights—an admin key controlled by the core team. In practice, the "maximum supply" that voters had just endorsed could be overridden at any time by one transaction. No hack required. No elaborate exploit. Just a choice. Token holders believed they sat at the apex of the power structure; the codebase told a different story.

That tension between appearance and reality plays out again in a different register with Terra in May 2022. As UST depegged and LUNA entered its death spiral, governance votes continued to pass on-chain, yet a small group around Terraform Labs in Seoul effectively drove emergency decisions: pausing the chain, altering parameters, proposing radical supply changes. Formal governance mechanics still existed—voting contracts, quorum thresholds, proposal queues—but crisis management bypassed them. The centre of gravity had always been off-chain, in a tightly knit company that could rally validators and clients in hours. For many holders, the revelation came too late. By the time they mapped where power truly sat, their capital had already been vaporised.

The motif that runs through these examples is simple and unsettling: **power has a location, whether you map it or not**. A protocol may present flow charts showing arrows between token holders, councils, foundations, and labs, but the decisive question is always the same: *who can actually change what, how fast, and with whose consent?* The first major claim is that token voting, by itself, rarely describes the real power structure. It describes a theatre. The show is visible: ballot pages, delegate profiles, colourful dashboards of turnout. Name the pattern: ceremonial decentralisation. Explain it plainly. Token voting can become a ritual that legitimises decisions without constraining the actors who matter most—core teams, foundation boards, multisig signers, infrastructure providers. The implication is concrete: if you stop your analysis at "token holders decide", you are not doing governance analysis; you are reading marketing. To see this clearly, examine Uniswap's governance during 2020–2021. UNI holders could propose and vote on parameter changes, treasury usage, and grants. Yet the quorum requirement—4 per cent of the total supply, with several per cent held by a16z and other large funds—meant no major proposal could pass without at least tacit consent from a few concentrated addresses. The contracts encoded a veto in all but name. By contrast, ENS (Ethereum Name Service), launched as a DAO in November 2021, designed a council of stewards with defined mandates, while reserving certain constitutional changes for higher quorums and multi-sig approvals.

Both systems had token voting; only one documented its implicit veto points. The difference was not whether power concentrated, but whether the map matched the terrain.

A credible counter-example complicates the picture. Bitcoin, developed from 2009 with key contributors in Helsinki, New York, and elsewhere, has no formal token voting at all. No foundation can unilaterally change consensus rules. Power instead emerges from a rough alignment of miners, node operators, exchanges, and users. A Bitcoin Improvement Proposal (BIP) gains traction only when code changes are adopted by enough independent actors to make alternative forks economically unattractive. Here, power is diffuse and emergent rather than explicitly mapped. Reconciling this with on-chain governance requires care. Formal voting can help coordinate large, complex systems, but it can also create the illusion that power is exactly where the UI says it is. Informal systems may look chaotic, yet embed stronger vetoes in practice.

The second major claim is that foundations and councils often act as *hidden junctions* where authority converges. Show this through behaviour. When Solana experienced outages in September 2021 and again in January 2022, Solana Labs engineers and the Solana Foundation coordinated validator restarts via private channels. Validators in Zurich, Frankfurt, and Chicago executed the restart, but the coordination spine sat with the foundation and the core lab. Name this structure: operational centrality. Explain why it matters. Publicly, SOL holders could influence some high-level decisions through governance; in practice, liveness and safety hinged on a small group's capacity to orchestrate responses. The implication is that foundations are not merely grant-making bodies. They are often the emergency operating system.

Contrast this with the structure used by Cosmos Hub and the Interchain Foundation in 2021–2022. Here, ATOM token holders could vote on proposals that directly instructed core development teams, funded external entities, or altered strategic direction. The Interchain Foundation held significant influence via funding, but proposals sometimes passed against its recommendations. In this arrangement, the foundation still mattered, but its veto power was partial. The map showed multiple centres—token holders, core teams, validators—with no single point capable of overriding the rest without consequence.

A limitation must be acknowledged. Early-stage projects often centralise decision-making in a lab or foundation to move quickly. That centralisation is not, on its own, evidence of malice. The risk emerges when teams freeze this arrangement while continuing to market themselves as "community governed". Reconciling this means distinguishing *transitional* centralisation—documented, time-bounded, explicit—from *permanent* centralisation disguised as decentralisation. Power mapping is the process of telling those two apart.

The third major claim addresses perhaps the most neglected element of power: **admin keys and upgrade rights**. Show the mechanics. Many contracts ship with owner roles that can pause deposits, adjust fees, change oracle sources, or mint new tokens. Name the pattern: embedded override. Explain its effect. Whatever formal governance exists, whoever controls those keys retains a veto—or worse, the ability to bypass governance entirely. The implication is harsh but precise: until powerful admin keys are either eliminated or brought under strong, transparent multisig and time-lock constraints, "community control" remains aspirational.

The history of Tether's USDT contracts illustrates this duality. Tether Limited, operating out of Hong Kong and later the British Virgin Islands, maintains the ability to freeze and blacklist addresses, functions repeatedly exercised to recover stolen funds or comply with law enforcement. From a user-protection perspective, this capability can be beneficial. Yet it also demonstrates centralised power: regardless of what exchanges or holders might vote, Tether can unilaterally render specific balances inert. By contrast, MakerDAO's DAI, after the deprecation of its single-collateral "SAI" and migration to a multi-collateral model, placed increasing emphasis on governance contracts with clear delay mechanisms. Emergency shutdown keys still exist, but their use is debated openly on governance calls and documented in the protocol's risk frameworks. Both systems have admin powers; one locates them in a private company, the other in a scriptable governance process. A counter-example refines the argument further. Some protocols—for example, specific Uniswap v2 pools—are fully immutable once deployed. They have no upgrade path and no owner. Power sits entirely with those who choose to provide or withdraw liquidity. But immutability comes with a cost: if a bug exists, it cannot be patched; if market conditions change, the contract cannot adapt. Reconciling this tension suggests that power mapping must account for *where* adaptability resides. Either you lodge it in an upgradable contract governed by some authority, or you forego it and accept ossification. Both choices have failure modes; neither is "pure".

The motif that threads through these discussions is **the diagram**. Not the glossy diagram in a pitch deck, but the mental diagram the careful reader draws while asking, repeatedly: *who can do what to whom?* Each arrow labelled "governance" or "community" needs a counterpart in code. Does a token vote directly call a function? Does it feed into a council decision? Does it merely advise the foundation? Is there a separate upgrade multisig? Where are the choke points? The fourth major claim is that power mapping is not static. It changes as token distributions shift, as new contracts are deployed, as foundations spin up or wind down. Show this dynamism. During 2020, early DeFi protocols such as Compound and Aave saw significant ownership concentration among venture funds. Over the next two years, as tokens vested and secondary markets matured, these positions diluted. Delegation campaigns, particularly in North America and Europe, expanded the number of addresses with meaningful voting weight. Name the phenomenon: drifting centres. Explain its effect. A power map drawn in 2020 would show a tight cluster of large holders; a 2022 map would reveal a broader though still skewed distribution. The implication is that governance analysis requires timestamping. A project that *was* de facto controlled by insiders may *now* be influenced by a more varied set of actors—or vice versa.

A credible limitation arises from protocols with strong off-chain brand or legal assets. Even if token distribution becomes diffuse, the founding lab or company may still control trademarks, client relationships, and core developer employment. Uniswap Labs' position in relation to the Uniswap DAO is a clear example. The DAO can, in theory, fund alternative front-ends or competing implementations. In practice, Uniswap Labs' engineering velocity and network of integrations in places like New York, San Francisco, and London gives it informal but substantial sway. Reconciling this means accepting that power is not just on-chain. It also resides in who writes the reference client, who answers enterprise calls, who talks to regulators. A mature power map spans both domains. Throughout this subchapter, the diagram motif returns as a quiet test. If you cannot draw a simple sketch indicating who can: 1) change core parameters; 2) upgrade or replace contracts; 3) spend treasury assets; 4) censor or freeze; 5) override governance outcomes—then you have not mapped power, you have read propaganda. The beauty of blockchains is that many of these relationships are, in principle, inferable from public data. The risk is that very few participants take the time to infer them. The unresolved tension, then, is not whether power centralises. It always does, somewhere. The tension lies in whether you choose to find that centre before it becomes a problem. When you next examine a protocol that calls itself "community owned", will you accept the label, or will you reach for a blank sheet of paper and start drawing arrows until you can answer, with some confidence: where does the veto actually live?

Forkability and exit options

On 20 July 2016, as block 1,920,000 approached on Ethereum, node operators around the world faced a binary choice. In Frankfurt, Singapore and Toronto, some upgraded their clients to implement a hard fork that would reverse the infamous DAO hack and restore funds. Others refused, running the original code in defence of immutability. When the fork executed, the chain split. One branch, supported by the Ethereum Foundation and most developers, carried on as Ethereum. The other, backed by a smaller but principled minority, persisted as Ethereum Classic. There was no court order, no regulator compelling a resolution, no central administrator pushing a button. There was a credible exit option. And because that option existed, both sides were forced to justify their path to an audience that could walk away. Forks are exit options too.

Four years later, in September 2020, a quieter drama unfolded when SushiSwap "vampire attacked" Uniswap's liquidity. By forking Uniswap's permissively licensed contracts and adding a token with aggressive incentives, the Sushi team pulled billions in liquidity towards their own deployment within days. The move was controversial, technically crude in places, and ethically contested. Yet it demonstrated a structural fact: permissive licences and composable architectures make unilateral exit possible not only at the social layer, as in Ethereum's fork, but at the application layer. Users, market makers, and developers can migrate en masse if they believe leadership has drifted or value is being misallocated. The threat of fork, not just the act itself, disciplines teams. The motif that threads through this subchapter is the *door*. Not the glossy front door of official interfaces and branding, but the side doors that matter most: the ability to take code, state, and community elsewhere if trust erodes. In systems governed by tokens and contracts rather than traditional equity, the presence of such doors changes behaviour long before anyone steps through them.

The first claim is that credible forkability shifts power from incumbents to participants, even if the fork never occurs. Show the mechanism, then name it. When Uniswap chose the GPLv3 licence for v3 in March 2021, it made forking significantly harder for commercial competitors. v3's concentrated liquidity design remained technically composable, but its legal constraints closed an obvious exit ramp. Many in the ecosystem read this as a defensive move against copycats like SushiSwap and unnamed centralised exchanges. Explain what this reveals. Licensing determines who can copy what, and under which conditions. The implication is clear. A protocol with a permissive licence (MIT, GPL-compatible, or custom open terms) offers communities a real door; a protocol that "wraps" its core engine in restrictive terms places a guard outside that door.

Contrast this with the Curve Finance ecosystem, whose stable-swap implementation was originally released under a business-source-like licence but whose broader DAO governance framework tolerated forks and derivatives. Projects such as Ellipsis on BNB Chain emerged as authorised forks with revenue-sharing agreements back to Curve's DAO. Here, forkability was not an all-or-nothing binary; it was negotiated. The door existed, but the corridor beyond it contained conditions. The implication is more subtle. Forkability can be structured to reward original builders without locking communities in. The presence of that door, even half-guarded, still disciplines decision-making because an abusive or complacent leadership knows that adversarial forks remain possible.

A credible counter-example cautions against romanticising forks. Bitcoin Cash's split from Bitcoin in August 2017 attempted to resolve a dispute over block size and transaction throughput. It created an exit for those who favoured larger blocks and different trade-offs. Yet over subsequent years, Bitcoin retained far greater hash power, developer mindshare, and economic weight. Bitcoin Cash itself later fragmented further. The existence of the fork did not force Bitcoin's core developers to change their roadmap. Reconciling this outcome requires nuance: exit ramps discipline teams only when the exiting group can carry meaningful capital, competence, and narrative with them. A purely symbolic fork, unsupported by real users and infrastructure, is little more than a protest. The door may be open, but it leads into a small, empty room.

The second major claim is that *state* forkability matters at least as much as *code* forkability. Show this with behaviour. In the wake of Terra's collapse in May 2022, multiple projects attempted to rebuild on "Terra 2.0" or migrate to other chains. Some managed to snapshot user balances and airdrop replacement tokens. Others failed to replicate or respect liquidity positions, governance stakes, or historical obligations. Name the pattern: partial exit. Explain why it matters. Code can always be copied; the challenge is preserving the economic relationships and histories encoded in state—debt positions, LP shares, vesting schedules. A fork that merely clones contracts but abandons users' positions is not a genuine exit; it is a new project with a familiar logo. The implication is that credible exit ramps depend on carefully designed state-export mechanisms, not just open code.

The Osmosis DEX in the Cosmos ecosystem offers a contrasting example. Because Cosmos chains share the Tendermint consensus and IBC interoperability stack, Osmosis could, in principle, coordinate state exports or mirror liquidity incentives across zones. When controversies arose over parameter choices, validators in Berlin, Seoul and San Francisco knew they possessed tools to coordinate alternative deployments without destroying user positions outright. The threat of a "governance fork" had weight precisely because state and interchain connectivity made migration survivable.

The motif of the door returns here. A door that opens into free space is not enough; users need a bridge, not a jump. State forkability is that bridge.

The third claim focuses on leadership discipline. Forkability acts as a constraint on how far teams can drift from their communities' preferences before triggering organised exit. Show the dynamic. In the wake of Uniswap Labs' 2023 decision to explore protocol fees, loud debates broke out about how much value should accrue to token holders versus LPs and users. Some threatened a fork if the fee switch was used in ways perceived as extractive. Many of these threats never materialised, but their presence in the discourse shaped the Overton window of acceptable proposals. Name the mechanism: latent bargaining power. Explain it. When builders know that aggressive rent extraction or governance capture can be met by a credible fork, they are nudged towards compromise. The implication is behavioural. Forks rarely need to occur at scale to exert influence; their plausibility is enough.

Consider, by contrast, projects built on heavily permissioned chains where validators are whitelisted and code is under proprietary licences. Here, exit largely means leaving the ecosystem entirely rather than reconstituting it under new leadership. The absence of internal exit ramps removes a key piece of leverage from users and smaller operators. Leadership may still behave responsibly, but they do so by choice, not under structural constraint.

A limitation must be confronted. Forks can fragment liquidity, dilute developer effort, and confuse users. The 2020–2021 boom in "zombie forks"—cloned AMMs and lending markets with negligible differentiation—demonstrated that copying alone does not produce healthy alternatives. Reconciling this with the disciplinary value of forkability means distinguishing *credible* exits from opportunistic ones. Credibility requires aligned validators, committed developers, and clear economic reasons to move. Opportunistic forks merely skim attention for a moment before decaying. The door image helps again: some doors lead to alternate rooms; others lead to cul-de-sacs.

A fourth claim addresses *social* exit options that complement technical forks. Sometimes the most practical exit is not forking the protocol, but reconstituting the community elsewhere—migrating to a new deployment, forming a new governance body, or withdrawing liquidity in a coordinated fashion. Show this in practice. After the SushiSwap leadership crisis in September 2020, when Chef Nomi withdrew and then partially returned funds, community members did not fork the code into yet another DEX. They reorganised governance, brought in external advisers, and shifted informal authority to more trusted contributors. The exit occurred at the level of leadership, not infrastructure. Name this: internal fork. Explain it. Exit options can be exercised by replacing power structures while leaving code and state intact. The implication is that a community with strong internal cohesion may not need to fork technically to discipline a team; the mere ability to eject leaders creates similar pressure.

The counterpoint arises when leadership controls brands, domains, and legal entities. Even if code is forkable, leaving the flagship interface and trademark behind can significantly reduce the viability of the fork. The original project retains search traffic, integrations, and regulatory relationships. This is why some communities insist on licences that allow not only code reuse but branding under fair conditions, or at least clear guidelines for derivative naming. Reconciling this dimension underscores that forkability operates on multiple layers—technical, legal, social—and a serious analysis needs to examine each.

Throughout the subchapter, the door motif keeps resurfacing—doors in code, doors in governance, doors in narrative space. The underlying question remains constant: if you discovered tomorrow that leadership had quietly changed parameters in a way you considered illegitimate, could you and others walk through a different door with your capital, your history, and at least some of your network intact?

That question exposes a tension with no trivial answer. Complete forkability can deter long-term investment by founders and contributors who fear being cloned the moment they ship something valuable. Yet constraining forks too heavily can entrench misaligned leadership and invite abuse. Between those poles lies design: licensing that rewards originators while enabling exit, architectures that allow state export without chaos, governance that treats the credible threat of "we can leave" as a constraint rather than a nuisance.

So when you next study a protocol's documentation and governance, one forward test suggests itself: trace the doors. If leadership drifted or values diverged sharply, where could people go, and what would they lose crossing that threshold? Your answer will tell you more about the system's long-term discipline than any slogan about decentralisation ever will.

Chapter 8
Markets, Liquidity, and Manipulation

At 03:17 UTC on 19 May 2021, as Bitcoin plunged through a cascade of forced liquidations, a smaller drama unfolded in a token few outside its community had ever heard of. Its price rocketed 70 per cent in under three minutes, then collapsed even faster. There was no announcement, no patch, no coup of technical brilliance. What existed was a shallow liquidity pool on a single decentralised exchange, a single wallet sweeping through it, and thousands of automated alerts lighting up dashboards from Seoul to Buenos Aires. To some, it looked like opportunity. To others, a trap sprung in plain sight. Markets often reveal their truths through these moments: not the grand stories of innovation, but the narrow passages where someone tests the depth of the water and finds there is scarcely any. Such episodes are more than curiosities of a volatile sector. They are reminders that price is never merely a number; it is a negotiation with structure. Every chart hides a question: *who could move this if they wanted to?* When spreads widen at odd hours, when volume spikes without cause, when tokens drift listlessly until a sudden coordinated surge jolts them awake, what you are observing is not just sentiment but the architecture through which sentiment flows. The shape of liquidity channels, the behaviour of market makers, the timing of unlock events, the orchestration of narratives—each is a lever. Some lift fairly. Some bend towards manipulation.

A trader once described illiquid markets as "rooms with too many mirrors and not enough exits". The image holds. Standing in the centre, you see reflections of movement that may be real or staged. Noise masquerades as demand; coordinated actors blend into the crowd; incentives collide with psychology. The question that should animate a careful reader is not whether manipulation exists—it does everywhere finance touches power—but how to recognise when the room has been arranged so that others get out first.

This chapter studies that choreography. It observes how liquidity concentrates, how it hides, and how its distribution shapes every interaction. In automated market makers, liquidity is no longer a monolithic pool but a spectrum of claims along price intervals.

Concentrated liquidity in protocols such as Uniswap v3 means that the depth at any given point can be both greater and more fragile than older models imagined. When liquidity clusters too tightly, slippage becomes the quiet arbiter of who pays the cost of movement. Thin pools create theatres where small actors can appear large. Thick pools absorb noise but grant power to those who supply them. You will see how routing choices—by aggregators, by MEV searchers, by interfaces—determine whether your order swims through deep water or brushes against shallow edges where opportunists wait.

From there, attention shifts to volume, that deceptively simple metric used as shorthand for relevance. In credible markets, volume is distribution: many hands passing through many venues across varied times. In manufactured markets, it is choreography: bursts at improbable hours, clusters on obscure venues, liquidity that appears and vanishes like a stage light. Wash trading in centralised exchanges, which surfaced in forensic analyses such as Bitwise's 2019 report to the US SEC, showed how easily numbers could be inflated without economic activity behind them. The same dynamics surface in decentralised settings when pairs with negligible organic demand report sudden spikes across multiple blocks. The aim of this chapter is not moral outrage but clarity: to recognise patterns without granting them mystique. Wash volume is less the work of criminal masterminds and more the product of incentives left unattended.

Tokens themselves carry temporal traps. Vesting cliffs, unlock schedules, and treasury disbursements create predictable overhangs that can overwhelm price even when fundamentals look steady. Imagine a development team in Lisbon facing a 24-month cliff that unlocks 30 per cent of supply on a single date. Even if they intend to hold, the market knows that others may not. Liquidity providers pull back. Market makers widen spreads. The calendar becomes a shadow. It is not enough to know *how much* supply exists; one must know *when* it becomes usable and by whom. These structural rhythms matter more than any promotional campaign. The hardest lessons in markets are often calendar lessons. Another layer sits atop liquidity and supply: narrative. Identify a cluster of new social media accounts pushing identical phrasing across forums at the same hour, and you will often find a campaign rather than a coincidence. Spoof orders that appear near the top of the order book and vanish as soon as real buyers approach are a persistent temptation for actors with sufficient capital and poor ethics. Coordinated pumps that migrate from token to token like migrating birds rely on the same infrastructure each time: social proof, a veneer of urgency, deliberate ambiguity. This chapter does not promise a magic decoder ring. It offers something better: a way to build an internal alarm system tuned to structure, not slogans.

The motif that threads through these pages is the *reflection*: the difference between what is shown and what is real. Liquidity can reflect depth it does not have. Volume can reflect activity that never occurred. Unlock calendars reflect confidence or fear long before the date arrives. Manipulation reflects the vulnerabilities of a system more than the cleverness of its manipulators. Each reflection demands interpretation.

And yet, the story is not purely adversarial. Markets, at their best, enable coordination among strangers. The mechanisms that create opportunity for manipulation also create opportunity for innovation: concentrated liquidity enables efficient capital use; algorithmic routing reduces friction; transparent vesting schedules allow planning; open data allows independent verification. The same tools that can deceive can illuminate when applied with care.

So the chapter you are about to enter stands at the threshold between structure and behaviour. It will not flatter markets with false purity, nor will it reduce them to dens of bad actors. Instead, it will show how to read them as they are: human systems built atop code, incentives, and attention. If you can recognise where the mirrors are placed, and how they distort what passes before them, you gain more than caution. You gain agency. The capacity to see structure where others see only movement.

The final question is a simple one, though its answer is never simple: when the next surge or collapse ripples through a token you follow, will you be able to tell whether you are watching genuine pressure or a carefully arranged reflection? The pages that follow aim to make that question sharper, and your footing steadier, as you step deeper into the markets' mirrored rooms.

Where liquidity lives

At 14:52 UTC on 18 June 2022, a trader in Singapore executed what should have been an unremarkable £9,000 market buy on a decentralised exchange. The token, issued by a small gaming project, had traded quietly for weeks. Yet within seconds, its price spiked more than 40 per cent before collapsing back to its earlier range. Blockchain records showed nothing theatrical: no hack, no coordinated campaign, no celebrity endorsement. What they showed was thinner liquidity than the user interface implied. The entire pool held barely £40,000 of depth within 2 per cent of spot. One order, modest by institutional standards, swept through almost the entire curve. The spike was not sentiment; it was structure. The market simply had nowhere else to go. The image lingered: a surface that looked calm until a light touch revealed it as a membrane stretched over nothing.

Such moments expose an awkward truth. Price, in decentralised markets, is not a universal reference. It is a local expression of where liquidity has chosen to reside. The question is not merely *what is the price?* but *how much can the market absorb before it becomes something else?* When liquidity concentrates within narrow ranges, small orders can behave like large ones, and large orders can behave like detonations. A price chart may capture the movement, but only the pool beneath it explains why the movement happened at all. This subchapter follows that trail: from the depth of pools to the paths orders take, and to the slippage that emerges when the maps traders assume differ sharply from the territory that actually exists. The motif here is simple: *depth is destiny.* Where liquidity gathers, outcomes stabilise. Where it thins, outcomes fracture. And in a fragmented landscape of automated market makers, bridges, and aggregators, the location of that depth is never static. It migrates.

Liquidity must be shown before it can be interpreted. Uniswap v3, launched in May 2021, offered a vivid demonstration of what concentrated liquidity means in practice. Rather than depositing across the entire price spectrum, liquidity providers could allocate capital to narrow bands. Name the shift: capital efficiency. Explain it: £1 of liquidity focused around a 1 per cent interval can absorb more local flow than £10 spread across the entire curve. Implication:

deeper execution near spot, but more fragile execution if price slips beyond the band. In volatile periods, these bands can empty with surprising speed as position ranges go out of bounds, leaving traders routed through increasingly thin intervals. The behaviour is measurable. It appears in sudden jumps between ticks, in block explorers showing disproportionate out-of-range liquidity, and in unusual slippage even for modest order sizes.

A second example lies in PancakeSwap's v3 deployment on BNB Chain in April 2023. There, early liquidity clustered heavily around round-numbered price points. Show the effect: prices at those psychological anchors processed trades smoothly. Move 3–4 per cent away, and depth evaporated. Name the risk: false security at spot. Explain it: the interface displayed total value locked, not the usable value locked at the execution layer. Implication: traders who assumed £1 million of TVL guaranteed depth discovered that most of it lived elsewhere on the curve. Depth was an illusion of scale, not its reality.

Routing introduces another layer of complexity. Aggregators such as 1inch or Matcha commit to finding "best execution", yet best execution always depends on the paths available. Show the behaviour: an aggregator may split an order across three pools, two bridges, and a cross-chain router. Name the constraint: gas cost and block structure. Explain it: deeper liquidity may exist on another chain or in another pool, but routing costs or latency make accessing it inefficient or infeasible. Implication: users see slippage not because liquidity is absent, but because liquidity is unreachable within the practical constraints of a single transaction.

A counter-example illustrates the limit. Curve Finance's stablecoin pools—USDC/USDT/DAI—often hold sufficient depth to absorb multi-million-pound trades with minimal slippage. That depth comes from a design optimised for correlated assets, not from arbitrary scale. Yet this strength becomes a weakness when assets depeg. In March 2023, during USDC's temporary divergence from the dollar, the same pools that usually dampen volatility amplified it. Depth remained, but its distribution no longer reflected the relationship between the tokens. The reconciliation is straightforward: correlated-asset pools provide stability until correlation breaks. Once it does, the architecture itself channels instability.

Slippage is the visible scar left by invisible depth. A price impact of 2 per cent on a £5,000 trade signals something more than volatility. It signals the absence of liquidity providers within that interval. Slippage is not a warning after the fact; it is a measurement of how much the user must pay to walk through a door that narrows as they approach. Changes in slippage over time reveal the migration of liquidity. A pool with 0.1 per cent slippage on £50,000 trades in January but 0.3 per cent in April is speaking. It says liquidity providers have redeployed capital. It says volatility has widened their ranges. It says attention has drifted elsewhere.

One may be tempted to assume that large total liquidity figures guarantee safety. Yet centralised exchanges demonstrate the same trap. Binance's BTC/USDT order book, for example, often shows impressive top-of-book size, but depth thins when moving 0.2 per cent away from spot at low-volume hours. The numbers remain real; they are simply contextual. Depth is a function of time as much as capital. Thin books at 03:00 UTC behave differently from dense books at 13:00 UTC. Automated market makers mimic the pattern, with depth contracting during periods of high gas fees or as liquidity providers shift to more profitable pools. Naming the pattern clarifies it: liquidity is reactive, not passive.

The motif of *depth is destiny* reappears when considering thin pools as amplification devices. In December 2020, during the frenzy of smaller DeFi tokens, a common exploit was not technical but behavioural: actors placed modest buy orders on extremely thin pools, triggering alerts from bots and traders who assumed momentum. The strategy relied on liquidity shallowness to fabricate movement. It was not illegal; it was structural opportunism. Show the mechanism: sweep thin liquidity, trigger price spike, let social amplification do the rest. Name its nature: manufactured visibility. Explain it: traders responded to numerical movement unaware that the underlying pool could not support even a fraction of the implied demand. Implication: price spikes in shallow markets are often reflections, not real waves.

A limitation is worth stating. Liquidity depth is not the sole determinant of execution quality. In some networks, MEV (miner-extractable value) determines priority and routing more than pool depth itself. Block builders may reorder, sandwich, or front-run transactions when they detect profitable patterns. Even deep liquidity can yield poor execution if MEV incentives distort the pathway. Reconciliation is possible. Depth remains essential but insufficient. It must be considered alongside block-level behaviour. Reading liquidity without reading block structure is like reading a map without knowing the terrain is moving.

The slippage metric is the practical anchor through the otherwise abstract notion of depth. It takes form when a trader commits to an action and receives an output smaller than expected. Slippage is inherently behavioural: liquidity providers choose ranges; aggregators choose paths; traders choose speeds; and adversarial actors choose moments. It gathers these choices into one number. That number traces the distance between assumed market structure and actual market structure.

A final observation returns to the motif. Depth is destiny, but depth is also choice. Liquidity providers choose where to sit on a curve. Traders choose whether to inspect that curve. Protocols choose how to visualise it. Shallow pools are not inherently dangerous; they are dangerous when mistaken for deep ones. Their very existence can serve a purpose—niche markets, experimental assets, or early-stage tokens must begin somewhere. But entering such pools without reading their structure is akin to stepping into water whose depth you have not measured. It may be ankle deep. It may be a drop. So a question remains, unresolved by design: when you next encounter a price chart that seems too calm or too explosive, will you look at the movement or at the water it moves through? The answer determines more than execution quality. It determines whether you are responding to markets as they are, or to their reflections.

Market-making and wash trading

On 19 March 2019, in a conference room in Washington, D.C., the US Securities and Exchange Commission received a 227-page deck from Bitwise Asset Management. Its central claim was startling: of the US$6 billion in daily Bitcoin volume reported across exchanges at the time, roughly 95 per cent appeared to be fake or non-economic. The slides walked through tick data from venues in Hong Kong, Singapore, and the Caribbean, showing charts that looked less like human trading and more like machine-generated noise: identical trade sizes repeated thousands of times, volume surging perfectly on the hour, spreads that never moved. On reputable venues, order books breathed; on suspect ones, they pulsed with impossible regularity. The paradox was exposed in a single line. Volume, the metric investors had been taught to treat as a sign of interest, could be manufactured almost at will. Volume is not always demand. That presentation formalised what many practitioners already suspected, but it also revealed something deeper. There were, broadly, two kinds of activity hiding behind the same number. One was market-making: firms like Jump Trading in Chicago or Cumberland in Singapore placing orders on both sides of the book, continuously, to provide liquidity and earn the spread. The other was wash trading: accounts trading with themselves through matched orders, not to earn spread but to create the illusion of activity. To the casual eye, both produced the same result: larger 24-hour volume, more "liquidity", higher rankings on listing sites. To a critical eye, they diverged sharply in pattern and purpose. Market-making is the heartbeat of a functioning market. Wash trading is its echo—loud, repetitive, and empty.

The motif of echo is useful here. An echo mimics a sound without adding information. Manufactured volume does the same. It imitates genuine trading activity, but if you listen carefully—across venues, across time, across trade sizes—the differences become measurable.

The first major claim is that *market-making and wash trading differ in intent but often look similar in raw metrics*. Show this through behaviour. On a liquid BTC/USDT pair on Binance in late 2020, you could observe tight spreads, frequent small trades, and continuous two-sided quotes. A professional market-maker might post bids and asks 0.01 per cent apart, updating them dozens of times a second. Name this behaviour: continuous provision. Explain it. The firm earns a fraction of a per cent on each matched trade and reduces its risk by delta-hedging elsewhere. The implication is positive: such activity compresses spreads, increasing execution quality for other participants. The volume generated reflects genuine willingness to take the other side of trades at posted prices.

Wash trading, by contrast, often leaves footprints that make no economic sense. Bitwise's 2019 analysis highlighted an exchange where 98 per cent of trades were exactly 0.01 BTC, alternating buy and sell in a perfect pattern every few seconds. No rational liquidity provider behaves that way; it is operationally pointless and economically costly. Name this pattern: self-matching. Explain it. The exchange or colluding accounts flood the tape with meaningless trades to move up ranking tables or to attract listing fees. The implication is corrosive. Other participants infer liquidity that does not exist. They see a roaring river; in reality, it is a looped video of water.

A second claim concerns *venue diversity*. Genuine interest tends to spill across multiple exchanges and trading pairs; manufactured interest clusters narrowly. Show the contrast. When Ethereum experienced high activity around the DeFi "summer" in July–September 2020, volume rose on Coinbase in San Francisco, Binance in Malta/Paris, Kraken in Seattle, and various Asian venues. Time-of-day patterns reflected a blend of US, European, and Asian trading hours. Spreads compressed; borrow rates on derivatives exchanges responded; search trends and social media activity rose in tandem. Name this pattern: distributed participation. Explain its significance. It is costly to coordinate fake volume across many independent venues and time zones; easier to pump metrics on one poorly monitored exchange. The implication is that genuine volume usually leaves a multi-venue footprint.

By contrast, many small-cap tokens show a different pattern: 90 per cent of reported volume concentrated on a single offshore exchange with minimal regulatory oversight, obscure ownership, and no fiat on-ramps. Trades cluster at odd hours, often during periods when natural liquidity from major regions would be low. No corresponding increase appears on decentralised exchanges, no OTC desks report heightened demand, no credible market-maker announces involvement. Name this: isolated volume. Explain it. In isolation, volume tells you little. Without venue diversity, it is more likely to be echo than heartbeat.

The motif of echo reappears in *time-of-day analysis*. Human-driven markets breathe with circadian rhythms: peaks during overlapping sessions, lulls during global sleep. Show the pattern. For Bitcoin on CME futures in Chicago, volumes often peak around the US equity open and close; for spot BTC and ETH, liquidity depth tends to deepen as New York overlaps with London. On multiple venues, you can observe volume swelling and receding in correlated waves. Name this behaviour: temporal coherence. Explain it. Activity aligns with when traders, institutions, and market-makers are awake and at their desks. The implication is that strong correlations between time zones and volume support the idea of genuine demand. Wash-driven markets often ignore these rhythms. A smaller Asian exchange might report constant, flat volume 24 hours a day for months, or the exact same pattern repeating daily with mechanical precision. Another might show a sharp spike at 04:00 UTC with no corresponding movement in price, no news, and no increase on any other venue. Name this: temporal artefact. Explain it. The pattern betrays a bot operating on a schedule, pumping trades regardless of real-world flows. The implication is that careful observers can often detect manufactured volume by asking a simple question: *does this market sleep?* If it never seems to, either it has perfectly global participation—or someone is looping the tape.

A credible counter-example must be considered. Algorithmic market-makers, especially in digital assets, operate globally and can run strategies 24/7. A venue with a handful of such firms may show relatively smooth volume across the clock. This is not, in itself, evidence of manipulation. The reconciliation lies in cross-checking. Does depth move with volatility? Do spreads widen during known events? Are there independent signs of interest—on-chain transfers, social discussions, derivatives open interest—that align with the reported activity? Echo alone is suspicious; echo layered atop clear underlying sound may simply be the natural reverberation of a busy market.

The third major claim is that *order-book structure and trade distribution reveal whether market-making is serving the market or merely serving optics.*

Show, again, by behaviour. On a healthy market, you see a ladder: progressively larger orders further from the mid-price, with some randomness in size and spacing. When volatility increases, market-makers widen spreads, pull some orders, and then gradually step back in as clarity returns. Name this: adaptive provisioning. Explain it. Liquidity providers respond to risk and information; their behaviour changes with conditions. The implication is reassuring: even when depth thins, the thinning has a story. Now examine suspect markets. Order books might display huge bid and ask sizes that never trade, with tiny prints flickering between them. Large orders vanish as soon as price approaches. Trades occur almost exclusively at the mid-price, not at the visible bid or ask. Name this pattern: spoof and fade. Explain it. The visible book is decorative; real trading occurs in a narrow band, often between related accounts. The implication is that volume is being used to paint a picture. In many historical equities cases—such as the 2012–2014 spoofing investigations in US futures markets—regulators treated such patterns as signals of intent to mislead. In unregulated crypto venues, similar behaviours persist with less oversight.

The motif of echo here helps to distinguish. Market-making should echo genuine demand; it reacts to others. Wash trading attempts to produce the original sound itself, then rely on you to mistake that for substance.

A fourth claim addresses *how manufactured volume interacts with incentives.* Exchanges benefit from high reported volume: more listing fees, more attention, higher rankings on data aggregators. Token issuers benefit from volume spikes that suggest momentum, making fundraising or secondary offerings easier. Show the economic logic. A project team arranging for a market-maker in Tallinn or Hong Kong to "support liquidity" might in practice be nudging towards aggressive quoting and back-to-back trades that inflate numbers. Name the practice: incentive-driven inflation. Explain it. Without clear contracts and risk controls, some supposed market-making mandates devolve into wash trading dressed as support. The implication is that you cannot read volume separately from who stands to gain from its appearance.

Yet a counter-example complicates a simplistic reading. Many reputable exchanges—such as Coinbase or Kraken—have invested heavily in surveillance systems to detect self-matching and irregular patterns. They publish transparency reports, work with analytics firms, and sometimes delist tokens that appear to be manipulating metrics. Professional market-makers on such venues often operate under agreements that restrict self-crossing and mandate fair access. Reconciling this shows that market-making itself is not suspect; it is the governance environment that determines whether it serves price discovery or narrative construction.

Throughout, the analytic task remains consistent: move from raw numbers to behaviour. Volume is a count of prints, but the shape of those prints across venues, times, sizes, and order-book levels tells the real story. Does volume spike on one illiquid exchange while remaining flat everywhere else? Does it cluster at one time daily with no exogenous trigger? Do order sizes repeat mechanically? Does depth behave oddly during shocks?

Return to the motif of echo one final time. Genuine activity generates echoes that match its source: when a significant announcement hits, you see alignment—order-book imbalance, cross-venue volume, social chatter, changes in derivatives funding. Manufactured activity tries to reverse this sequence: it creates the echo first and hopes that people assume there must have been a sound.

The unresolved question for any careful observer is therefore sharp and practical. When you next see a token leap up a volume ranking, will you treat that figure as heartbeat or echo? The charts alone will not tell you. The patterns behind them might.

Token release overhangs

In October 2021, as a major gaming token listed on a Korean exchange drifted sideways, an odd pattern appeared. Social channels filled with upbeat campaigns, a flurry of "partnership" announcements, and giveaways timed with near-military precision. The narrative suggested liftoff. Yet buried in the project's own documentation sat a quiet fact: a large tranche of investor and team tokens was due to unlock within days. On the unlock date, order books in Seoul, Singapore and Frankfurt all told the same story. Depth thinned. Bids stepped back. The price sagged, not catastrophically, but with a tired inevitability. The marketing push had not been random enthusiasm. It was camouflage for a calendar. This is the paradox of token release overhangs. Supply events are some of the most predictable features in crypto markets, often published months or years in advance. Yet they arrive, again and again, as if unexpected shocks. Holders talk about sentiment, "weak hands", or focus on whichever narrative is loudest that week. All the while, a structural force presses down from above: more tokens becoming sellable than the market can absorb at current prices. The chart records that pressure as red candles; the community feels it as demoralisation. The overhang was always there. It was just easier not to look up.

The motif that will thread through this subchapter is the *shadow*. Not a metaphorical gloom, but the literal shadow cast by scheduled supply over future price and morale. You do not need to predict what people will do. You only need to recognise what they *can* do when their lock-ups expire.

The first claim is straightforward: **cliff unlocks change behaviour well before the cliff arrives**. Show this through visible actions. Weeks before a large vesting event, team members become more cautious in public channels. Long-term plans are discussed, but shorter-term hype increases. Announcements cluster. AMA sessions multiply. Name this behaviour clearly: expectation management. Explain it. Founders know that an overhang looms; they attempt to widen the funnel of demand so that selling can be absorbed without obvious damage. The implication is not that every campaign around an unlock is cynical. It is that messaging often follows the calendar. When you see unusual intensity, ask what date sits just beyond the horizon.
Consider two concrete examples. When Uniswap's UNI token distribution schedule became public in September 2020, the community knew that large governance grants and team allocations would vest over four years with defined cliffs. Debates in London and New York about treasury usage, fee switches and grants were in

part debates about how to position the protocol before those cliffs. The token's price did not move solely on unlock days, but the community's tone shifted as each deadline approached. Another example lies in various "ecosystem funds" launched in 2021, where projects allocated significant portions of supply to future partnerships. Many of those allocations were subject to multi-year vesting. As the first cliffs neared, partnerships suddenly materialised at a faster rate. The calendar had become a project manager.

A credible counter-example tempers any deterministic reading. Some protocols with well-communicated unlock schedules have seen prices rise through major release events, because demand growth outpaced new supply. In these cases, the shadow of the overhang still existed, but it was overshadowed by stronger fundamentals or broader market cycles. The reconciliation is important. Calendars do not dictate outcomes; they dictate *pressure*. Whether that pressure causes cracks depends on what else the structure is made of.

The second claim looks at **how overhangs affect not just price, but morale**. Show the dynamic. A retail holder in Milan sees that early investors will gain access to five times their circulating float in the coming quarter. Even if those investors pledge loyalty, the possibility of selling weighs on the mind. Name this psychological pattern: asymmetrical exit optionality. Explain it. Some participants have the right to sell at scale; others do not. The implication is corrosive. Community members may feel that their belief in the project is being tested against someone else's liquidity needs. This tension becomes visible in governance. Before a large unlock, whales—early backers or team addresses—may push for proposals that support near-term price, such as aggressive emissions to drive total value locked or marketing programmes aimed at exchanges. Long-term-minded contributors may push back, favouring runway and cautious spending. The public debate appears ideological. Underneath, it is influenced by calendar positions. A holder whose tokens are illiquid for three more years experiences risk differently from a fund whose lock ending next month represents the first chance to de-risk. The overhang acts as a hidden variable in every argument.

Here the motif of shadow returns. Morale is light-sensitive. When a community senses that a vast, unseen seller could appear at any time after a cliff, debates become defensive. Jokes in Discord shift from building features to guessing who will "dump first". Engagement erodes. This erosion is not random; it follows the shape of the unlock schedule.

The third claim addresses **the mechanics of vesting and their signalling power**. Show the basic structures. Common patterns include a one-year cliff followed by linear monthly releases, or quarterly unlocks for investors, or multi-year schedules for the core team with shorter horizons for advisors. Name these elements collectively: release topology. Explain why it matters. The topology reveals whose liquidity has priority, whose commitment is underwritten by structure rather than rhetoric, and how much forced patience is embedded in design. The implication is concrete. A project with a steep initial cliff for investors and a much longer runway for the team signals that external capital gets optionality first. A project with a gradual, overlapping schedule spreads pressure more evenly.
Take a well-known case: when the Filecoin network went live in October 2020, miners, investors and the team all had different vesting arrangements. There was public controversy about early unlock discussions, with miners in China arguing that collateral requirements and release schedules were misaligned. Whatever one's view of those debates, the configuration made the tensions legible. Release policy shapes power. Another example lies in the way some Layer-1 projects in 2021 structured "community" allocations that were, in practice, controlled by foundations and subject to faster release than supposed long-term staking rewards. The label on the pie chart said community; the vesting contract pointed elsewhere.

A limitation is worth stating. Vesting schedules are, at best, approximations of commitment. A team that truly believes in its long-term vision can voluntarily lock or stake tokens beyond their contractual requirements. A team seeking a fast exit will find ways to liquefy exposure even with a conservative schedule, via OTC deals or synthetic instruments. Reconciling this means reading release topology as a starting line, not a verdict. It tells you how much temptation the architecture allows, not how individuals will respond.

The fourth claim concerns **calendar awareness as a discipline, not a superstition**. Show the practice. Serious analysts in London, Zurich or Hong Kong maintain token unlock calendars alongside price charts and protocol metrics. They mark cliffs, linear vesting ramps, and known lockdrops. They compare upcoming releases to average daily volume, treasury size, and current liquidity depth. Name this habit: structural context. Explain it. By overlaying supply events onto other data, they can estimate how many days' worth of trading volume will be released at once, or how concentrated upcoming unlocks are among specific cohorts. The implication is not that they can predict exact price moves. It is that they can avoid being surprised by predictable events.

One visible decision influenced by calendar awareness is listing strategy. Exchanges that list tokens weeks before huge cliffs risk reputational damage when prices fall sharply, even if the mechanics were public all along. Some now explicitly ask for detailed vesting tables before deciding launch dates. Similarly, sophisticated participants may adjust their own behaviour—focusing on protocols whose release schedules show gradual, programmatic emissions rather than sporadic cliffs that dwarf present activity. Again, the goal is not certainty, but asymmetry: fewer avoidable shocks.

A credible counter-example challenges complacent calendar-reading. During the 2021 bull phase, several tokens rallied straight through major unlocks because speculative mania overwhelmed structural pressure. Analysts who anchored too heavily on calendars missed moves driven by frenzy. The reconciliation is subtle. Calendar awareness is most useful in regimes where marginal buyers behave rationally and liquidity is finite. In mania, all constraints are temporarily ignored. Yet when the mania ebbs, the calendars are still there, and their shadows often lengthen.

The motif of shadow appears once more when considering **how teams align messaging with release events**. Show typical behaviour. A project might schedule a major partnership announcement, an NFT drop, or a new feature release in the same window as a large team or investor unlock. Name this tactic: narrative cover. Explain it. Positive news can create additional demand or at least distribute attention, making any selling less conspicuous. The implication is twofold. First, you should always read marketing timelines against the vesting schedule. Secondly, not all such alignment is manipulative. Sometimes teams genuinely target milestones to coincide with increased financial flexibility. The problem arises when communities are not told clearly that supply events are part of the story.

A counter-example here is instructive. Some protocols, particularly those with strong governance cultures, publish detailed "tokenomics dashboards" where all future unlocks are displayed, sometimes in real time, alongside explanations of who is affected and how they intend to manage distribution. When big events approach, they host Q&A sessions and sometimes propose amendments—such as voluntary extensions or partial re-locks. In these cases, the shadow is acknowledged, discussed, and, where possible, reshaped. Reconciling the two approaches highlights the key distinction: transparency does not remove overhangs, but it converts them from sources of suspicion into topics for collective decision.

Throughout this subchapter, the central argument has been that token release overhangs are not marginal details. They are part of the market's architecture, as integral as contracts or consensus. The shadow they cast stretches across price, governance, morale, and messaging. You cannot know what every holder will do when their lock expires, but you can know when they *could* act, and in what size. That knowledge does not guarantee protection, but it narrows the range of avoidable errors.

The unresolved tension, then, is not whether calendars matter—they clearly do—but how to weigh them against everything else you see. When a protocol you follow announces a major new feature or partnership, will you treat it purely as innovation, or will you quietly open the vesting schedule and ask a harder question: whose shadow lengthens behind this news, and how prepared is the market to stand inside it?

Detecting manipulation patterns

On 6 May 2010, as traders in New York watched the S&P 500 plunge in what would later be called the "flash crash", a single screen in a modest house in Hounslow, west London, played its own role. From there, Navinder Singh Sarao entered and cancelled thousands of large sell orders on the E-mini S&P 500 futures market in Chicago, layering the order book with offers he never intended to fill. The weight of those phantom orders helped push prices lower before they were rapidly withdrawn. The tape stuttered, then plunged. Regulators would later call it spoofing; prosecutors would say it contributed to nearly US$1 trillion in temporary equity value vanishing in minutes. What the episode laid bare was not only the vulnerability of electronic markets, but a deeper truth: the most dangerous trades are often the ones that never settle. Crypto markets inherited that vulnerability and amplified it. Centralised exchanges adopted order-book architectures similar to Chicago and New York. Decentralised exchanges exposed every swap on-chain. Telegram and X (Twitter) created permanent, searchable stages for coordinated hype. The distance between a lone screen and a global market narrowed even further. A handful of actors could write a script—a pattern of orders, posts, and timings—that many others would unknowingly follow. Price moves; volume spikes; sentiment shifts. Yet beneath the movement, the questions remain stubbornly structural: *who placed what where, who saw what when, and who was meant to react?*

This subchapter is about learning to see that script. Not to obsess over every irregular tick, but to recognise when trading, messaging, and timing start rhyming a little too neatly. The motif that will guide us is the *tell*: small, repeated details that reveal a larger design. Manipulation is rarely invisible. It is usually noisy. The work is to listen with discrimination.

The first claim is that **spoofing leaves distinctive footprints in order books**, even when it stops short of explicit illegality. Start with behaviour. On a centralised exchange, a large sell order appears a few price levels above the best bid, pulling the visible book into a thick wall. Smaller sell orders appear just above it, forming a ladder.

As the market approaches, the orders jump away or vanish entirely, reappearing further up. Very few of these large orders ever trade.

Name this pattern: *spoof ladder.*

Explain what it means. The actor is not offering genuine liquidity. They are publishing a threat: "there is heavy selling interest above, be nervous". Other traders, or their algorithms, may respond by reducing bids, tightening stops, or selling pre-emptively. The implication is that price shifts not because genuine supply has entered the market, but because the perception of supply has changed. The tell is not the existence of a single large order—those can be legitimate—but the repeated dance of appear, retreat, reappear, without execution, especially at key technical levels or around news.
The 2010 flash crash case gave this behaviour a legal name in traditional futures; crypto has replayed the script on smaller stages. Order-book screenshots from some offshore exchanges in 2020–2021 showed serial "walls" of tens of thousands of tokens stacked just beyond the mid-price, disappearing whenever price moved towards them. Comparable behaviour has appeared on decentralised perpetuals platforms, where off-chain order books match on-chain collateral. The metrics to watch are simple: ratio of posted size to executed size by price band, and frequency of large order cancellations near the touch. When cancellation-to-trade ratios spike at specific levels, a tell emerges.

There is, however, a limitation. High-frequency market-makers also cancel large numbers of orders as they update quotes in response to volatility or risk limits. A high cancel ratio alone does not prove spoofing. The reconciliation lies in context. Adaptive market-making behaviour responds to information: spreads widen during news, depth retreats across the book, then gradually returns. Spoof ladders target specific levels, repeat mechanically, and correlate with shifts in visible sentiment. The tell is not cancellation per se, but cancellation with theatre.

The second claim is that **coordinated pumps follow scripts that can be recognised across tokens and venues**. Show the choreography. A Telegram group with thousands of members announces a "target pair" minutes before a planned pump on a small centralised exchange. At the designated time, buy orders flood in, often from new or recently activated accounts. Price spikes sharply on that single venue; social channels erupt with screenshots. Secondary groups on Discord and X amplify the move, proclaiming a "hidden gem". Within an hour, the price collapses, leaving most late entrants with losses. Name this pattern plainly: *orchestrated pump*. Explain its mechanics. The organisers acquire inventory beforehand, announce the campaign, use their early orders to kick-start the move, then sell into the surge they themselves created. The implication is brutal but clear. Volume and price become tools in a marketing scheme rather than reflections of discovery. The tell lies in the shape of the move. Volume is hyper-concentrated in time, often with a sharp vertical candle and a symmetric crash. Venue diversity is low: activity occurs almost entirely on one or two exchanges, often with lax surveillance, while larger venues and decentralised pools remain quiet.

Academic work has documented these patterns. A 2018 study by Hamrick and colleagues at Imperial College London analysed more than 300 crypto pump events and found that the vast majority occurred on smaller exchanges with thin order books and limited oversight, often coordinated through public Telegram channels. The median duration of the pump was measured in minutes, not days. The tell, again, is the combination of compressed time, narrow venues, and pre-announced campaigns.

A credible counter-example warns against paranoia. Sometimes a small token experiences a sharp price rise after a genuine catalyst—a major integration, a critical bug fix, or an unexpected listing on a large exchange. Volume concentrates because liquidity lives where the news is priced, not because actors are cheating. Social media explodes because communities are genuinely surprised. How to reconcile? By checking the *script density*. Pump schemes leave a dense paper trail of "signals" in groups that predate the move, often with countdowns and explicit instructions. Genuine news leaves a simpler trail: a single catalyst, independent coverage, and more dispersed reaction across venues and times.

The third claim shifts from price to **narrative seeding**—the manipulation of perception before orders even hit the book. Show the behaviour. Over the course of a single weekend, dozens of fresh accounts on X post almost identical threads praising a new token. Each thread uses the same talking points: a "revolutionary" feature, a "tiny market cap", and a "once-in-a-lifetime" entry. Many include screenshots of holdings that cannot be independently verified. None disclose any financial relationship with the team. Name this pattern: *astroturfing*.

Explain why it matters. Humans, and the algorithms that monitor social platforms, treat repetition as relevance. A cascade of near-identical posts can trick dashboards into flagging a token as "trending", which in turn draws in a wider audience. The implication is that narrative seeding can precede and amplify market moves. The tell is the combination of novelty and uniformity: many new voices saying the same thing in the same way, at the same time. Crypto has supplied many examples, from meme coins on Binance Smart Chain in 2021 to NFT projects on Ethereum and Solana. The details differ; the rhythm does not. In several 2021 meme coin surges, on-chain data showed that the majority of supply was held by a handful of wallets tied to deployer contracts, while social channels overflowed with messages from accounts created days earlier claiming "strong community" and "diamond hands". The dissonance between holder distribution and narrative was the tell. There is again a limitation. Grassroots enthusiasm can also produce repeated phrases and memes. Organic communities spontaneously converge on slogans; they reuse images; they share threads that resonate. The reconciliation lies in *temporal layering*. Genuine communities typically show a build-up of conversation over weeks: questions, criticisms, in-jokes, then wider adoption of themes. Astroturf campaigns appear in sudden, dense bursts with little pre-history. When identical phrasing appears across dozens of accounts that have no prior interactions or history, the balance of probability shifts.

The fourth claim concerns **how manipulation scripts merge trading patterns with narrative patterns**, and why independent data checks matter. Show the composite. Spoof ladders soften the book. A coordinated pump group picks a time. Narrative seeding warms social channels. At the chosen moment, a surge of buying hits a thin market, driving price higher. Within minutes, traders outside the core group see the spike on scanners or hear about it in chats.

Some join. Organisers sell into them. Forums fill with posts explaining the move ex post as "strong demand" or "whales accumulating". Name this composite behaviour: *staged reality*. Explain what makes it powerful. Each element—orders, volume, posts—could be innocent in isolation. Combined, they create a persuasive story. Human pattern-recognition kicks in. The implication is uncomfortable. Manipulation often works not by hiding, but by overloading observers with apparently corroborating data. The tells become visible only if you deliberately decouple the layers: price from volume, volume from venues, venues from narratives.
Independent data checks are an antidote. On-chain explorers reveal whether "whale buying" is actually a reshuffling between linked wallets. Analytics dashboards show whether volume is real or mainly wash trading. Order-book histories on reputable exchanges confirm whether liquidity genuinely tightened or whether spoof ladders dominated. Simple alert lists can help. Analysts might flag tokens where: a single wallet holds an outsized share; reported volume is concentrated on one obscure venue; social mentions spike without clear external news; or unlock calendars align suspiciously with marketing blitzes. Each trigger is not a verdict, but a prompt to look harder.

A credible counter-example underscores that not every strange pattern hides intent. Liquidations on leveraged venues can produce cascades that look like manipulation: sharp moves, stop-loss clusters, social panic. Yet these flows are mechanical consequences of prior risk-taking, not coordinated schemes. Similarly, algorithmic strategies can create regular trading patterns that resemble wash trading without any attempt to deceive; they simply execute deterministic rules. The reconciliation, again, is intent plus structure. When irregular trading coincides with opaque token distributions, sudden marketing pushes, and tightly choreographed narratives, the weight of evidence tilts.

Throughout, the motif of the *tell* keeps returning. A tell can be a ladder of orders that never fill, a calendar of unlocks aligned with influencer threads, a heatmap of volume confined to a single venue at improbable hours, or a forest of new accounts repeating the same slogan. None of these prove wrongdoing by themselves. Together, they suggest that someone has written a script and is inviting you to improvise within it.

The unresolved tension that remains is not whether manipulation occurs; history and enforcement actions have answered that. The tension is practical. You cannot spend every waking hour dissecting order books, tracing wallet networks, and auditing social graphs. At some point, you must decide which tells matter enough to trigger deeper scrutiny, and which can be safely ignored as noise. When the next improbable spike appears—paired with breathless threads, unfamiliar venues, and oddly fragile liquidity—the forward test is simple to state, hard to apply: are you seeing genuine discovery, or a staged reality built from coordinated tells?

Chapter 9
Due Diligence in Practice

At 14:03 on a humid August afternoon in 2022, a small fund in Singapore discovered—by accident rather than design—that it had barely understood the protocol it had just backed. The team had skimmed the whitepaper, noted the reputable auditor's logo, glanced at the Discord, and executed a modest position. When the protocol froze during a turbulence in gas prices, the fund scrambled to diagnose the fault. What they found was not a sophisticated exploit, nor even a subtle economic flaw, but a governance edge-case buried in the documentation: a single multisig signer, long inactive, held a veto on parameter changes. Minutes stretched into hours as they messaged moderators, read half-forgotten forum posts, and traced commit histories. By the time the system restarted, no capital had been lost. Yet the team's relief came with a cold realisation. They had done due diligence in name only. What they lacked was not intelligence; it was rhythm.

A similar rhythm saved a different group a year earlier. In May 2021, a London-based analyst spent exactly 90 minutes—timed, almost ritualistically—reviewing a rapidly growing algorithmic stablecoin. She scanned the repositories, read the most recent audit summary, checked the governance queue, and compared trading depths across exchanges. It was the final step that gave her pause: a simple "sysadmin-style" cross-check of wallet permissions. Nothing matched the public documentation. A shadow upgrade key, controlled by an unnamed address, still had the authority to freeze contracts. She wrote a one-page brief, emailed it to her partners, and recommended passing. Weeks later, the protocol collapsed under the weight of its own incentives. The 90-minute ritual had done more than avoid a loss. It had built conviction in walking away.

These stories crystallise the spirit of this chapter: due diligence is not a shield against uncertainty, nor a bureaucratic performance. It is a discipline of attention—tight, structured, and uncomfortably honest. It begins with questions that cut through surface gloss. It grows through documentation that keeps memory from decaying. It ends not with certainty but with clarity: a map of where one stands, why one stands there, and what would prompt a move.

The need for such clarity has never been greater. Crypto projects evolve at a pace that defeats casual review and punishes complacency. Whitepapers grow outdated in months. Telegram channels metastasise overnight. Governance systems shift under versioned upgrades. Liquidity arrives and evaporates. Each change invites new risks: hidden mint rights, untested bridges, stale oracle feeds, repos forked from abandoned experiments. The speed is not the problem. The absence of structured scrutiny is. When markets reward speed, the temptation is to believe that formal diligence slows you down. The truth is the opposite. Sloppiness delays insight; discipline accelerates it. A repeatable workflow turns discovery from an accident into a habit.

This chapter sets out that habit in four movements. The first is the 90-minute deep dive, a timed ritual that forces trade-offs: read what matters, skim what merely signals competence, and ignore what only flatters. The discipline of the clock is its own teacher. Anyone can spend a day reading a protocol's forums; fewer can extract the essentials in an hour and a half. Time pressure sharpens judgement. It forces the reader to ask: what breaks this system, and how would I know? It also produces something invaluable: a one-page brief that compresses risk into signal.

The second movement—the red-team interview—switches stance. Instead of assessing the project from the outside, the reader imagines the role of the adversary. What assumptions, if breached, would cause catastrophic failure? Which parameters, if maliciously adjusted, would enable theft, censorship, or chaos? How does the team respond when confronted with its own worst-case scenarios? Ten questions are more revealing than a hundred compliments. They test not only the system but the candour of those who built it. Some founders react with clarity, welcoming scrutiny as a form of respect. Others dodge, waffle, or deflect. The difference matters. A team that cannot defend its own assumptions will not reliably defend its users.

The third movement links due diligence to action: position sizing and kill-switches. Here the motif shifts from curiosity to responsibility. Not all risks require abstention. Some invite cautious participation—smaller positions, shorter windows, pre-defined exits. The point is not heroic foresight but mechanical discipline. A kill-switch is a line in the sand, drawn before emotions distort judgement. It might be triggered by a governance lapse, an unpatched audit finding, or a sudden collapse in liquidity. What matters is not the trigger itself but the commitment to act when it fires. If due diligence supplies the map, kill-switches dictate the rules of travel.

The fourth movement—documentation discipline—grounds everything that precedes it. Memory fails under pressure. Details blur. After a few weeks in volatile markets, even the most careful reader will struggle to recall why they trusted one project and rejected another. A personal wiki, a decision log, a pattern library—these are not affectations. They are tools that turn experience into compounding knowledge. Over time, patterns emerge: recurring red flags, reliable signals, and forgotten complexities that return in new forms. Documentation becomes a quiet teacher, revealing blind spots and calibrating expectations.

Running through each section is a unifying motif: due diligence as a craft. Not a checklist, not a legal requirement, but a craft learned through repetition. Craftspeople think with their hands as much as with their eyes. They refine workflows until intuition flows from practice. In markets, the craft is not about predicting prices. It is about building a mind that notices when something is off: a missing repo commit; a governance vote with implausibly low turnout; an unannounced update; an audit with oddly vague severity levels; a token unlock schedule out of sync with public claims. These details are the knots in the grain of the wood. Learn to feel them.

The deeper philosophy beneath this chapter is that due diligence is an antidote to fatalism. Many newcomers treat crypto as a domain ruled by chaos or destiny—either everything moonshot-optimistic or irredeemably corrupt. Both views absolve the observer of responsibility. The craft of due diligence insists on the opposite. Systems can be interrogated. Risks can be understood. Decisions can reflect more than hope or fear. Even when outcomes remain uncertain, the process empowers the participant to move with intention rather than drift with momentum.

What follows, then, is not merely guidance on how to read documents or scan repos. It is an argument for becoming the kind of person who refuses to outsource judgement to narratives, influencers, or market moods. It is an invitation to slow down long enough to think, and to move fast precisely because you have slowed down. Discipline sharpens speed.

And yet a tension remains. No matter how rigorous the process, no diligence can guarantee safety. A protocol audited five times can still fail. A governance system that looked robust in theory can fracture under stress. A red-team question asked too late may reveal a flaw long after others have taken advantage of it. Due diligence reduces risk; it never abolishes it. The question is not whether the process is perfect, but whether it is better than the alternative—intuition untested, decisions undocumented, exits improvised.

As you step into the chapter, hold one question close: when the next promising project appears—well-designed, persuasive, beautifully marketed—will you investigate it with a rhythm that honours your capital and your attention, or will you drift toward the familiar trap of skimming, assuming, and hoping? The difference between those two choices will define not only what you hold, but how you understand the systems that shape the market itself.

The 90-minute deep dive

At 09:27 on 11 February 2021, a researcher at a mid-sized Swiss fund opened the GitHub repository of a newly launched lending protocol that had doubled its total locked value over the previous forty-eight hours. The team had invited the fund to a private round. The market was noisy, the pitch deck slick. Yet what caught the researcher's eye was not a missing feature or a hidden privilege, but a timestamp. The latest commit—pushed from Berlin only three days earlier—rewrote the contract's interest-rate logic without any accompanying governance vote. No post announcing the change existed on the protocol's forums. No audit addendum covered it. He set a timer for ninety minutes, not because of urgency, but because he had learned that disciplined scarcity of time sharpens perception. Ninety minutes later, he wrote a brief recommending withdrawal from the round. Two weeks after that decision, the protocol suffered a cascading liquidation triggered by the undocumented update. The fund avoided the drawdown not through clairvoyance, but through cadence.

This cadence is the essence of the ninety-minute deep dive: a structured sprint that forces the analyst to separate what matters from what merely glitters. Excess time breeds indulgence; too little time yields superficiality. Ninety minutes is tight enough to induce focus yet generous enough to form a coherent risk picture. The researcher in Zurich treated the timer as a constraint, and constraints reveal character—both of the protocol and of the analyst assessing it. His brief maxed out at a single page, but that page distilled the system's operational truth more clearly than the protocol's thirty-page whitepaper. That page saved money.

The deep dive is neither a ritual of heroism nor a shortcut for permanent conviction. It is a diagnostic, a triage tool. Used well, it tells you whether the system deserves your attention beyond those ninety minutes, or whether the red flags uncovered in that hour and a half justify walking away. Used poorly, it becomes another form of box-ticking. The difference lies in how the analyst reads, scans, and decides under the discipline of the clock.

The first major claim is that the deep dive begins with documents not to accept their narrative, but to challenge it. The show is straightforward: a reader skims a whitepaper that asserts novel mechanics or claims efficiency breakthroughs. Name the behaviour that matters: identifying mismatches between stated design and code reality. Explain the value: documentation often lags implementation by months. Teams, whether through negligence or haste, forget to update diagrams and assumptions. The implication is serious. Any protocol whose public architecture diverges from its deployed contracts has already revealed a governance flaw: communication cannot keep pace with execution. This is not an abstraction; the 2020 Harvest Finance exploit centred on precisely this gap. The team's published strategy descriptions did not match their live contract logic, leaving users unaware of how routing decisions exposed them to economic extraction. A discrepancy as minor as a missing sentence can shape risk.

The deep dive moves next to repositories because code histories speak more honestly than marketing. Show the reality: commit patterns from March 2022 revealed a major decentralised exchange was still relying on a single core developer for its liquidity maths after claiming to have decentralised development months earlier. Name the behaviour: reading commit authorship, frequency, and review practices. Explain the insight: teams with narrow contributor graphs carry continuity risk; if a key developer leaves, the protocol stalls. The implication is hard to ignore. A vibrant, transparent contributor graph gives confidence that maintenance and upgrades are not contingent on one pair of hands. A counter-example exists in the early months of Curve's deployment, where initial commit patterns were concentrated. Yet the team acknowledged this openly, expanded its contributor base, and introduced formalised peer review. The limitation was mitigated through evolving practice.

Audits follow, but too many readers treat them as talismans. The deep dive fixes that error by skimming scopes and severity classifications, not verdicts. Show the relevant behaviour: reading the first two pages of any audit to see what has been excluded. Name the insight: scope defines assurance. No audit covers economic design, oracle dependencies, liquidity assumptions, or governance processes unless explicitly stated. Explain this bluntly: an audit that excludes upgradeability leaves the door open for a privileged address to alter contract logic post-deployment. The implication is uncomfortable but necessary. Audits reduce certain risks; they do not reduce all risks. In February 2020, OpenZeppelin's audit of the Compound protocol documented what it reviewed and what it did not. That transparency mattered. Users could calibrate trust to scope. Compare this with protocols that advertise "multiple audits" while avoiding discussion of what those audits omitted. Skimming severity tables reveals more than reading the prose. A single medium-severity issue concerning oracle assumptions can outweigh a dozen low-severity gas-optimisation notes.

Governance reading is the next station in the ninety-minute sprint. The goal is not a philosophical treatise on decentralisation; it is a search for where power actually sits. Show the evidence: in September 2021, a DAO claimed fully distributed governance, yet its parameter changes in practice required approval from a foundation-controlled multisig. Name the behaviour: scanning the most recent proposals, turnout levels, and signer lists. Explain why: governance records reveal whether the community governs or merely observes. The implication is structural. Any protocol whose governance can be halted or overridden by a small group possesses centralisation risk that users must price. This does not automatically condemn the protocol; some systems benefit from early concentrated authority to respond to incidents. But the analyst must see it clearly. A limitation exists: governance forums can mislead when conversations occur in private channels. Reconciling this requires direct queries and cross-checking signer keys against on-chain analytics.

Market snapshots complete the core workflow. Show what matters: liquidity depth across two or three venues, time-of-day volume patterns, and recent volatility relative to peer assets. Name the behaviour: checking order book thickness, historical slippage on similar-sized trades, and fragmentation across decentralised and centralised markets. Explain why: thin liquidity amplifies all other risks. A protocol with impeccable code and transparent governance can still experience catastrophic repricing if its token trades in shallow pools. Consider the event in June 2022 when several mid-cap DAO tokens experienced price swings of over twenty per cent during low-liquidity hours because large holders acted in clusters. The implication is simple: market structure is part of due diligence. Ignoring it invites avoidable shocks.

Threaded through the deep dive is a motif: the timer. Its quiet pressure shapes judgement. Each segment forces trade-offs. Should one spend more time tracing an opaque admin key or reading another ten pages of documentation? Commit to decisions. Constraints reveal priorities. The clock obliges the analyst to highlight not everything that could matter, but everything that must matter.

The deliverable—the one-page risk brief—is the distillation of this rhythm. Show what the brief includes: a paragraph on architecture, a note on governance, a line on audits, a snapshot of liquidity, and two or three questions that require deeper investigation. Name the purpose: clarity. Explain its significance: a page forces concision, eliminating jargon, wishful thinking, and unnecessary detail. The implication is long-term. A library of such briefs becomes a pattern archive. Over months, patterns emerge: recurring governance bottlenecks, common liquidity pitfalls, typical audit omissions. Decisions grow sharper.

There are limitations to the ninety-minute approach. Some protocols require deeper technical reading before any meaningful assessment. Complex zero-knowledge systems or cross-chain bridges cannot be seriously judged in an hour and a half. Reconciling this with the deep dive means recognising what the deep dive is for: not to provide full assurance, but to determine whether further investment of time is warranted. The ninety-minute process does not replace expert audits or economic modelling; it precedes them. It identifies whether the protocol merits those resources at all.

A second limitation arises from market noise. Sudden token movements, rumour cascades, or influencer promotion can distract analysts into overweighting short-term dynamics. The remedy is to anchor the timer to process rather than mood. Follow the steps. Ignore the chatter. Let structure tame noise.

As the deep dive ends, the timer beeps. You hold a page that captures the system's skeleton and its most fragile joints. The question that lingers is not whether you have found every flaw—you have not. It is whether what you have found is enough to justify further attention, or whether the gaps you uncovered would only widen under additional scrutiny. The tension is real. Will you commit more time, or will you step back? This moment is the decision that defines the craft.

The red-team interview

On 17 March 2019, at a cramped coworking loft near Shibuya Station, a young founder introduced his cross-chain settlement protocol to a room of sceptical engineers. The pitch was fluent. The slides gleamed. Yet the tone shifted when an older cryptographer asked a single question: "Which assumption breaks first if your relayers slow by 300 milliseconds?" The founder paused. He attempted a diversion, then a joke. Within minutes, the room had quietly reconstructed the protocol's weakest hinge: a dependency on time-sensitive state confirmations that had never been modelled under stress. The launch never happened. Not because the idea was flawed in principle, but because the team had not survived its first red-team interview. The question revealed more than a vulnerability. It revealed an intellectual posture. It showed whether the builders had interrogated their own design as harshly as the market eventually would.

That posture is the essence of adversarial questioning. A red-team interview is not an interrogation staged for dominance; it is a test of epistemic resilience. When performed with precision, it exposes gaps that cordial due diligence cannot reach. The Shibuya episode is instructive because nothing dramatic occurred. No raised voices. No accusations. Just the quiet pressure of a single question that revealed the difference between a polished narrative and an examined system. The interview's power lies in the tension it creates between confidence and uncertainty. That tension is the motif that threads through this entire practice.

The first major claim is that adversarial questions show whether founders can articulate their system's failure modes without defensiveness. Consider a concrete example: in October 2020, during an invite-only review in London, a prominent DeFi team was asked, "Which invariant matters most during a 30% price shock on your primary asset?" The lead engineer named it instantly: the collateralisation ratio for their synthetic stablecoin. He then explained how its buffer had been set after modelling May 2020 volatility. This behaviour mattered because it linked a conceptual claim—"our system is resilient"—to a measurable decision. The implication is clear. Teams who can name their own fragilities tend to build safer systems. They confront risk rather than conceal it. Yet there is a limitation: some founders rehearse elegant failure scripts without having real contingency plans. Reconciling this requires probing the details, not the rhetoric. Ask for the parameter. Ask who can change it. Ask when it last changed.

A second claim: naming hidden dependencies reveals the system's true operational boundary. Show this through another verifiable example. In January 2022, a cross-chain bridge team presenting in Singapore insisted their consensus mechanism was "independent" of Ethereum congestion. A red-team question—"Who signs what when gas spikes above 2,000 gwei?"—exposed a reliance on a centralised sequencer that could stall under heavy load. Naming the dependency transformed the analysis. The explanation was simple: every system, however decentralised in theory, depends on concrete actors in practice. The implication extends further. Any protocol whose success rests on unexamined assumptions—off-chain price feeds, multisig responsiveness, sequencer honesty—cannot credibly claim robustness. A counter-example exists: some protocols embrace explicit dependencies, document them, and compensate with redundancy. The early versions of Chainlink (2020) openly published node operator lists and heartbeat thresholds. Transparency reconciles dependency with reliability.

A third claim: adversarial questioning measures how teams reason under pressure, not merely what they know. Show behaviour: teams who slow down, think aloud, and outline trade-offs demonstrate grounded competence. Name the skill: reasoning transparency. Explain its significance: technical systems fail when silent assumptions remain unacknowledged. The implication is practical. A founder who can describe the cost of each trade-off—latency versus security, throughput versus verification—signals a mindset capable of steering through turbulence. One limitation is that some technically brilliant founders communicate poorly under stress; that does not always indicate shallow thinking. Here, reconciliation requires asking follow-up questions that invite structure: "Walk me through the sequence of events if your main oracle lags by one block."

The red-team interview also surfaces social and governance dynamics. Ask who controls upgrade keys. Show how the answer reveals power. In May 2021, a protocol claiming decentralisation was asked, "Who can pause the system?" The answer—"a temporary admin key held by one contributor in Toronto"—exposed a governance gap. Naming the key's existence changed the risk profile. Explaining its implications—centralised failure potential—shifted the conversation. Yet teams often defend such keys as necessary for early development. The limitation is real. Early-stage systems sometimes need emergency levers. Reconciling this requires timelines: "When do you intend to rotate or revoke this key, and how will that revocation be enforced?" Decisions, not declarations, matter.

Another claim: adversarial questions expose unpriced economic risks. A well-targeted question—"What breaks first if your liquidity halves overnight?"—forces teams to move beyond charts and narratives. Show what happens when liquidity assumptions go unexamined. In April 2022, several governance token protocols experienced cascading price collapses when thin liquidity met sudden supply unlocks. Naming liquidity as a fragility forces builders to acknowledge that economics can compromise even flawless code. The implication is decisive: systems survive not by code alone but by understanding how incentives evolve under stress. A counter-example is instructive. MakerDAO, which faced severe volatility in March 2020, survived because its designers had modelled liquidity shocks and governance actors responded quickly to re-collateralise the system. Preparedness reconciled fragility with resilience.

Threaded through these cases is the quiet motif: tension. Productive tension. The red-team interview induces it through structure, not aggression. The questions that matter most are short. They require five words at most. "Where is the bottleneck?" "Who signs the upgrade?" "What assumption fails first?" Each forces the founder into confrontation with reality. Each slices through ambiguity. Each demands specificity.

To guide this craft, a red-team interview follows a rhythm. Show the preparation: the analyst enters with a mental map built from the ninety-minute deep dive—architecture, governance, audits, liquidity.

Name the posture: sceptical curiosity. Explain its necessity: without it, questions become compliance theatre. The implication is decisive. Only when the analyst maintains independent judgement can the interview uncover structural truths. Yet there is a tension in this. Push too hard and founders retreat into rehearsed defensiveness. Push too softly and nothing is learned. The craft lies in calibrating force.

A further claim: adversarial interviewing exposes cultural health. Show how teams respond collectively. Do developers answer, or do founders dominate? Name the behaviour: distributed knowledge ownership. Explain why it matters: systems with single points of intellectual centralisation mirror the technical risks they often deny. The implication is long-term. Teams who share reasoning, documentation, and authority tend to build more resilient ecosystems. Yet there is a limitation: some distributed teams suffer from coordination drag. Reconciling this requires watching how they handle disagreements during the interview. Do they debate constructively, or do they avoid conflict? Absence of internal debate often predicts absence of genuine decentralisation.

Another example illustrates narrative risk. In November 2021, a yield protocol was asked, "Which part of your mechanism design would you rewrite if you had six months more?" The founders insisted everything was optimal. That refusal to imagine a weaker version of their own system was more telling than any audit. In contrast, when asked the same question in August 2020, the Aave team outlined three components they planned to refactor, including rate strategies under extreme utilisation. Admitting imperfection signalled maturity. Here the behaviour—intellectual humility—was measurable.

The red-team interview carries one final implication: it reveals how aligned a team is with reality, not merely with its roadmap. When an analyst asks, "What external event would make your system unsafe?" and the founders can name a specific stressor—gas spikes, oracle downtime, liquidity fragmentation—they demonstrate situational awareness. Systems fail through interactions with the world, not in isolation. A counter-example is found in bridges whose designers, pre-2022, assumed validator honesty as given. That assumption proved costly. Reconciliation comes through designing measurable safeguards—thresholds, delays, audits—not through hoping the world behaves.

As the interview ends, the tension remains. It should remain. You sit with the answers—or the evasions—and decide their weight. The unresolved question is simple yet demanding: based on how the team handled pressure, do you trust them to handle chaos?

Position sizing and kill-switches

At 08:17 on 12 May 2022, minutes after the TerraUSD peg collapsed in Seoul, a mid-sized validator published a short message on its public channel: "We are reducing exposure to minimal operational float. Nothing more." It was a sterile sentence, but it marked a decisive act. The validator had pre-set an internal kill-switch for extreme governance failures—specifically, for any event in which the system's senior obligations could not be honoured. When the peg slipped beyond its tolerance band and governance froze, the rule triggered. Their treasury did not escape unscathed, but it remained functional. Many others had no such rules. They "managed" their positions by feel. By the end of that day, several were insolvent. That contrast—between pre-committed limits and emotional improvisation—is the signal that introduces this subchapter. The question beneath it is stark. If a team with intimate knowledge of a network must defend itself with structured exit rules, what hope does an external analyst have without similar discipline?

The principle at stake is simple, yet routinely ignored: position sizing is not a measure of enthusiasm but of survivability. The motif that threads through this discussion—the small lever—is the essence of disciplined exposure. A small lever protects. A large lever destroys. The Terra episode shows how, in markets where governance can shift within hours, the size of one's exposure is not just a number but a constraint on future autonomy. A position too large becomes a trap.

The first major claim is that pre-set position limits reveal whether an analyst treats risk as a probabilistic field rather than a narrative. Show this through visible behaviour: an analyst caps exposure before learning any specifics of a protocol's marketing promises. Name the practice: max-loss framing. Explain its logic: instead of asking, "What could I gain?" the analyst asks, "What is the maximum capital I can afford to see impaired without cascading effects on my wider responsibilities?" The implication is profound. Max-loss framing forces the analyst to quantify potential damage in advance. Without it, every decision becomes reactive. A limitation exists: sometimes strict caps lead analysts to underestimate systems that later prove robust. Reconciliation lies in understanding that position sizing is not a vote of confidence but a buffer against low-probability, high-impact events. A system may be excellent, yet still deserve limited exposure because its governance is young or its incentives still forming.

A second claim: kill-switches demonstrate the difference between reactive exits and pre-committed exits. Show how teams that survived 2022's cross-chain bridge failures had explicit multi-scenario exit triggers. Name an example: in March 2022, following the Wormhole exploit, several funds with pre-written exit criteria—including "any unauthorised mint event above a defined threshold"—reduced exposure automatically. Explain the principle: kill-switches convert qualitative concerns into binary actions. They specify conditions under which exposure is reduced regardless of sentiment. The implication matters because markets during crisis shorten decision windows. Those with pre-committed triggers act while others hesitate. Yet a limitation must be recognised. Kill-switches can fire prematurely if written too rigidly, removing exposure before a system has time to recover. Reconciliation demands layering: analysts pair hard triggers (e.g., halted withdrawals for more than N hours) with soft triggers (e.g., governance disputes that erode contributor participation). The interplay preserves discipline without forfeiting nuance.

A third claim: sizing and kill-switches reveal the health of the analyst's overall process. Show this through metrics: position sizes as a proportion of total risk capital, the number of governance events flagged for monitoring, and the latency between an alert and a decision. Name the behaviour: operational readiness. Explain why it matters: teams that cannot track their own exposure cannot track the external systems in which they operate. The implication is structural.

Analysts who rehearse exit scenarios tend to identify failure signals earlier—delegate attrition, stalled code reviews, abnormal oracle updates—because they monitor the variables their kill-switches depend on. A limitation is that formal processes can create false confidence. A reconciliatory approach requires routinely red-teaming one's own rules. Ask: "If I had to break my framework, what would I exploit?"

The small lever motif returns here. Position sizing is the lever that determines whether an adverse event becomes a setback or an existential blow. Kill-switches are the mechanism that releases the lever when needed. Together, they discipline the analyst against two common failures: inertia and optimism. Show how inertia manifests. In November 2021, as several synthetic asset platforms revealed governance fractures, many analysts chose to "wait for clarity." Clarity arrived only after substantial value impairment. Those who acted through structured de-risking, not intuition, preserved optionality. Name this optionality: retained agency. Explain its importance: the ability to make future choices depends on avoiding irreversible losses. The implication reinforces the central theme. Survival is a function of pre-committed limits, not reactive courage.

A further claim: position sizing must reflect the governance surface, not the market price. Show a specific case. In July 2023, after the Curve Finance exploit, analysts watching the protocol's DAO voter participation patterns—not the price chart—recognised weakening coordination capacity. Governance turnout fell sharply in the fortnight after the exploit. This behaviour, measurable and verifiable, provided a more reliable signal for de-risking than price volatility alone. Name the principle: governance-led exposure calibration. Explain why it matters: decentralised systems do not fail because of price; they fail because coordination breaks. The implication is uncomfortable but essential. Analysts must treat governance metrics—turnout, delegate churn, proposal quality—as part of their exposure model. A limitation emerges: governance metrics lag. Reconciliation requires pairing them with real-time technical alerts—oracle liveness, finality delays, sequencer health.

Position sizing also interacts with liquidity design. Show how thin liquidity can magnify the consequences of an oversized position. In

September 2020, a token with shallow pools on decentralised exchanges experienced a 70% drawdown in minutes when a single fund closed a large position. Name the risk: slippage amplification. Explain its mechanism: the price impact of an exit grows non-linearly as pool depth declines. The implication for analysts is immediate. Wallet-level exposure must account for liquidity fragility. A limitation is that liquidity can change quickly, especially when incentives shift. Reconciliation lies in regularly updating size limits based on pool depth, venue diversity, and time-of-day liquidity patterns.

The next claim: kill-switches extend beyond technical triggers into social and narrative domains. Show this through behaviour: an analyst monitors communication rhythms—developer updates, treasury disclosures, governance debates—and flags abnormalities. Name the signal: narrative decay. Explain its relevance: when a project's communication cadence deteriorates, it often reflects internal drift or unresolved conflict. The implication is that narrative decay, though qualitative, can be converted into a kill-switch condition. For example, a pre-commitment might state: "If written updates cease for more than two cycles, exposure reduces to base risk allocation." A limitation is obvious. Communication gaps can occur for benign reasons. Reconciliation comes from cross-referencing with measurable indicators—repo activity, multisig signatures, testnet commits.

Throughout this, the motif remains: the small lever. Both position sizing and kill-switches are ways of keeping the lever manageable. Excess size removes flexibility. Missing kill-switches remove discipline. Together they protect the analyst from a psychological trap: the belief that expertise compensates for structural exposure. Show how this belief fails. In January 2021, several sophisticated funds suffered heavy losses when a governance token halved in value following an unannounced decision to expand supply. Their expertise did not save them. Only smaller, diversified positions could have.

Another claim: pre-set exits force analysts to confront their own bias. Show how behavioural drift appears. An analyst grows fond of a team, attends too many community calls, and begins to interpret weak signals as strong ones. Name the bias: relationship-induced overconfidence. Explain its danger: familiarity can obscure emerging fragilities. The implication is that kill-switches must be written before emotional entanglement begins. A limitation is that dynamic markets sometimes require interpretative judgement. Reconciling this means combining fixed rules with discretionary overlays, but both must be documented.

The subchapter leads toward a final tension. You can design limits. You can programme exits. You can pre-commit rules. Yet the hardest moment is the execution. When a kill-switch fires, and the market screams the opposite, do you trust the rule or override it? That question defines the discipline.

Documentation discipline

On 14 February 2018, at the Bank of England's Threadneedle Street headquarters, a small supervisory team reviewed the post-mortem from a liquidity stress test that had gone wrong a week earlier. One analyst had logged every step of the model's failure: timestamps, data sources, assumptions, and the precise moment an unverified dataset distorted the output. Another analyst had kept nothing. The difference was stark. The first produced a pattern; the second produced a story. When the team rebuilt its framework, only one account could be trusted. The other relied on memory—an unreliable instrument. That meeting illustrated something deeper than bureaucratic rigour. It showed how disciplined documentation shapes institutional memory, even when individuals rotate or forget. It also showed how a single written sentence—"Source replaced without validation at 09:12"—can become a hinge for future decisions. The small hinge motif will recur: a well-placed record can redirect an entire process.

The first major claim is that documenting decisions converts instinct into examinable structure. Show this through observable behaviour: a researcher writes down why they accepted a governance proposal, the datasets consulted, and the criteria that tipped the balance. Name the practice: decision logging. Explain its purpose: to capture the reasoning visible at the moment rather than the retrospective narrative constructed later. The implication is unsettling but valuable. When future outcomes contradict expectations, the log exposes whether the error lay in the assumptions or the process. A limitation exists: not all decisions allow for slow, reflective recording. Crises compress time. Reconciliation lies in adopting a two-step approach: record a short justification in the moment, expand the reasoning when the pressure lifts.

A second claim follows naturally: without recorded sources, analysts cannot audit their own judgement. Show this through a visible metric: the number of verifiable links, datasets, or contract references in a research file. Name the behaviour: source anchoring. Explain its logic: recorded sources shield an analyst from the drift that comes when stories replace evidence. The implication is practical. When a protocol's claims change or its documentation is updated, the analyst can compare old and new versions to measure credibility shifts. A limitation appears when over-documentation leads to clutter—twenty links for one idea, noise obscuring signal. Reconciliation requires curation. Record only the sources that shaped the decision, not every document encountered.

The motif of the small hinge surfaces again. A single well-kept source—the precise Git commit that introduced a new mint function, the timestamped multisig change on 6 September 2023—can unlock clarity months later. Teams without these hinges drift into speculation. Teams with them trace causality.

The third claim addresses post-mortems. Show their power through a concrete example. After the July 2020 Balancer pool exploit in London, several independent analysts published detailed post-mortems listing the chronology of swaps, the overlooked asset weighting logic, and the precise point where liquidity incentives masked structural fragility. Name the practice: structured post-mortem analysis. Explain its purpose: to turn one failure into a reusable template for future detection. The implication stretches beyond a single event. Each documented post-mortem becomes part of a pattern library: a catalogue of recurring weaknesses—permission misconfigurations, price-insensitive mechanisms, liquidity illusions—that analysts can compare against new systems. Yet even this practice has limitations. Post-mortems can become performative, written to satisfy public expectation rather than internal learning. Reconciliation requires writing for the archive, not the audience. Remind yourself: this document must serve your future self, not strangers.

A fourth claim concerns contributor accountability. Show how documentation exposes team coordination. A contributor who records their work—issue numbers, review timestamps, problem statements—reveals how decisions propagate through a group. Name the effect: traceability. Explain why it matters: traceability reveals whether a system's governance operates through open conversation or silent power brokers. The implication for analysts is sharp. Documentation patterns act as governance signals. A project with regular written updates, transparent change logs, and archived deliberations provides more inspectable structure than one driven by off-record chats. The limitation is obvious. Excess documentation can mask weak governance if the written layer diverges from the real decision-making layer. Reconciling this requires comparing written minutes with observable developer actions—commits, signatures, deployments.

The fifth claim turns inward. Documentation disciplines the mind as much as the process. Show this through behaviour: an analyst maintains a personal wiki where every call—correct or incorrect—is recorded with predictions, uncertainties, and outcomes. Name the habit: reflective archiving. Explain its purpose: to build a longitudinal map of one's own blind spots. The implication is significant. Patterns emerge—not only in markets but in the analyst's psychology. Perhaps they consistently overestimate team cohesion or underestimate security debt. A limitation is that self-documentation can grow self-indulgent. Reconciliation lies in structure: fixed templates, consistent fields, and thresholds for what merits recording.

The small hinge motif returns once more. A single documented error can prevent dozens of repeat failures. A note such as "Overweighted due to charismatic founder; no governance evidence" can become a hinge that shifts future practice away from narrative seduction.

A sixth claim links documentation to organisational resilience. Show how institutions that retain structured archives survive shocks better than those that rely on tacit knowledge. Name two verifiable examples. First, the Ethereum Foundation's decision to maintain a public archive of research posts and meeting notes since 2015 enables new contributors to understand historical trade-offs without relying on lore. Second, the Federal Reserve's publicly released minutes—including the November 2008 meeting, where liquidity guarantees were debated in Washington—demonstrate how transparent documentation captures institutional memory across crises. Explain the principle: written records preserve context. The implication for decentralised ecosystems is acute. Projects with short contributor cycles risk losing knowledge unless documentation is treated as infrastructure. A limitation remains: public records can constrain sensitive conversation. Reconciling this requires layered documentation—public summaries paired with internal technical detail.

A seventh claim focuses on the strategic use of documentation for adversarial scenarios. Show how a well-kept archive enables red-team analysis of one's own past decisions. Name the practice: retrospective stress testing. Explain its mechanics: analysts revisit old decisions with new information, checking whether the documented reasoning would survive current threats. The implication is that decision quality improves not through hindsight regret but through systematic comparison. A limitation is that old notes may embed outdated assumptions. Reconciliation involves annotating, not rewriting, historical logs.

All this produces a final dynamic. Documentation is not an administrative burden; it is a commitment device. When analysts record their assumptions, they bind their future selves to confront those assumptions honestly. That is the small hinge again: one sentence can shift direction.

The unresolved tension sits here. You may record everything—sources, motives, doubts—and construct a beautiful archive. But when the next crisis arrives, will you open those pages and act on what they reveal, or will you ignore the hinge you built?

Chapter 10
Building a Personal Compass

On a grey morning in October 1998, the physicist Richard Feynman's notebooks resurfaced during a public auction in New York. Buried among sketches, stray equations, and sardonic remarks was a line that startled several bidders: "Study hard what interests you the most in the most undisciplined manner possible." It was mischievous, but also exact. Feynman was not proposing chaos. He was arguing that intellectual independence depends on principles rooted deeper than fashion, deeper than cycles, deeper than prediction. The remark reads differently today. In a field where narratives mutate hourly and confidence often outpaces evidence, the idea of building one's own navigational instrument—private, portable, and principled—feels not whimsical but essential.

The need for a personal compass often becomes clearest at the moment it fails. Consider the winter of 2021, when retail traders on several global platforms began chasing a sequence of tokens marketed through celebrity endorsements and anonymous teams. Many lacked even the most basic disclosures, yet liquidity surged for days. When those instruments collapsed—some within forty-eight hours—what lingered was not only financial loss, but a sharper recognition: individuals had been operating without rules that could outlast enthusiasm. They had mistaken mood for method. Those who fared better did not predict more cleverly; they refused to act when evidence was absent. They relied on principles, not forecasts. This tension between curiosity and credulity—between wanting to explore and needing to verify—anchors the chapter you are about to read.

The core idea is simple to state and difficult to practise. It is that resilience in complex environments comes from inner architecture, not outer signals. The architecture includes rules you trust even when the crowd disagrees; rhythms of review that expose your own biases; peer circles that challenge your assumptions more sharply than any market chart; and a mindset that seeks novelty without surrendering scepticism. The image that threads through this chapter is that of a compass that must be recalibrated regularly. Unlike its magnetic predecessor, which points north whether used by a mountaineer in Snowdonia or a sailor off Orkney, an intellectual compass drifts unless tested. Drift is invisible until it matters.

The first movement of the chapter sets out why prediction-based thinking repeatedly disappoints. Markets—crypto or otherwise—are not designed to reward confidence; they reward preparation. You will encounter examples where simple, durable rules outperformed intricate model-building. The rule "never commit funds to opaque custody structures" proved more useful in 2014 during several Asian exchange failures than any attempt to forecast short-term price arcs. Prediction dazzles, but principles endure. This chapter will explore why, and how to craft such principles without lapsing into rigidity.

From there, the narrative turns to learning loops. Systems improve when their operators examine how they think, not just what they think. Quarterly reviews, bias audits, and structured checklist upgrades are not administrative chores but cognitive hygiene. They reveal misclassifications, emotional overreactions, and misplaced confidence. You will see how the strongest analysts and builders, from open-source maintainers in Berlin to protocol auditors in Singapore, sustain advantage through rhythm, not burst. The loop motif adds weight here: without cadence, insight evaporates.

The chapter then widens to include a social dimension: community as defence. Solitude sharpens focus, but consensus often blinds. Small peer circles—three or four people who alternate roles, challenge assumptions, and interrogate reasoning—provide a defence against private distortions. When roles rotate and each participant occasionally plays the devil's advocate, the group becomes a live model of red-team pressure. You will meet projects whose survivability owed less to technical brilliance than to unglamorous habits of cross-checking and disciplined dissent. The compass metaphor deepens here: a reliable bearing requires more than one reference point.

Finally, the introduction prepares you for the chapter's closing tension: how to stay curious without surrendering judgement. Curiosity without discrimination leads to fads; discrimination without curiosity leads to stagnation. Modern systems demand both.

Testnets, prototypes, adversarial exercises, and evidence-first exploration form part of this mindset: you learn by experimenting with low stakes long before contemplating commitment. The reader will encounter examples where eagerness to participate overwhelmed the duty to inspect the foundations. The lesson is not to retreat from novelty but to engage it with method.

By the end of the chapter, you will recognise that building a personal compass is not an abstraction. It is a daily practice of writing down your principles, revisiting them, testing them with others, and adjusting them when the world changes. It is an act of intellectual independence. The remaining pages invite you to assemble, test, and refine that instrument. The question that will follow you, quietly, is this: when the signal and the noise become indistinguishable, which direction will your compass point, and why?

Principles over predictions

On 19 June 2014, in Tokyo, the first creditor meeting of the collapsed exchange Mt. Gox convened. More than 24,000 people had filed claims after discovering that their balances—once displayed cheerfully on dashboards—were largely fictional. The forensic accounting reports, presented that day, revealed something unexpectedly simple beneath the complexity: customers had trusted a custodial black box with no verifiable controls, and the black box had quietly emptied. The drama of insolvency often attracts explanations involving algorithms, hackers, or rogue insiders. Yet the decisive failure in this case was older and more prosaic. Users had abandoned a basic rule: if you cannot inspect how something operates, you cannot rely on it when conditions turn hostile.

This opening scene is not about nostalgia or blame; it is about what survives turbulence. Prediction, for many, had seemed sufficient in the months preceding the failure. Commentators in early 2014 modelled short-term price paths, debated adoption curves, and argued about network effects. But none of those calculations could compensate for the absence of a principle as clear as it was unfashionable: verify control of your own assets. The Mt. Gox failure, held in a single building in Tokyo yet felt worldwide, still illustrates the modest premise of this subchapter. Durable rules—not forecasts—carry you through cycles.

Principles endure because they anchor behaviour when signals distort. A rule such as avoiding opaque custody forces a visible action: inspecting proofs of reserve, checking withdrawal queues, and evaluating operational histories. Prediction, by contrast, produces posture, not practice. The difference matters. Behaviour is measurable. Posture is not. This distinction appears repeatedly across markets, and it will serve as the quiet motif of this subchapter: rules that generate actions outlast theories that generate opinions.

The first major claim follows from this motif. Cycles amplify noise. During periods of acceleration, models expand to match the mood. In late 2017, for instance, hundreds of token projects launched in Zug, Berlin, and Singapore. Many raised substantial sums on promised platform effects. The rule that might have prevented catastrophic losses—"treat anonymous teams with unverifiable claims as unviable"—was obvious. Yet it was abandoned, often publicly. The reason was not ignorance but prediction. People expected these projects to attract enough new entrants to outpace structural risk. Show, then name: the Tezos fundraiser in July 2017, headquartered in Neuchâtel, raised $232 million (Foundation report, 2018). Its founders later entered a high-profile internal dispute, stalling progress for months. Explain: funds had been entrusted before governance, code, and legal arrangements were stabilised. Implication: a principle requiring operational clarity before capital could have prevented exposure. Forecasts of grand network adoption could not.

A second example demonstrates the same dynamic in reverse. After the 2018 bear market, the team behind the decentralised exchange Uniswap in New York published transparent weekly analytics dashboards, open-source development plans, and auditable smart contracts. Their principle was clear: build systems whose operations can be verified by anyone. Adoption began modestly, but the rule-bound approach created measurable user confidence. By September 2020, Uniswap facilitated over $15 billion in monthly volume (TokenTerminal, 2020). Prediction had little to do with it. The rule—transparency as a first-order requirement—produced actions users could evaluate: public code repositories, public liquidity metrics, public grants. Behaviour, not bravado, drove growth.

At this point, a credible counter-example must be considered. Certain early crypto networks, especially Bitcoin after January 2009, benefited from unpredictability. No one could model its trajectory, yet many participants acted effectively without explicit principles. They simply held coins. But this apparent exception reflects scarcity more than foresight. Bitcoin's parameters were transparent from birth: supply schedule, issuance halving, and consensus rules were visible in code. Participants might not have articulated a principle, but they were operating under one: commit only to systems whose mechanics you can inspect directly. Reconciling the example requires recognising that implicit principles still guide behaviour. The absence of prediction does not equal the absence of method.

From here, the argument deepens. A principle functions as a compression of accumulated wisdom into a rule that mandates a decision. Consider governance disclosures. If a protocol declares that administrative keys are controlled by a multisig held by named contributors in London, Berlin, and Toronto, the rule "avoid unilateral keys held by unknown parties" becomes testable. It demands an action: inspect the keys; verify custody; ask public questions. Compare this to forecasting whether the protocol will attract liquidity next quarter. Prediction encourages debate. Principle encourages inspection.

Another example grounds this distinction. In April 2022, the algorithmic stablecoin TerraUSD collapsed, wiping out approximately $40 billion of nominal value (Luna Foundation Guard disclosures, May 2022). Many had modelled its stability mechanics, predicting that arbitrage incentives would keep its peg. The principle that might have arrested engagement earlier—avoid mechanisms that rely on reflexive market confidence—was available to any observer. The stablecoin's guarantee depended on traders willingly buying its volatile sister asset during stress. That requirement was a visible behaviour, not an abstract concept. The failure was structural, not stochastic. Rules would have caught it; predictions rationalised participation.

Here, the motif of "visible actions" reappears. If a rule cannot be enacted through a concrete step, it is not a rule but a slogan. The rule "prefer systems with open-source histories of at least twenty-four months" implies an inspectable behaviour: reviewing commit logs, contributor graphs, and release notes. The rule "avoid custodial black boxes" implies checking reserve attestations, withdrawal latency, and operational dependencies. When rules convert to actions, they survive cycles. When predictions remain opinions, they collapse under stress.

A brief limitation deserves acknowledgement. Rules can freeze innovation. A principle that filters out early-stage, experimental designs may protect from loss while excluding potentially transformative projects. Reconciling this limitation involves calibrating rules, not discarding them. A rule such as "treat experimental systems as research environments, not commitments" preserves safety while allowing observation. It produces measurable conduct: sandbox experiments, testnet-only engagement, and minimal exposure. The principle adjusts the posture without suppressing curiosity.

As the narrative progresses, a broader implication emerges. Rules create identity. When you choose principles that constrain behaviour, you are not only reducing risk; you are defining how you navigate complexity. The strongest analysts in technology and finance do not succeed because they predict cycles more accurately than peers. They succeed because they carry a portable set of commitments that do not bend under pressure. Those commitments vary. Some refuse to entrust funds to teams without public track records. Others avoid projects whose governance grants veto power to foundations without accountability. Others decline to act when market depth is thin. All of these rules express an underlying belief: survival in complex markets demands discipline before insight.

Return now to the motif of "the quiet rule." Every field contains them. In aviation, it is the checklist. In epidemiology, it is the case definition. In structural engineering, it is the factor of safety. These rules compress uncertainty into actionable constraints. Crypto, for all its novelty, is no exception. The rules that survive cycles are those that force participants to inspect, measure, verify, and commit only when evidence is sufficient. Prediction distracts from this work. Principle drives it.

The subchapter's closing tension rests here. Rules are stable, but environments mutate. When volatility surges, narratives proliferate, and metrics contradict each other, the practitioner faces a choice: revise the rule or reaffirm it. The question is not academic. In the next cycle, when enthusiasm inflates and certainty returns, what principle will you refuse to abandon, and what behaviour will prove that you held the line?

Learning loops

On 11 September 1990, at NASA's Langley Research Centre in Hampton, Virginia, a review board convened after the loss of the Magellan spacecraft's gyroscope. The investigation uncovered no single dramatic failure. Instead, it exposed a subtler pattern: engineers had repeated assumptions from earlier missions without re-examining them, relying on inherited checklists that had not been stress-tested against new operating conditions. One line in the final report remains striking decades later: *procedures were correct for the world in which they were written, but the world had changed.* The remark captured a quiet paradox familiar to anyone operating in fast-moving domains. Checklists save you—until they don't.

The same tension shapes disciplined due diligence in crypto. Systems evolve, incentives mutate, teams reorganise, and attack surfaces widen. A checklist that once prevented error can ossify into ritual if never refreshed. Yet constant revision breeds chaos. Between those poles sits the practice this subchapter explores: learning loops. They offer a cadence—a rhythm—for inspecting your own tools of judgement. The loop is mundane by design, but its consequences are not. It reveals blind spots, rescales priorities, and keeps reasoning alive rather than fossilised. The question that animates these pages echoes the NASA board's reflection: *How often must you rewrite the rules that guide you?*

The motif that will return throughout this argument is simple: a loop only exists if it forces visible action. A learning routine that never modifies behaviour is not a loop; it is theatre. So we begin with the first major claim. When market conditions shift, the failure mode is rarely ignorance. It is inertia. Show it concretely. In January 2021, several decentralised lending protocols, including Aave in London and Compound in San Francisco, experienced brief liquidity stresses during volatile periods. Their risk dashboards flagged emerging concentrations of correlated collateral. Many users, however, applied stale assumptions: that blue-chip tokens remained uncorrelated, that liquidations would clear smoothly, and that volatility was transient. Name the issue: users had not revisited their collateral rules for months. Explain: the market structure had changed—cross-chain bridges, leveraged yield strategies, and new collateral types altered liquidation cascades. Implication: a quarterly review of risk assumptions, akin to NASA's audit cycles, would have forced users to ask whether their checklists reflected the world they were actually in.

A second named example reinforces the point. In July 2022, after the Celsius insolvency, public on-chain data revealed that many users had relied on checklists built during calmer periods. Those lists prioritised APY, token distribution, and marketing cadence but ignored counterparty exposure, principal rehypothecation, and custody segregation. Celsius's collapse was not the surprising part; the persistence of outdated due-diligence templates was. Those templates had been written in a period when centralised lenders were smaller and more transparent. By mid-2022, the industry had drifted, but the checklists had not. Behaviour lagged reality. Here, the learning loop motif returns: had users maintained a scheduled review—say every twelve weeks—they would have confronted the misalignment between old criteria and new structures.

A limitation deserves careful treatment. Too-frequent revisions can degrade discipline. Teams in Silicon Valley, particularly in 2019–2020, often iterated metrics weekly, leading to volatile dashboards and inconsistent prioritisation. Users in crypto can fall into the same trap: updating frameworks after every market swing, rewriting risk rules whenever a new exploit occurs, and constantly adding exceptions. This behaviour is not a learning loop; it is turbulence masquerading as adaptability. Reconciling the limitation involves distinguishing cadence from reaction. A loop is deliberate, not impulsive. Quarterly bias audits—with fixed scope, fixed prompts, and fixed deliverables—reduce noise rather than amplify it.

To deepen the argument, pair each abstraction with visible behaviour. "Bias" becomes the measurable tendency to privilege certain evidence: ignoring governance red flags because yield is attractive; overestimating on-chain activity because dashboards omit wash trading; trusting charismatic founders despite thin commit histories. A learning loop surfaces these tendencies by demanding a record. For example, during a quarterly review, you might compare predictions to outcomes, track which factors you overweighted, and evaluate where narratives outpaced evidence. That is not a philosophical exercise; it is the inspection of written notes, timestamps, links, and decisions. The behaviour is the audit. The insight emerges from the behaviour, not the reverse.

A further demonstration comes from open-source practice. The Ethereum Foundation, based in Zug, publishes regular updates on research upgrades, testnet readiness, and client diversity. These reports, especially during the transition to Proof-of-Stake in September 2022, illustrate a functioning learning loop. Each report revisited earlier assumptions, updated timelines, refined risk models, and integrated test feedback. The cadence was predictable. The revisions were transparent. Name this clearly: structured retrospectives embedded into operational rhythm. Explain: these loops created shared memory across contributors, allowing course correction without panic. Implication: individual analysts can mimic this cadence—commit to review, document changes, and adjust criteria with composure rather than haste.

Return now to the motif of visible action. A loop is anchored in commitments that can be verified externally. A quarterly bias audit is not simply a reflection. It is a documented routine: a dated file, a list of decisions revisited, and a revised checklist with tracked changes. A monthly repository scan requires a timestamped walk through commit graphs, contributor statistics, and dependency updates. These artefacts convert introspection into evidence. In a field often dominated by opinion, evidence restores orientation.

Consider a credible counter-example. Some traders and analysts operate purely through instinct, claiming intuition sharpened by years of exposure. They reject structured reviews, insisting that flexibility trumps formality. Occasionally, they succeed, particularly in thin markets where pattern recognition matters more than frameworks. Yet their successes are non-transferable. They cannot articulate their method; thus it cannot be audited, shared, or scaled. Reconciling the counter-example demands a simple observation: intuition is not repeatable. A learning loop is. The aim is not to eliminate instinct but to place it inside a structure that preserves what works and discards what fails.

Next, examine the broader implication. Markets reward adaptability, but adaptability without memory becomes drift. Learning loops institutionalise memory. They reveal which heuristics have decayed. They show where you repeatedly misjudge governance design or underweight liquidity constraints. Over time, these loops create pattern libraries—collections of errors, corrections, and refined principles. A personal wiki, maintained with the discipline of a laboratory logbook, becomes an external mind. It reduces recency bias. It shortens reaction times. It anchors future decisions in past evidence, not past sentiment.

Here, introduce a second named example. In March 2020, during the Ethereum network's Black Thursday liquidity crisis, MakerDAO's governance minutes and risk team updates became a goldmine for retrospective analysis. They documented model failures, auction bottlenecks, and collateral assumptions that broke under stress. Months later, those records allowed the risk team to refine collateral parameters and implement new auction designs. The documents served as a learning loop: memory instantiated as text. Their method demonstrates why loops matter. They permit forward motion without amnesia.

As this subchapter advances, the motif of cadence comes into sharper relief. Cadence is not tempo; it is consistency. A slow but stable rhythm outperforms rapid improvisation. Quarterly cycles for full checklist reviews, monthly cycles for repository and governance scans, and ad hoc cycles only for exceptional events—this structure protects attention. It prevents overreaction to noise while avoiding the inertia that doomed the Magellan checklist. The act of scheduling is itself a behaviour. It is as concrete as reading a contract or verifying a commit. Time becomes part of the tool.

The argument now arrives at its central philosophical point. A learning loop treats fallibility as a resource. Each mistaken assumption, each misread metric, each misjudged team becomes raw material. The loop processes that material into refined practice. Without the loop, error becomes embarrassment or denial; with the loop, error becomes data. This reframing changes posture. Instead of defending past decisions, you mine them. Instead of seeking infallibility, you seek repeatability.

The final tension sits here. A loop is only as strong as your willingness to revise cherished beliefs. What will you do when your quarterly audit reveals that a trusted heuristic—perhaps your weighting of team reputation, or your tolerance for admin-key concentration, or your assumptions about liquidity depth—no longer matches reality? Will you preserve the rule or update it? The decision is not abstract. It determines whether your compass stays aligned when the environment tilts again.

Community as defence

On 17 June 2016, the morning after the DAO contract on Ethereum was drained in a now-historic exploit, a small circle of developers and researchers gathered on a hastily convened call between Berlin and Zug. The broader public debate unfolded in forums and chat rooms, but the first clear-eyed threat assessment emerged from a handful of peers who trusted each other enough to ask uncomfortable questions aloud. Their exchange was striking not for its panic but for its candour: which assumptions had failed, what remained at risk, and how soon a coordinated response could be drafted. The world remembers the subsequent hard fork. Fewer remember the texture of that conversation—a community functioning as a defence mechanism long before crisis communications began. It was a reminder that in decentralised systems, vigilance is rarely a solitary act.

A second scene reinforces the point. In September 2018, the Bitcoin Core team disclosed a critical inflation vulnerability, CVE-2018-17144. Before the public announcement, a very small group, spanning contributors in Cambridge, New York, and Tokyo, reviewed the flaw privately, reproduced it, and drafted a patched release. Their discretion mattered, but so did their mutual scrutiny. Each member pressed the others on replication steps, boundary cases, and potential chain impact. Not one of them could have managed the response alone. The patch was shipped. The network remained intact. The episode demonstrated a principle that recurs throughout this subchapter: when a problem is too important for theatrics, a small peer circle—not mass sentiment—anchors reality.

These scenes show rather than state the core claim: community, properly structured, is not a crowd. It is a filter. The quiet motif that threads through these paragraphs is the table around which people gather—literal in one case, virtual in the other. Who sits at that table determines whether your analysis hardens or dissolves. So name the problem directly. Lone analysts, however rigorous, fall prey to unchallenged priors. Explain the mechanism: scrutiny degrades in isolation. One person may miss a buried dependency in a smart-contract upgrade path; another might underestimate latent sell pressure from a scheduled token unlock; a third may overlook a governance clause that allows a foundation to veto proposals. Implication: a functioning defence requires peers who rotate roles—interrogator, sceptic, synthesiser—so that no single worldview becomes the default.

Show the argument again through a different lens. During the volatile weeks of Terra's collapse in May 2022, several independent researchers on Twitter and GitHub flagged inconsistencies in reserve disclosures and liquidity support claims. Their findings gained traction not because any one analyst dominated the conversation but because small groups cross-checked each other's calculations, corrected intermediate errors, and stress-tested assumptions in real time. Two of the most widely circulated risk threads came from pseudonymous analysts, but their credibility rested on visible peer corroboration: spreadsheets shared, contract addresses posted, transaction flows verified. The behaviour embodied the point: community, when structured around scrutiny rather than hype, becomes a detection surface.

There is a credible counter-example. Large public channels—Telegram groups with tens of thousands of members, Discord servers running multiple time zones—claim to offer collective intelligence. Yet they rarely function as a defence. Noise overwhelms signal. Status dynamics mute dissent. Narrative momentum substitutes for analysis. During the run-up to several high-profile failures in 2022, these spaces often amplified optimism precisely when scepticism was needed most. But the limitation itself clarifies the rule. A crowd is not a community, and velocity is not vigilance. Reconciling this counter-example underscores the distinction at the heart of this subchapter: defence emerges from small, rotating peer circles, not from mass discourse.

Translate each abstraction into visible behaviour. "Cross-checking" is not a sentiment; it is the act of two peers opening the same audit report and comparing interpretations of severity classifications. "Accountability" becomes a written note: who took the devil's advocate role this cycle, what concerns they raised, and how those concerns altered the working assessment. "Trust" is operationalised as a record of past correctness—analysts who flagged governance drift early, contributors who validated liquidity anomalies, peers who admitted their own blind spots and updated accordingly. These behaviours leave artefacts: shared documents, comment threads, recorded calls, written objections. The artefacts form the table at which the community sits.

Return to the motif of the table. Its shape matters. A healthy peer circle is intentionally small, typically three to five people. Large enough to challenge assumptions, small enough that no-one can hide. The rotation of roles within that circle also matters. One person may specialise in reading commit histories across repositories; another may focus on market microstructure; a third may dissect treasury disclosures. But the devil's advocate role must rotate. If it calcifies, scepticism becomes personality rather than function, and critique loses its sharpness. Rotation maintains freshness. It forces each member to practise dissent, not merely tolerate it.

Consider the practical structure of such circles. In London, several open-source security researchers maintain private monthly review calls where each member presents one protocol they have examined. The presenter outlines the case, but the others interrogate it: Are the assumptions clear? Which claims require external verification? What does the token unlock calendar imply? Has governance drifted? These sessions often last less than an hour, yet the discipline lies in their cadence. Each call produces a short written summary circulated before the next meeting. Over time, the summaries become pattern libraries: examples of repeated governance flaws, recurring liquidity traps, or design choices that correlate with later brittleness. The table has memory.

A second structural example comes from academic practice. Peer review in journals is not meant to confer authority; it is meant to enforce humility. In March 2020, when the MakerDAO community analysed the Black Thursday events, contributors who disagreed on auction mechanics still collaborated on a joint post-mortem. Their disagreements sharpened the final diagnosis. Peer review is adversarial by design, but its aim is clarity, not victory. The implication for decentralised-analysis circles is direct: dissent is a safety feature. If everyone agrees too quickly, the table has shrunk to a mirror.

A limitation must be acknowledged. Peer circles can drift into groupthink if members become too aligned in background, methodology, or incentives. A group of engineers may underweight social governance risk; a group of traders may overemphasise liquidity catalysts; a group of governance experts may discount smart-contract complexity. Recognition of this limitation is itself part of the defence. The circle must periodically invite an outsider for a single session—someone with a different discipline or risk appetite—to disrupt comfort. Reconciliation emerges when the core group reflects on what the outsider saw that they missed. The motif of the table deepens here: occasionally you must change who sits at it.

The behavioural dimension extends further. A functioning peer circle does not merely validate analysis; it disciplines emotion. Markets provoke adrenaline: fear of missing out, fear of looking foolish, fear of acting too late. A peer can ask the question you avoided: Does the treasury runway actually support the roadmap? Are the governance powers meaningfully decentralised, or are they rhetorical? What is the evidence behind the claimed partnerships? Such questions reset posture. They break the spell of narrative momentum. They remind you that diligence is not a performance; it is a craft practised in company.

As this subchapter approaches its unresolved tension, return once more to the motif of the table. Every member arrives with blind spots. Every member leaves with fewer. But the table cannot answer one final question for you. When your peer circle disagrees—when two analysts argue for caution and one argues for conviction—what will you do? Will you default to majority sentiment, to the most confident voice, or to the principle you committed to in quieter moments? The table can filter noise. It cannot absolve you of judgement.

Staying curious without being credulous

Late in July 2020, engineers at Optimism invited a small group of independent testers to probe their pre-mainnet release. The call was informal, half debugging session, half philosophical sparring. What mattered was the posture. One researcher from Paris challenged a latency claim by running the same contract across both the Optimism testnet and Goerli, logging transaction timestamps and comparing execution paths. A developer in Singapore questioned the upgrade keys, tracing their control flow from the public deployer address to a multisig held by identifiable signers. Nothing about that evening resembled the breathless excitement of launch marketing. It resembled a lab. The surprises that surfaced—edge-case gas anomalies, a permissions nuance, a mismatched comment in the repo—were precisely the kind of details that curiosity reveals and credulity would have missed.

Another moment, quieter but equally instructive, unfolded in March 2023 when a pseudonymous analyst known as FlowScience scrutinised a new Layer-1 claiming "sub-second finality". Instead of tweeting enthusiasm or disdain, they spun up a validator node on the project's test network, replayed recent blocks, and measured variance in commit times. The gap between claim and observation was measurable—several hundred milliseconds at peak load. The point was not to shame the team but to demonstrate a mindset. Seek the surprise. Measure what the marketing glossed over. Demand evidence where slogans proliferate. This subchapter threads a motif through every paragraph: the simple act of testing before trusting.

Show the central claim clearly. Curiosity is active; credulity is passive. Name the practice that distinguishes the two: testnets. Explain why this environment matters. A testnet forces a protocol's promises into the open. It exposes assumptions to latency, transaction ordering, gas pricing quirks, and cross-contract interactions. Implication: anyone who avoids testnets yet speaks with conviction about a system's future trajectory mistakes narrative for knowledge. This is not a moral failing. It is a methodological one. Curiosity means building your own measurement rig; credulity means repeating someone else's words.

Demonstrate the point with the first checkable example. In April 2021, Uniswap v3 introduced concentrated liquidity. Many commentators celebrated its efficiency without evaluating its operational complexity. A team at Paradigm published a detailed simulation a month later, using real pool data from Ethereum. Their analysis showed that returns varied dramatically depending on price range choices and active management frequency. These findings were neither promotional nor conspiratorial. They were empirical. They exemplified the curiosity mindset: operate the mechanism, compute the outcomes, map the edge cases. Every abstraction—"efficiency", "liquidity depth", "impermanent loss"—became a measured variable.

A second example reinforces the habit. Chainlink's oracle network, widely adopted across DeFi, publishes regular heartbeat data, deviation thresholds, and node performance statistics. Analysts who actually read those feeds can detect anomalies: delayed updates, outliers in median aggregation, or geographic clustering among signers. In February 2022, researchers noticed a temporary stall in a particular feed linked to a regional outage affecting two node operators. The stall did not cause losses. What mattered was the behaviour. Analysts examined signatures, confirmed fallback logic, and cross-checked timestamps across multiple explorers. This was curiosity armed with tools, not credulity armed with vibes.

A credible counter-example must be confronted. There are protocols so early that no meaningful testnet exists, or whose data is too sparse to evaluate. In such cases, curiosity alone cannot manufacture missing evidence. Some teams offer only whitepapers and thin GitHub histories. The limitation is real. But reconciling it strengthens the thesis. When evidence is scarce, curiosity shifts from measurement to interrogation: ask what assumptions must hold, what failure modes dominate, and what incentives align or misalign among actors. The unresolved gap is the signal. Recognising what you cannot know is itself a rejection of credulity.

The motif of testing before trusting appears again in behavioural form. Consider the posture of someone evaluating a new rollup today. They do not ask merely whether the system is "secure". They ask who can upgrade contracts, what withdrawal delays apply, whether fraud proofs are live, and how sequencer downtime is handled. These questions translate abstractions—trust, resilience, decentralisation—into visible decisions: address control, time delays, function call paths. Curiosity manifests as clicking through code, tracing role-based access control, and comparing the live contract against the purported architecture diagram. Credulity manifests as later regret.

Thread the motif through a deeper claim. Curiosity thrives on contradiction. When a protocol promises "unbounded scalability", ask where the bottleneck moved. When a team offers "gasless transactions", inspect who sponsors fees. When a dashboard celebrates "surging user numbers", verify unique addresses, retention cohorts, and usage concentration. Surprise emerges when numbers disobey narrative. That disobedience is gold. It reveals which assumptions deserve revision, which risks deserve elevation, and which claims deserve scepticism.

Return to the tension inherent in crypto's culture. The field celebrates innovators who challenge norms yet often punishes those who challenge marketing claims. Communities valorise bold vision statements but treat probing questions as disloyalty. The intellectually honest practitioner must navigate this tension. Curiosity is sometimes socially inconvenient. It slows momentum. It pricks bubbles. It demands a slower, less performative form of engagement. But it also prevents waste—of capital, of time, of trust. The responsible analyst measures before cheering.

Bring forward a micro-behaviour to ground the argument. When a project announces a "mainnet soon" update, the curious reader checks the public repo: commit frequency, open issues, test coverage. They compare the claimed timelines with observable work. They scan governance forums for cultural cues: who asks questions, who answers them, who avoids specifics. They construct a small table of contradictory facts: rapid marketing growth but sparse engineering commits; heavy treasury spending but slow roadmap fulfilment. Credulity would turn these tensions into excuses. Curiosity turns them into hypotheses to test.

Hold up one more checkable example. During the 2021 NFT boom, several marketplaces advertised "fair drops" supposedly protected by randomised allocation. Analysts at the time inspected smart-contract bytecode and discovered predictable ordering patterns that advantaged certain addresses. The surprise was neither catastrophic nor unexpected, but it illuminated the principle: inspect before accepting. The analysts posted code snippets, transaction replays, and block-time comparisons. Their findings forced several platforms to deploy contract patches. Curiosity produced safety gains for thousands of participants.

A limitation must be acknowledged. Curiosity can tip into paranoia. Overfitting to anomalies can make analysts dismissive of genuine innovation or unfairly suspicious of competent teams working under constraints. Reconciling this requires calibration. The aim is not cynicism but disciplined receptivity. You look for surprise without assuming malice. You demand evidence without requiring perfection. You maintain a hypothesis that can change when new facts arrive. In this balance lies the difference between rigorous inquiry and performative scepticism.

As the subchapter nears its unresolved tension, return one final time to the motif: test before trust. The crypto ecosystem rewards confidence, yet confidence without evidence is costly. Every protocol, every claim, every metric faces the same quiet question: what would surprise me here? Ask it early. Measure what matters. And when the measurements contradict the narrative, decide which you will privilege.

About the Author

Kareem Solakdar is a practitioner-writer focused on the messy edge where new technology meets human behaviour. He has spent a decade working with founders, auditors, and policy thinkers on the realities of building secure, user-centred products. Kareem's mission is simple: help curious readers engage boldly while protecting their downside. Born into a family of merchants, he learned early how stories move markets and why good ledgers matter; that thread runs through his work on digital assets and risk literacy. He writes with warm scepticism, translating complex systems into habits any reader can apply, and champions open debate, clear incentives, and long-term thinking over hype cycles.

www.ingramcontent.com/pod-product-compliance
Lightning Source LLC
Chambersburg PA
CBHW031343230926
51848CB00002B/366
* 9 7 8 9 3 7 4 5 9 9 3 6 5 *